An Age of Wonders

MANCHESTER
UNIVERSITY PRESS

An Age of Wonders

Prodigies, politics
and providence in England
1657–1727

WILLIAM E. BURNS

Manchester University Press

Manchester and New York

distributed exclusively in the USA by Palgrave

Published by Manchester University Press
Oxford Road, Manchester M13 9NR, UK
and Room 400, 175 Fifth Avenue, New York, NY 10010, USA
www.manchesteruniversitypress.co.uk

Distributed exclusively in the USA by
Palgrave, 175 Fifth Avenue, New York,
NY 10010, USA

Distributed exclusively in Canada by
UBC Press, University of British Columbia, 2029 West Mall,
Vancouver, BC, Canada V6T 1Z2

British Library Cataloguing-in-Publication Data
A catalogue record for this book is available from the British Library

Library of Congress Cataloging-in-Publication Data applied for

ISBN 0 7190 6140 7 *hardback*

First published 2002

10 09 08 07 06 05 04 03 02   10 9 8 7 6 5 4 3 2 1

Typeset in Palatino
by SNP Best-set Typesetter Ltd., Hong Kong
Printed in Great Britain
by Bell & Bain Ltd, Glasgow

Dedicated to my mother and father

Contents

Acknowledgements

This project began as a doctoral dissertation at the History Department of the University of California at Davis under the direction of Paula Findlen. Over the years, she has been as fine a mentor and adviser as a young scholar could wish for. The late Betty Jo Teeter Dobbs and Margaret Jacob also contributed heavily to the shaping of the project. I also appreciate the help of Clarence Walker, Kay Flavell, Richard Schwab, and Winfried Schleiner, all at Davis. The Davis History Department generously supported dissertation research with fellowships and grants.

I thank the Clark Library and the Center for Seventeenth and Eighteenth Century Studies at UCLA for their financial support. I am also grateful to my family, for support both financial and emotional.

This project has benefited from numerous conversations with other early modernists, including Kathryn Brammal, Marvin Breslow, Lori Ferrell, Ulrike Gleixner, Deborah Harkness, Howard Hotson, Bruce Janacek, Lorraine Madway, Margaret Osler, Lynda Payne, Matthew Vester, Kathleen Whalen and Dave Woods.

Outside of the early modern field, I thank Marie Bolton, Chi-Kong Lai, Mark Eifler, Jeff Kolnick, Jeff McClurken, Carl Sjovold, Jon Sumida, and Madeline Zilfi.

I thank the librarians at the Clark Library and the University Research Library at UCLA, the Folger Library, the Franklin Library of the University of Pennsylvania, the Huntington Library, the Library of Congress, the McKeldin Library of the

University of Maryland at College Park, the Shields Library of the University of California at Davis, and the Simpson Library of Mary Washington College.

Across the Atlantic, I thank the librarians and archivists at the Bodleian Library, the British Library, the Cambridge University Library, Dr Williams Library, the Public Record Office, and the Royal Society. Margaret Notley, with typical generosity, provided me with a place to stay and transportation in Britain, for which I thank her. Finally, I thank the people of early modern Britain, for being a never-failing source of fascination.

Abbreviations

Add. MSS	Additional manuscripts
Birch, *History*	Birch, Thomas. *History of the Royal Society of London for improving of natural knowledge.* Four volumes. London, 1756–57.
BL	British Library
Boyle, *Works*	Royle, Robert. *The Works of the Honourable Robert Boyle,* ed. Thomas Birch. Six volumes. London, 1772.
CUL	Cambridge University Library
DNB	*Dictionary of National Biography*
DWL	Doctor Williams Library
Heywood Diary	Heywood, Oliver. *The Rev. Oliver Heywood B.A., 1630–1712. His Autobiography, Diaries, Anecdote and Event Books,* ed. J. Horsfall Turner. Four volumes. Brighouse, 1882–85.
HMC	Historical Manuscripts Commission
Mather Papers	*The Mather Papers.* Collections of the Massachusetts Historical Society Fourth Series no. 8. Boston: Massachusetts Historical Society, 1868.
POAS	*Poems on Affairs of State.* General editor Lord George DeF. Seven volumes. New Haven: Yale University Press, 1963–75.
RBC	Register Book Copy
SP	State Papers, Public Record Office.

Introduction

A woman gives birth to a monster. An army of mice invades a rural area. Three suns are seen in the sky. Today, such phenomena epitomize the intellectually marginal, relegated to the journalism of the supermarket checkout line. There have been, however, many societies where these events were not marginal, but important clues to understanding the nature of the cosmos and the destiny of human society. The transformation of this attitude to one resembling ours in a particular society, that of late Stuart England, is the subject of this book.

One term that the people of seventeenth-century England used to refer to such bizarre natural phenomena was 'prodigy'. The word had many uses, but its core meaning was that of a strange and aberrant event, the occurrence of which appeared to be outside the usual order of nature. The category of *the prodigious* linked such disparate phenomena as monstrous births, when like did not bring forth like but a monster, unusual rains, when instead of water blood, wheat, or frogs fell from the sky, and violations of the celestial order such as comets or apparitions of battles in the sky. While most educated contemporary Westerners would divide these events into those which could possibly occur, such as comets or deformed births, and those which are impossible, such as rains of blood, in early modern England all of these events were widely considered possible. When they did occur, they were considered not merely bizarre oddities but meaningful events.

The most important status a prodigy could have was that of a providential sign from God. Prodigies had been interpreted as divine messages since ancient times. The Bible is replete with prodigious events which function as signs of the divine will, from Noah's rainbow in Genesis to the signs and wonders of the 'last days' in Revelations. Greek and Roman sources as well as Christian and Jewish contributed to the providential or divinatory interpretation of prodigies. The frequently invoked works of classical poets, historians and natural philosophers such as Ovid, Suetonius and Pliny the Elder were well-stocked with prodigies and omens. Although medieval historians never had for early modern writers the canonical authority that classical and biblical sources did, prodigies had also continued to be incorporated into histories and chronicles throughout the Middle Ages.[1]

As providential signs of future events, prodigies did not all have the same relation to historical time. An important division existed between those prodigies that took place in annalistic time and those that took place in apocalyptic time. Annalistic prodigies, going back as far as Livy and common in the annals of medieval monks, were related to specific political or social events that would take place in the future. Annalistic prodigies appear in many works of history in the seventeenth century, such as the popular history of England by Sir Richard Baker. Annalistic prodigies built to no particular end, and theoretically were equally distributed through all periods of history, clustering at the great events of which they were signs. Apocalyptic prodigies were Biblical in origin. They were related not to other events in the sequence of historical time, but to the end of time itself. The various wonders described in the apocalyptic books of Daniel and Revelations, as well as elsewhere in the Bible, were interpreted by early modern Christians as harbingers of the millenium or the last judgement. As such, they came in ever-increasing numbers as the end of history was thought to grow near. This meant that the mere act of listing contemporary prodigies or asserting that the contemporary era was marked by a particularly large number of them could bear apocalyptic meaning.

The prodigious was a loosely bounded category, overlapping with many other types of phenomenon or event. On one side the prodigious was bordered by the miraculous, a category that generally included events that were even more dramatically striking, more directly explainable by supernatural intervention, and more blatant violations of the normal order of nature. In England, as in other Protestant countries, this relationship was particularly problematic in that many (although not all) mainstream Protestant religious thinkers held that miracles had ceased after the first centuries of the early church.[2] On the opposite side, prodigies bordered on those phenomena which were merely odd or remarkable, such as giants or dwarfs. Prodigies were also related to omens, seemingly trivial events which portended other, significant events, as when the lord treasurer's secretary fainted in the middle of a debate in the House of Commons in 1601, and men debated whether this was a good or bad omen.[3] Omens differed from prodigies in that they were not in themselves necessarily striking or remarkable. Finally, prodigies were also connected with 'judgements', divine providential punishments of individual sinners or groups of sinners. These punishments were sometimes prodigies, as when a sinful woman was punished by giving birth to a monster. Sometimes, however, judgements were merely common diseases or accidents. Collected accounts of judgements, such as Thomas Beard's very popular and frequently reprinted *The Theatre of God's Judgements*, sometimes included prodigious material under the overall rubric of 'remarkable providences'. All of these phenomena were part of a providential culture common to English Protestants in the first half of the seventeenth century, and have recently been explored by Alexandra Walsham.[4] This study will deal with events from these other categories when they are germane to the argument.

Prodigies were a particularly important site for competing discourses concerning God, nature, and politics because England lacked an official body or profession charged with the investigation and interpretation of alleged wonders – a College of Augurs on the ancient Roman model or an Inquisition on the contemporary Catholic one. Lacking authoritative resolution, prodigies and wonders remained open for competing interpretations. The most obvious profession to fill this role was the clergy of the established Church, but, lacking even the ability to perform the everyday miracle of transubstantiation, mainstream English Protestant clergy made much more modest claims of supernatural power than did their Catholic (or sectarian) counterparts. Lacking authoritative interpreters, English society allowed a variety of groups and individuals to assign meanings to prodigies. During the Civil War and especially after the Restoration, this lack was felt to be a problem. The response to this problem was a series of projects for creating such an authoritative body or profession of interpreters based on such different already existing professions as the clergy, astrologers or natural philosophers. None of these projects was entirely successful.

Contests over the significance and interpretation of prodigies became bound up with other contests over authority, particularly political and religious authority, in seventeenth-century England. After escaping the direct impact of the devastating Thirty Years War, England became a particularly volatile country in the mid-to-late seventeenth century, suffering civil war (precipitated and accompanied by wars in the satellite kingdoms of Scotland and Ireland), regicide and restoration, reaching a somewhat stable, although still fiercely contested, religous and political settlement only after the revolution of 1688. In this situation of the continuous questioning and construction of authority, prodigies and their interpretation were connected to a range of political and religious issues. For this reason, it is necessary to look beyond prodigy tracts and compilations themselves, and examine the roles prodigies played in journalism, polemic and everyday life.

Historians of ideas and historians of science since the Enlightenment have usually treated providential prodigy belief as a superstition that was displaced by 'scientific', or natural philosophical, explanations of anomalous phenomena, and have explained this displacement simply by the fact that the scientific explanations were superior. That such stars of the standard narrative of early modern secularization as Niccolo Machiavelli believed significant earthly events to be preceded by celestial prodigies has until recently been passed over in silence.[5] Distinctions had not been made between various ways of interpreting prodigies, and the varieties of early modern thought about prodigies were not explored or even known to exist. This approach is not dead, as can be seen in Jerome Friedman's recent study of prodigy writing and other forms of popular pamphlet literature in the Civil War, *The Battle of the Frogs and Fairford's Flies: Miracles and the Pulp Press during the English Revolution*. Friedman's analysis relies almost solely on the category of *superstition*. He argues that the cheap prodigy literature of the Civil War and the Interregnum reflected a growing sense of a chaotic world. The shock and horror felt at the prodigies was a result of the challenge that the Civil War and regicide presented to the ordinary English person, whose political stance, Friedman asserts, was one of conservative royalism. Although the sense of a chaotic world is indeed characteristic of much Civil War prodigy writing, Friedman underestimates the degree to which prodigy stories were used by parliamentarians as well as royalists. Not every denunciation of instability was a declaration of support for the king! Friedman's frequently inaccurate book also claims that an interest in prodigies and other supernatural events was incompatible with interest in the political and religious issues dividing the two sides, a claim not borne out by the extensive evidence of interest in prodigies on the part of people with strong ideological positions on the issues of the war.

However, more sophisticated treatments than Friedman's have emerged, often in the context of intellectual history and the history of science. The pioneer of the study of the early modern prodigious was the French scholar Jean Céard, whose 1977 classic study of the learned literature on prodigies of sixteenth-century France, *La nature et les prodiges: l'insolite au 16e siècle, en France*, associated prodigies with the idea of nature as inexhaustibly fecund and varied, and showed that some of the revered names of Renaissance France had taken an interest in them.[6] Following Céard, scholars such as Katharine Park, Lorraine Daston, and Ottavia Nicolli have studied prodigies and their reception in the early modern world.[7]

Studies of the prodigious by modern scholars can be divided into two groups. The first are by those primarily interested in popular culture, such as Niccoli and Friedman, who see providential prodigy belief, along with other beliefs such as that in ancient prophecy, as characteristic of ordinary people in early modern Europe. The second are by those interested in the relation of the prodigious to the development of early modern natural philosophy, such as Céard, Park and Daston. Park and Daston, in their pathbreaking article '"Unnatural conceptions": the study of monsters in France and England' and Daston's 'Marvelous facts and miraculous evidence' have given accounts of the evolution of seventeenth-century attitudes towards prodigies and related phenomena based on an internalist history of science. Daston argues that prodigies and monsters were one area from which the notion of a 'scientific fact' emerged. These scholars have done much less on the continued history of the prodigy as message from God, with direct political relevance, in the post-Reformation period. Park and Daston treat the Reformation as the high point of the interpretation of monsters as religious signs, and assert that this tradition declined rapidly during the seventeenth century.[8] '"Unnatural conceptions"', particularly influential in that for many years it was one of the very few English-language historical works on prodigies and monsters in the early modern period, argued a steep decline in the providential interpretation of prodigies from the mid-sixteenth century onwards, at least on the learned level. Park and Daston substantially, and correctly, modified this position in their recent book *Wonders and the Order of Nature, 1150–1750*, which gives a far more complex picture of the role of providential interpretation, acknowledging its continued strength into the seventeenth century. Providential prodigy interpretation flourished during the English Civil War of the mid-seventeenth century, and the theological and providential interpretation of prodigies continued to play a role in learned and popular culture through the late seventeenth century. But Park and Daston are uninterested in politics, and the 600-hundred year narrative sweep of their history precludes close study of local political contexts.

The most important work on the role of prodigies in European popular culture has been Niccoli's study of early sixteenth-century Italy. Niccoli associates providential prodigy interpretation with popular prophecy and astrology, finding all three common in the epoch of the Italian wars, and all suppressed with the ending of the Italian wars and the 'liberty of Italy' after 1530. Like many early modernists, Niccoli finds associates interest in prodigies and prophecies to have closely tracked civil unrest. Periods such as the wars of religion in France, the Thirty Years War in Germany and the wars of the three kingdoms in the British Isles have attracted much scholarship on prodigies and prophecies. Periods of relative peace, on the other hand, have been assumed to exhibit low interest in such phenomena. This model, as I shall demonstrate, does not fit the English case, where interest in prodigies continued long after the end of the civil unrest.

The lack of interaction between those studying prodigies in popular culture and those studying prodigies in natural philosophy has meant a lack of awareness of the interchanges between the two. Nowhere is this more marked than in Restoration England, where natural philosophers and their intellectual allies viewed the tradition of providential prodigy interpretation as an active threat to their own hopes of establishing a position as authoritative interpreters of prodigies and nature in general. In this fear of prodigy belief, they functioned as allies of forces attempting to deprive prodigies of political significance, as part of the Restoration attempt to erect an intellectually stable political regime, whose relation to the growth of early modern science has been studied by Margaret Jacob, James Jacob, Simon Schaffer and Steven Shapin. The particular English development had been created by the political crisis of the Civil War and the subsequent attempts by leaders of the restored monarchy and the Church of England to find a new set of ideological bases for their regime. It required the destruction of some practices, such as that of providential prodigy interpretation, as well as the construction of an authoritative science.

The role of the new science in attacking politically destabilizing beliefs has been studied in other areas. Patrick Curry, in *Prophecy and Power: Astrology in Early Modern England*, gives an explicitly political narrative of the displacement of 'superstitious' astrological beliefs in the seventeenth century, relying on a Gramscian model of 'hegemony'. Curry argues that the displacement and marginalization of astrology as a particular form of magical belief was due not to its inferior 'rationality' but because it represented a democratic threat to the intellectual and political authorities of late seventeenth-century England, bent on reinstating the elite intellectual authority and political authority of the gentry after the Civil War and the Interregnum. These authorities, of whom Restoration natural philosophers formed an important segment, suppressed astrology by treating it as an irrational and superstitious form of belief that had been superseded by organized natural philosophy.

Christopher Hill, among others, has criticised Curry for excessive relativism, and for minimizing the degree to which the decline of astrology was related to its failure to produce testable results.[9] Curry has also been criticized for failure to give due weight to the opposition to astrology prior to the Restoration, and for exaggerating the powers of the magistracy and gentry, a group which he often treats as internally undifferentiated and as inter-changeable with the emerging group of natural philosophers. His work seems overly conspiratorial, and exaggerates the conscious political motivations of those combating astrological belief. Although many of these criticisms have force, Curry's overall thesis that certain forms of belief were stigmatized as part of a Restoration effort to reconstruct intellectual authority on new bases makes some sense when applied to the belief in prodigies as divine signs. However, there was one important difference between providential prodigy interpretation and astrology that affected how they were attacked and defended. While anti-astrological polemics could be directed at a defined class of 'astrologers', or at individuals within that class, there was no defined class of prodigy interpreters. Thus polemics against prodigy interpretation were much more diffuse, often aimed at habits of mind rather than particular groups or individuals.

There are more sophisticated analyses of the decline of certain kinds of 'supernatural' belief in the late seventeenth and early eighteenth centuries. Some of the best recent studies are those of the decline of witchcraft belief, in Stuart Clark's *Thinking with Demons* and Ian Bostridge's *Witchcraft and its Transformations, c.1650–c.1750.* Both treat witchcraft and demonology in terms of a 'fit' with the structures of early modern thought in other areas, particularly theocratic monarchy and the conception of society as a religious community. The decline of belief in witchcraft, then, was not brought about principally by its own inconsistencies, or its poor 'fit' with reality, but by the decline of a whole series of related beliefs and cultural practices. As such, Bostridge in particular points out the necessity of integrating witchcraft with the political history of the period, pointing out how various controversies over witchcraft cases and witchcraft legislation fitted with the politics of the time. Michael MacDonald and Terence Murphy's *Sleepless Souls: Suicide in Early Modern England* also shows the complexity of the different but parallel processes by which explanations of sucide became secularized in elite and popular culture.

Study of prodigy belief in England and Europe has not taken this approach, tending to avoid the Restoration and Augustan periods entirely. The most important studies of the prodigious in later seventeenth-century Britain have been studies of the

Puritans of New England. These are David Hall's *Worlds of Wonder, Days of Judgement* and Michael P. Winship's *Seers of God: Puritan Providentialism in the Restoration and Early Enlightenment*.[10] These works, particularly Winship's, show great awareness of the English context of seventeenth-century New England culture. Winship's analysis of the position of Cotton Mather on prodigies is a model for how to understand prodigy belief in the mind of a member of the cultural elite. But Hall and Winship are American historians whose principal concerns are with the culture of New England, and neither situates developments in prodigy belief in a detailed study of the English context.

Study of prodigies and writing about prodigies in the seventeenth century reveals that their political relevance did not end with the Civil War. Prodigies were involved in the major political crises of the late seventeenth and early eighteenth centuries in England, from the Restoration itself to the Popish Plot and the Exclusion Crises, to the revolution of 1688 and the accession of the House of Hanover. There were explanations for the occurrence of prodigies, including both the fecundity and the decay of nature, but the most important kind of prodigy in relation to politics was the providential prodigy. As providential phenomena, prodigies revealed the will of God, though often in an ambiguous fashion.

In the decades following the Restoration English views of prodigies and their appropriate roles were drastically reorganized. The unregulated talk about prodigy of the Civil War period was unacceptable to many of England's religious, political, and intellectual elite, and both supporters and opponents of the Restoration regime followed Poole in putting forth a variety of schemes for setting up bodies or professions that would regulate the gathering and interpretation of accounts of prodigies.[11] More radically, others, including the new philosophers and their allies, simply denied the providential meaning of prodigies entirely.

Notes

1 For the use of prodigies in the Middle Ages, see Benedicta Ward, *Miracles and the Medieval Mind: Theory, Record, and Event 1000–1215* (Philadelphia: University of Pennsylvania Press, 1982), pp. 206–7; and

William J. Brandt, *The Shape of Medieval History: Studies in Modes of Perception* (New Haven and London: Yale University Press, 1966), pp. 52–65.

2 D.P.Walker, 'The cessation of miracles', in Ingrid Merkel and Allen Debus, eds, *Hermeticism and the Renaissance* (Washington: Folger Library, 1988).

3 Keith Thomas, *Religion and the Decline of Magic* (New York: Charles Scribner's Sons, 1971), p. 625.

4 Alexandra Walsham, *Providence in Early Modern England* (Oxford and New York: Oxford University Press, 1999). Walsham discusses Beard's *Theatre* on pp. 70–5.

5 For a recent discussion of Machiavelli's use of prodigies and astrology, see Anthony J. Parel, *The Machiavellian Cosmos* (New Haven and London: Yale University Press, 1992). For an Englishman whose belief in the political significance of prodigies was largely derived from Machiavelli, see Clark Library Manuscript, John Bolles, 'Observations Political and Civill', fo. 92r. The Anglican divine Thomas Jackson in his *Treatise Concerning the Signs of the Times* (1637) also referred to Machiavelli's support for providential interpretation. For Jackson's work on prodigies, see William E. Burns, 'Signs of the times: Thomas Jackson and the controversy over prodigies in the reign of Charles I', *The Seventeenth Century*, 11 (1996): 21–33.

6 Jean Céard, *La nature et les prodiges: l'insolite au 16e siècle, en France*, Series travaux d'humanisme et renaissance no. 158 (Geneva: Droz, 1977). For a much gloomier analysis of the monstrous and prodigious in the late sixteenth and seventeenth centuries which focuses on its relation to a sinful, fallen, and corrupt world see Jean Delemeau, *Sin and Fear: The Foundations of a Western Guilt Culture*, trans. Eric Nicholson (New York: St. Martin's Press, 1990), pp. 136–41.

7 Lorraine Daston and Katharine Park, *Wonders and the Order of Nature 1150–1750* (New York: Zone Books, 1998); Lorraine Daston, 'Marvelous facts and miraculous evidence in early modern Europe', *Critical Inquiry*, 18 (1991): 93–124; and Ottavia Niccoli, *Prophecy and People in Renaissance Italy*, trans. Lydia Cochrane (Princeton: Princeton University Press, 1990). Other recent works on prodigies in early modern Europe include Dudley Wilson, *Signs and Portents: Monstrous Births from the Middle Ages to the Enlightenment* (London: Routledge, 1993); and Michael T. Walton, Robert M. Fineman and Phyllis J. Walton, 'Of monsters and prodigies: the interpretation of birth defects in the sixteenth century', *American Journal of Medical Genetics*, 47 (1993): 7–13.

8 Niccoli, *Prophecy and People*, gives a similar interpretation for what she believes to have been a decline in the prophetic interpretation of prodigies after the sack of Rome in 1527.

9 Christopher Hill, 'New contributions to seventeenth-century social history', *Journal of British Studies*, 32 (1993): 76–83.

10 David Hall, *Worlds of Wonder, Days of Judgement: Popular Religious Belief in Early New England* (New York: Alfred A. Knopf, 1989) and Michael P. Winship, *Seers of God: Puritan Providentialism in the Restoration and Early Enlightenment* (Baltimore: Johns Hopkins University Press, 1996).

11 These attempts ran parallel with and involved some of the same people, such as the astrologer John Gadbury, as the conservative attempts to reform astrology discussed in Patrick Curry, *Prophecy and Power: Astrology in Early Modern England* (Princeton: Princeton University Press, 1989), pp. 57–78.

1

Organizing the prodigious: the Poole project and the *Mirabilis Annus* tracts

Matthew Poole (1624–79) was a strict Presbyterian clergyman, scholar and organizer, a minor figure of the great age of the 'intelligencer' in the seventeenth century – the age of Marin Mersenne, Samuel Hartlib, Henry Oldenburg and others who, in the infancy of the periodical press, maintained vast correspondences for the purpose of gathering and disseminating information. Poole's gentrified background gave him a small income to support himself, resulting in the leisure to come up with interesting projects. By 1657, Poole had conceived of a project for the collection and publication of prodigy accounts, initially in England and then throughout the British Isles. There was no shortage of prodigy stories to be collected and recorded. England was awash in prodigy accounts as during the recently concluded Civil War all sides had used the evidence of prodigies, in different ways, to demonstrate divine support for their respective causes.

The royalists' role model for the use of providential prodigies was the Roman historian Suetonius, whose *Lives of the Caesars* was full of prodigies showing the glamour of a certain individual marked out by fate, usually an emperor. Early modern prodigy writers frequently referred to Suetonius's story of the comet which heralded the death of Vespasian. Royalists used Suetonian prodigies to mark 'the divinity that doth hedge a King'.[1] Royalist writing about prodigies increased greatly after the execution of the king in 1649. Prodigies associated with Charles's death included unusual tides, monstrous births and three bloody suns.[2] Miracles worked by the king's blood were sometimes mentioned in royalist prodigy writings, and it was claimed that at his beheading the king had bled twice as much as an ordinary man.[3] The emphasis on royal glamour meant that royalist propaganda emphasized the similarity between Charles and Christ, and the execution and the crucifixion. Lesser royalist martyrdoms also produced prodigy stories, but the focus was always on the king.[4] Suetonian prodigies were annalistic rather than apocalyptic in their relation to time, and could be refurbished for subsequent generations of monarchs. Classical Suetonian biographical prodigies focusing on the lives and careers of individual emperors were easily adaptable to either King Charles, as royalists had claimed that the new star shining at the birth of the future Charles II showed a hopeful future.[5] Suetonian prodigies were used by opponents of the Stuart cause as well; the pamphlet *A True Relation of Some Passages at Madrid* (1655), describing the future Charles I's ill-fated journey to Spain in 1623 in search of a wife, recounted episodes of figureheads falling off ships' prows and bleeding statues in a catalogue reminiscent of Suetonius's.

For Puritans and parliamentarians generally, however, not Suetonius but the Bible was the principal guide to the application of prodigies to history. Parliamentarian prodigies tended to emphasise not the glamour of the leadership, but God's support of the cause. Biblical verses such as Psalm 105:5 – 'Remember his marvelous workes, that he hathe done, his wonders and the judgements of his mouth' – were often invoked to demonstrate the divine origin of prodigies and wonders and their function as direct signs from God.[6] Apparitions in the sky, as well as meteors and comets, particularly common types of prodigy, were easily linked to the divine will through the concept of heaven. The renewal of God's covenant with man after the Flood was signalled by a rainbow, the Israelites were guided in their flight from Egypt by a pillar of fire, and the Book of Revelations described in detail some wonderful and miraculous sights in heaven, such as a man enthroned on a cloud with a crown and sickle. Luke 21:25 spoke of 'signes in the sunne, and in the moone, and in the starres'. Joel 2:30–1 explicitly linked prodigies with the apocalypse: 'And I will shewe wonders in the heavens and in the earth: Blood and fyre, and pillers of smoke. The sunne shall be turned into darkness, and the moon into blood, before the great and terrible day of the Lord come.' The marginal notes to this passage in the Geneva Bible, the most popular English translation of the Bible among Protestants and especially Puritans in the late sixteenth and early seventeenth centuries, claimed that 'the order of nature shall seem to be changed' before the apocalypse.

Similar images of blood and fire were quite common in prodigy accounts, particularly in descriptions of apparitions in the sky. Scripture was not the only source of prodigies considered to be part of sacred history, however, and references to the prodigies which the ancient Jewish historian Josephus claimed had preceded the fall of Jerusalem to the Romans, including comets and monstrous births, were very common in prodigy literature on both the learned and popular levels.[7]

Parliamentarian prodigies therefore often involved more dramatic divine intervention than did royalist prodigies. The most dramatic example is probably that recounted in the 1642 pamphlet *A Blazyng Starre seene in the West*. This pamphlet recounted an incident alleged to have occured in Totness in Devonshire, when a royalist man attempted to rape a parliamentarian woman. Before he could do so, and just as he was taunting his intended victim by assuring her that no power on earth could save her, a comet appeared, from which descended a flaming sword that killed the would-be rapist.[8] One could hardly ask for a more irrefutable demonstration of the side God favoured.

Contestation over prodigies led to *ad hoc* investigations of particular prodigy accounts by authorities in Church and State. Noteworthy investigations included those of the Edgehill battle in the sky, the Kirkham monster and the royalist baby of London. In 1642 a number of rural workers interviewed by the local minister and justice of the peace claimed that for several nights, above the ground where the battle of Edgehill had been fought, they had seen the battle re-enacted by opposing celestial armies. So accurate was this image, which persisted for several weeks, that not only did the JP and the minister confirm it, but it was claimed that the king himself had sent two of his officers to view it, and that these officers had recognized the faces of some of their fallen comrades.[9] In the Kirkham case, a family of Roman Catholics attempted to conceal the birth of a headless monster after the mother had wished to give birth to a child with no head rather than a roundhead. The midwife, a Mrs Gataker, a pious Protestant, revealed the story to the local minister, a Mr Fleetwood.

Fleetwood and Gataker both spread gossip about the monster, and eventually word came to a 'Col. More', probably Colonel John More, MP for Liverpool and a future judge of Charles I. More wrote to Fleetwood asking for information. Fleetwood then questioned Gataker, and exhumed the monster's body. He sent an account to More in London, who showed it to other MPs, who ordered it to be printed.[10] A prophetic infant subsequently became a matter of concern for the government in 1650, when stories circulated of a nine-week old child in London crying 'A King! A King!' The official newspaper *A Perfect Diurnall* claimed that an investigation by the lord mayor had discovered that the parents of the child were brewers, and had made up the story to increase their custom.[11]

These investigations of prodigies owning the Civil War and the early Interregnum were followed by Poole's attempt to standardize and systematize their gathering and recording. Poole's project, had it actually been put into effect, would have resulted in a new kind of providential compilation. Previous compilers, such as Beard and Batman, had drawn their stories from a number of sources, including medieval collections of exempla, foreign compilations and pamphlet literature. The veracity of such stories was often impossible to verify. Poole's wonders would have been entirely British, had taken place at specific times and locations, and have been attached to the names of unimpeachable witnesses.

Although Poole did not cite Francis Bacon as an inspiration for his project, he drew on what may be termed a 'Baconian' tradition of fact-gathering as a way of enhancing knowledge as well as on the tradition of providential compilation. Francis Bacon's position on providential prodigy gathering had been ambiguous. On the rare occasions when he spoke of the providential interpretation of prodigies, he tended to disparage it, ranking it with the superstition of the interpretation of dreams and omens.[12] Reflecting his exalted position in the political hierarchy, Bacon frowned on divination and prophecy as politically destabilizing.[13] He tended to reject the analogical view of nature and natural phenomena which supported their use for divinatory purposes.[14] However, he also endorsed the 'History of Providences' as a subsection of ecclesiastical history, a call that could be interpreted as endorsing providential prodigy collections such as Poole's.

In its 'Baconian' emphasis on the systematic gathering and

compilation of information, Poole's project suited the mood of the time. Many intellectuals in the 1650s, sometimes inspired by Bacon, attempted to gather and organize information concerning the natural world.[15] These efforts were often associated with Samuel Hartlib and the circle surrounding him, and both Hartlib and one of his frequent correspondents, the Herefordshire cleric and natural philosopher John Beale, were aware of Poole's project.

Poole's plan for an English inquisition – though Poole would doubtless have been horrified to hear it described in those terms – is set forth in a document dated 1658 and titled 'A Designe for Registring Illustrious Providences'.[16] Poole, emphasizing the importance of observing God's actions in the world, planned for a network of ministers throughout every county in England, who would gather, examine, and report back to a secretary whatever 'remarkable providences &c., apparitions of spirits &c.' took place in their counties. He hoped that after the project was established in England it could be extended to Scotland and Ireland, at that time united with England in a single commonwealth. Each minister would establish in his county a correspondence with four or five men of 'judgement, activity, and zeall for God' to gather stories which could then be investigated. Each of these would enquire of ministers and others at public gatherings concerning stories of remarkable providences. Each story would be investigated by the minister, who would sift out the false from the true and get specific information as to the time and place of the incident and the names and veracity of the witnesses. He would write up a narrative of the account, and if possible get the witnesses to swear it before a justice of the peace. Then he would send it to Poole in London.

This plan, like Poole himself, is recognizably Presbyterian as well as Baconian. The Presbyterians, with their belief in the necessity of organization between churches, were the religious grouping during the Interregnum which placed the most emphasis on cooperation between ministers and groups of ministers, and had a higher idea of clerical authority than the Independents or the Baptists. As such, they were the most likely to be interested in this kind of clerically based institutional arrangement. Groups such as the Independents and the Baptists, which emphasized the separateness of 'gathered churches', could not claim to cover the nation in this way, while Erastian clergy might hesitate to set up an organization of a kind that could implicitly challenge the government.

Poole's view of ministers as the appropriate persons to carry out the project was, however, based on more than the convenience of a ministerial network. As 'trumpets and recorders of God's praises in ye earth', ministers had a special responsibility both to glorify God and to combat the growth of infidelity and atheism, a justification for this and similar projects which was to be frequently invoked in the following decades. To that end, the prodigies must be of undoubted veracity and unimpeachable testimony, and although Poole placed this project in a historical tradition of writing about providence he believed previous compilations of remarkable providences to be flawed by insufficient testimony to the alleged providences and by the mixture of legends and superstitions with true prodigies and providences. These failings made them vulnerable to 'the cavills of wanton, subtill, and self deceiving Atheists'. Poole's own project was therefore marked at each stage by a concern for veracious testimony, if possible from a number of witnesses, and the accounts of the prodigies were not merely to be gathered and stored at Sion College, but published for 'publick benefit'.

In 1657 Poole contacted his longtime associate, the eminent Presbyterian minister, Richard Baxter, who was quite enthusiastic for the scheme, suggesting that it be coordinated by a body of well-known Presbyterian ministers including Edmund Calamy and Samuel Annesley. Baxter also suggested that other conservative Presbyterian ministers such as John Bryan of Coventry be invited to collect and sift accounts of prodigies in their areas.[17] Baxter hoped that these accounts, if significant, could be sworn to before a Justice, indicating both the importance of exact descriptions of prodigies and some scepticism concerning the weight to be given to popular testimony.

The most enthusiastic and interesting reaction to the project, however, came not from Baxter but from Beale. Beale, the probable author of a commentary on the project preserved in Cambridge University Library, had been greatly impressed by the connection of prodigies to the events of the Civil War and wanted to use Poole's project to set up something like a college of augurs, a body that would study empirically the connections of prodigies and subsequent events, and place the foretelling of the future from prodigies on an empirical basis.[18] As he rhetorically inquired of Hartlib:

> Here I begin with my frequent expostulation. Are all Prodigyes, & Signes to bee despised, & neglected? If soe, Howe cam all Historians, inspired, holy, & prophane, soe constantly to record them? On the contrary if they ought to bee heeded, Where are the interpreters; what care to find them out? what publique notice is taken of them? what care is imployed for them? to trye them, to encourage them, to enable them, to informe them? Where is their colledge, what discipline appointed, or allowed? Is it a busines soe slight, That it deserves noe discipline, but must bee left, as it were only to chance?[19]

Beale departed from Poole's emphasis on moral reform and confuting atheism to one on understanding God's working in history, particularly the apocalypse. He also departed from Poole's plan to publish by suggesting the witholding of information not fit to be made public, either because it was too esoteric or because it might embarrass persons living. Impressed by the correlation between English prodigies and the events of the Civil War, Beale had already mentioned to Hartlib the idea of collecting accounts of prodigies from newsbooks to examine their connections with the events of the Civil War. Hartlib and Beale, along with many of their correspondents, were also interested in prodigies as a sign of the coming millenium, although Poole himself was not.[20]

Beale in particular believed that prodigies offered a way to understand the apocalypse. A bundle wrapper in Beale's hand among the Hartlib papers speaks of prodigies as *clavis apocalyptica* and hopes for the restoration of divine wisdom through a *collegio prophetarum* that would study prodigies and other ways, such as dreams and visions, in which God manifested himself to humans. Beale's theory of the historical development of astrology held that colleges of diviners in antiquity had been able to correlate 'new and extraordinary apparitions' with subsequent events, and that this knowledge had been the 'blameless subject of old astrology' and possibly handed down from God and the angels.[21]

Beale, a religious moderate who conformed after the Restoration, also hoped that the project could move beyond Presbyterian and Calvinist circles, particularly to moderate Anglican and Arminian divines. He suggested specifically the moderate Anglican leader Henry Hammond, the philosopher Ralph Cudworth and a Mr Lawson, probably the clergyman and political theorist George Lawson, indicating that Cudworth and Lawson were particularly fit to 'debate up the hidden and deep inquiriyes'.

An anonymous commentator who had seen both Poole's original design and Beale's commentary injected a note of caution, while generally approving of the project. Focusing on claims to spiritual inspiration or divine visitations rather than prodigies, he believed that an emphasis on remarkable providences led to false claims of divine inspiration and excessive individuality in religion, religious behaviours later known as 'enthusiasm'.[22]

Although Beale and Baxter, among others, were inspired to gather evidence of providences for Poole's use, the Poole project came to nothing, due to the heavy burden it would have placed on already busy ministers, Poole's lack of financial resources to pay for a scribe, the cost of sending and receiving letters, and the increasing pressure of his many other schemes.[23] The Restoration meant that many of the clergy Poole tried to recruit to his plan were deprived of their churches or were preoccupied with more urgent concerns of survival.[24] Poole went on to write a highly esteemed *Synopsis Criticorum* of the Bible, but he did not return to the collection of evidence of prodigies.

Despite the project's failure, however, Poole's idea of a massive, religiously oriented and clerically dominated effort to gather accounts of prodigies and other remarkable providences survived. Two of the most significant prodigy collections in the providential tradition published in the later seventeenth century were influenced by Poole. The New England Congregational minister Increase Mather claimed in his *Essay for the Collection of Illustrious Providences* (1684) to have been inspired by Poole, and by an anonymous manuscript connected with Poole's effort, to set up a similar scheme among ministers in New England. The Anglican divine William Turner's *Compleat History of the Most Remarkable Providences* (1697) would also claim Poole's work, and manuscripts surviving from it, as an inspiration.[25]

'Phanatick wonders': prodigies and politics in the early Restoration

Controversy over the legitimacy of the restored Church and monarchy made prodigies a major concern in the early Restoration. The early 1660s saw the most widespread and significant controversy over prodigies owning the early modern period, the *Mirabilis Annus* affair, as well as smaller conflicts leading up to it. These controversies would define the terms of debate over prodigies for the rest of the seventeenth century.

The controversy was precipitated by the minister-dominated remnants of Puritanism, now fragmenting into various dissenting groups and denominations. Prodigies were one way for English Dissenters to demonstrate that, despite outward appearance, their cause was still favoured by God. Royalists and Anglicans, some of whom had derived hope from favourable prodigies during the Interregnum, sometimes continued to interpret prodigious evidence in a sense favourable to the new order. More importantly, some intellectual defenders of the established regime elaborated a new theory which denied altogether the relevance of prodigies to religion and politics, and identified prodigies as principally the concern of natural philosophers.

In this controversy, Charles II's government took a stronger stand against subversive prodigy accounts than had previous monarchical or revolutionary governments. But forces other the remnants of Puritanism and the government and its intellectual defenders were involved in the struggle to control the interpretation of the *Mirabilis Annus* prodigies, and astrologers, natural philosophers and satirists also staked their claims. Throughout the later Stuart period, the *Mirabilis Annus* controversy set the bounds for discussion of prodigies and their meaning.

The storms that accompanied the coronation of King Charles in 1661 got the new regime off to a bad start as far as omens went, although pro-government propagandists put the best possible face on things.[26] Starting before the coronation in the first months of the restored monarchy, assaults on the new order in Church and State used accounts of the more bizarre, serious and deadly prodigies to demonstrate God's displeasure with the new rulers, in a continuation of the explicitly political prodigy literature of the Civil War and the Interregnum. This literature was widely distributed and served well enough to keep up the spirits of the defeated party and perhaps also to inspire fresh rebellion to cause the Restoration government serious concern.[27]

The struggle began with the anonymous pamphlet *Strange and True Newes from Gloucester*, published in the summer of 1660.

Reflecting religious divisions in the town of Fairford, it told of the disruption by 'Rude People' of religious services held by a 'Company of Christians met together lately, to serve, and worship the Lord according to their present apprehensions'. Some of the dissenters appealed to the local JP, William Oldisworth, who refused to disperse the hecklers. He was joined in this refusal by the 'Lord of the Town' – the lord of the manor Andrew Barker. Their failure to protect the dissenters was later 'punished' by the sudden appearance of masses of frogs and toads around their houses. These creatures carried a set of established cultural meanings. They were one of the plagues of Egypt referred to at the beginning of the pamphlet. Toads were often associated with witches, and frogs were also symbols of false doctrine due to the 'Unclean spirits, like frogs' issuing from the mouths of the dragon, the beast and the false prophet in Revelations 16:13. The Fairford beasts appeared in military ranks, not a disorganized mass. Their ranks parted only when Oldisworth declared he would go forth to make amends to the dissenters, and the frogs and toads vanished entirely once he had done so. The next section of *Strange and True Newes* was alleged to be a translation of a letter from France describing a recent earthquake and a few more French marvels including rains of blood, hailstones and more frogs. The concluding section described the death of a Brookington clerk's daughter, struck dead for mocking dissenters. All these prodigies were placed in the heavily providential context of the Lord defending his people and smiting their oppressors, the representatives of the new government.[28]

Strange and True News was quickly followed by the most important anti-royalist prodigy tracts of the early Restoration. A group of London printers and stationers, including Giles and Elizabeth Calvert, Thomas Brewster, Francis Smith and Livewell Chapman, known as the 'Confederacy press', had involvement in radical religion and politics dating back to the commonwealth.[29] These publishers were allied with radical London ministers including the Particular Baptist Henry Jessey and the Independent George Cokayn, and the Fifth-Monarchist layman and Interregnum colonel Henry Danvers.[30] This circle was more religiously radical, anti-establishmentarian and apocalyptically minded than the conservative Presbyterians of the Poole project. In the first years of the Restoration, this group was responsible for the distribution of a wide range of anti-government propaganda. Their seditious prodigy pamphlets included *The Lord's Loud Call to England* (1660) and the three tracts which appeared under the title of *Mirabilis Annus* (1661–62).

The first prodigy compilation published by the confederates, *The Lord's Loud Call to England*, could be seen from its title to be launched at a much wider target than *Strange and True Newes from Gloucester*, which had been firmly rooted in the politics of a particular locality.[31] Its target had been not the Restoration government in general, but the local leaders of Fairford. *The Lord's Loud Call* attacked the nation's sinfulness, a sinfulness specifically associated with the Restoration, the persecution of dissenters and society's libertinism. The title page credited the work to 'H.J.'. 'H.J.' was almost undoubtedly, by the consensus of both contemporaries and modern scholars, the London Particular Baptist minister and Fifth-Monarchist fellow-traveller Henry Jessey (1601–63).[32] Jessey, best known as one of England's leading philosemites and a leader in the effort to readmit the Jews to England during the Interregnum, never admitted to writing *The Lord's Loud Call*, but he was a religious radical who by his own admission participated in the circulation of prodigy accounts at this time.[33] *The Lord's Loud Call*, which on its title page named Chapman and Smith as publishers, mixed prodigy stories with other material demonstrating the corruption and ungodliness of the Restoration regime, such as a ten-page summary of William Prynne's 1628 tract against drinking healths, *Health's Sickness*, and stories of recent persecutions of Puritan preachers.[34] *The Lord's Loud Call* incorporated the story of the clerk's daughter and the French wonders from *Strange and True Newes* as well as the Fairford story itself, with the additions that the week after the frogs there was an invasion of flies, and that a minister in a neighboring town who had denounced the frog story as fraudulent had died shortly after.[35] Like the Fairford frog incident, many of the stories of persecutions included in *The Lord's Loud Call* were from Gloucester, indicating that Jessey had sources of information there independent of *Strange and True Newes*. Even less mistakable as a sign of divine wrath at the new order than an army of invading frogs was an incident taking place at Gravesend. On May 12, the king's proclamation day, a maypole, an object banned by the Puritan regimes of the Civil War and the Interregnum and widely accepted as a symbol of the Restoration, had been erected by the townspeople. This sinful act had been followed by the mass death of the town's dogs.[36]

Unlike *Strange and True Newes*, which set forth its wonders plainly, not attempting to defend their authenticity, *The Lord's Loud Call* explained how its accounts of prodigies were gathered and their fitness for inclusion determined. Jessey insisted that he had followed the strictest criteria possible. 'I forebore the longer, desiring to get the clearest evidence that I could, of the things related herein, forebearing many things that are spoken of, for want of clearer evidence.'[37] He went on to extenuate any possible mistakes that may have crept into his text by pointing out that reputable historians had also made errors. Interestingly, the historians whom he used as examples were Josephus, Eusebius, the early church historian Socrates, and John Foxe.[38] These writers had all dealt with important episodes in the struggle of true religion against false, and by likening himself to them Jessey implied that he was dealing with another episode in this conflict. He also placed himself in the context of sacred history by paralleling the events of which he spoke with passages from scripture.[39]

Royalists answered *Strange and True Newes* and *The Lord's Loud Call*, and their responses set forth themes which would play a central role in royalist discreditings of anti-government prodigies. These themes included the suspect motivations of those putting forward the prodigies, the fraudulent nature of the prodigies themselves and the preferability of explanations based on natural causes.

The earliest and least intellectually sophisticated responses to *Strange and True Newes* and *The Lords Loud Call* were a broadside ballad and a newspaper story that came out in the August of 1660. The ballad, entitled *The Phanaticke's Plot Discovered*, dealt only with the Fairford frog story, trying both to place it in a national, rather than a local, political context and to provide an alternative explanation for the presence of the frogs.[40] Its royalist position was made clear in the first verse:

> Kind Friends I am resolved to discover a thing
> Which of late was invented by Foes to our King
> A Phanatical Pamphlet was printed of late
> To fill honest hearted Affections with hate
> But here lies the thing, God hath sent us a King

> That hath Wisdom enough to extinguish their Sting;
> And therefore I wish all Allegeance be given
> To Him that directly was sent us from Heaven.

The ballad identified *Strange and True Newes* not as a plea for tolerance on the part of humble Christians, but as an anti-government propaganda ploy by 'phanaticks.' The presence of the frogs and toads was part of the same plot. They had been gathered and placed there by the fanatics themselves, and then dispersed through the area by the JP's maid, who was working with the fanatics. Both the creation of the 'prodigy' and its dissemination were part of the same plot attempting to discredit the king's government and bring back the days of the Interregnum, here stigmatised as a time when 'a Brave Kingdom' was turned to a 'base State'. Metaphorically, in fact, the fanatics *were* frogs and toads:

> Yet I'le not deny but that there was store
> Of Frogs and of Toads at the Justice his dore
> Which was Anabaptists, Brownists, and those,
> Which ever were known to be the Kings foes.

The newspaper story, in the government organ *Mercurius Publicus*, concentrated its fire on Livewell Chapman, referring to 'the most impudent, dull, and senceless [sic] pamphlet that even Leiden itself hath known', and asserting that the work was full of 'pretty, bottomless, impossible fictions'.[41] (The reference to Leiden was an attempt to link Chapman to the sixteenth-century revolutionary John of Leiden, leader of the shortlived but infamous Anabaptist regime in Munster.) However, the newspaper did not present specific evidence as to the falsity of the material; nor did it attempt counterinterpretation in the manner of the ballad.

The ballad's picture of fanatics possessing the mysterious power to convoke and disperse masses of amphibians at will strained credulity itself, and was not greatly superior to *Mercurius Publicus'* tactic of simple denial. A more sophisticated approach was taken by the most thoroughgoing response to *Strange and True Newes*, Robert Clarke's *The Lying Wonders, or Rather the Wonderful Lyes* (1660).[42] (Although *The Lord's Loud Call* was mentioned on the title page, Clarke's text discussed only the wonders recounted in *Strange and True Newes*.) Clarke, a local minister, dedicated his tract to the slandered Fairford leaders, and unlike the author of *Strange and True Newes* he identified them by name. He put the alleged prodigies in the context both of popular credulity and political subversion, beginning: 'It hath amazed me how a lying pamphlet will amaze the poore ignorant people of the Land.'[43] Like the anonymous balladeer, Clarke assumed throughout that the real purpose of the pamphlet was not to plead for tolerance from local leaders, but to overthrow the king's government and restore a Puritan regime. This enabled him to make the obvious response to arguments that providence was on the side of the separatists by pointing out that, after all, the king had been restored and the Puritan regime overthrown.[44] Providence, therefore, was really against the separatists and for the king and the Church. Providence's royalism was also demonstrated by Clarke's version of the story of the death of the clerk's daughter, as he claimed that she was not railing at fanatics when struck down, but actually came from a family of fanatics.[45]

Clarke's willingness to invoke providence against the separatists does not mean that he was unwilling to use explanations based on secondary causes in opposition to those who invoked the primary cause, God's providential will. He gave alternative explanations for the frogs, claiming that they had fallen in rain from the clouds, having previously been drawn up in atoms, and brought to life by the sun. Or possibly the general swampiness of the Fairford area was responsible for the appearance of frogs and toads in great numbers.[46] Clarke asserted, supporting himself with a statement by Aquinas, that to be a miracle an event must be altogether out of the order of nature.[47] This was an important polemical move, as it put his opponents, who had not asserted that the presence of the frogs was miraculous, in the position of claiming that the Fairford frog story was on the same level as the miracles of the Bible and the early church, a very uncomfortable position for English Protestants who mostly held that miracles had ceased. The elimination of the category of events intermediate between the ordinary course of nature and the miraculous was one of the most significant aspects of royalist anti-prodigious polemic.

Like the anonymous balladeer, Clarke likened the promoters of the Fairford frog story to frogs themselves, describing frogs as animals which delight in filth, croak importunately, leap about from place to place, and the enemies of useful bees.[48] He made an even less flattering connection by linking the perpetrators of the frog story with the Devil: 'Observe the Workings of this Serpent, which is after the Working of Sathan, with all power, and signes, and lying wonders . . .'[49] The phrase 'lying wonders', which Clarke also employed in the title of his pamphlet, was often used in prodigy literature. It referred to a biblical description of the Antichrist (2 Thessalonians 2:9). For Clarke, the dissenting propagandists were the true followers of Antichrist.

Adding insult to injury, Clarke taunted the anonymous writer of *Strange and True Newes*, who was in all probability justifiably afraid of reprisals similar to the imprisonment Jessey suffered, with not revealing his name.[50] The advantage the pro-government side had in being able to openly avow its opinions was exploited by a shorter and cruder pamphlet appearing around the same time as Clarke's and also denouncing the Fairford frog story, *A Perfect Narrative of the Phanatick Wonders Seen in the West of England* (1660). This took a form common among prodigy tracts themselves, consisting of a letter from a gentleman attested by the local minister, churchwarden and constable. The argument added little to Clarke's, claiming that there were many frogs in Fairford every year after the first rain. However, the show of an investigation and the invoking of eye-witnesses as to the non-occurrence of a prodigy was a tactic that royalists would continue to use.

'The throws of Providence come extream thick': the *Mirabilis Annus* tracts

The best known of the radical prodigy pamphlets, *Eniantios Terastios, Mirabilis Annus, or The Year of Prodigies and Wonders*, appeared in 1661, with no publisher or author identified, although Francis Smith, the Calverts and Chapman were all involved and Smith eventually publicly admitted his contribution.[51] The origin of the tract is obscure. Smith claimed that the tract was printed at the behest of 'A Person of quality yet living' but gave no further information as to the person's identity. Most early modern governments devoted more energy to the capture of the publishers rather than the authors of seditious material, and this case was no exception. The identity of the author or authors is still mysterious. Jessey was accused by the authorities of being responsible for the *Mirabilis Annus* tracts, but denied it.[52] The astrologer and Fellow of the Royal Society Elias Ashmole, serving on this occasion as an informer, thought the London minister George Cokayn responsible.[53] Jessey claimed that Cokayn, along with Smith and Henry Danvers, were people with whom he exchanged prodigy accounts.[54] It is clear that manuscript accounts of prodigies with an anti-government import were being circulated among religious radicals, and in at least one case a manuscript account of a prodigy included in the *Mirabilis Annus* series survives.[55] The tracts in all likelihood originated as compilations of such oral and manuscript accounts.

Mirabilis Annus made clear its political point very early on. Rather than merely adducing specific prodigies to demonstrate divine displeasure, it adopted an apocalyptic tactic of delegitimizing the regime through the sheer quantity of prodigies alleged to have taken place in the preceding 'Year of Wonders':

> And if ... Prodigies and Signs are especially for the sakes of wicked and ungodly men, Aaron's Rod budded for a token against the Rebels, then from the vast disproportion of their number this year, to what they were for many years together in the times foregoing, we may easily guess at the prodigious increase of the most brutish Prophaneness, Atheism, Uncleannesse, murders, blasphemy, and superstition, that this single year hath produced, beyond all the precedents which former times have acquainted us with.[56]

Since the chronological period whose events were recounted in *Mirabilis Annus* extended from the summer of 1660 to that of 1661, this dramatic increase of sin neatly coincided with the Restoration, and the 'times foregoing', comparatively free of both sin and prodigies, with the Civil War and the Interregnum. The strategy of asserting that the mere existence of prodigies in such numbers showed God's displeasure with the royal government also enabled *Mirabilis Annus* to move away from its earlier tracts' exclusive focus on prodigies of punishment, to include strange sights, miraculous tides and other signal prodigies, many of which were represented in the Frontispiece.

Not only was the Restoration regime alleged to be rife with sin, but it was weak and on the verge of a new civil war. *Mirabilis Annus* avoided particular predictions of the course of events, which could have been disproved, instead attempting to create a

mood of uncertainty and impending doom, not difficult to do in
the early Restoration. The choice of examples in the following
passage is revealing:

> We shall be bold to hint this much, that accidents of this kind do
> protend the futurition or manifestation of some things as yet not
> existent or not known, which usually carry in them some kind of
> agreement or assimilation to the Prodigies themselves, as (accord-
> ing to the opinion of some learned men) the raining of blood may
> signifie much slaughter, the noise of Guns and the apparition of
> Armies in the Air, wars and commotions, great inundations,
> popular tumults and insurrections . . .[57]

The prodigies that *Mirabilis Annus* actually recounted, which
divided into the four categories of prodigies of air, earth and
water, and judgements on particular individuals, continued to
undermine the regime's legitimacy by depicting it as sinful and
weak. One prominent technique for this was the use of historical
parallels. After recounting a prodigy, the author referred in an
annalistic manner to identical or similar prodigies which had
accompanied episodes of weak government, civil discord and the
persecution of true religion in the past, usually the English past.
For example, the drying up of the river Derwent in November of
1660 was likened to the drying up of the Ouse in 1399 that had
preceded and presaged the Wars of the Roses.[58] Double suns in
Hereford were compared, via Sir Richard Baker's *Chronicle*, to
those in the reign of the persecuting Queen Mary.[59] A violent rain
in London 'the day before the Covenant was burned' did double
duty in signifying God's disapproval of the burning of the
Covenant and in providing a link to the great storms in the reign
of King Henry VI, 'the troublesomeness of whose reign is sufficiently known to all that have been ordinarily versed in our
English Chronicles and Histories'.[60]

Another specific parallel was drawn between an invasion of
mice in Norfolk in 1660 and one in Essex in 1580. 'The year
following Queen Elizabeth was much disturbed by Jesuites, of
which severall were executed.'[61] Considering that the most prominent foreign invaders in 1660 were a king suspected to have been
excessively influenced by the Catholic rulers with whom he had
been associating on the continent, and his court of exiles and for-
eigners, this parallel was extremely inflammatory.

The most dangerous historical parallels in *Mirabilis Annus* were those that suggested a revival of the recent Civil War. A report on drums and guns heard in the air in various parts of England was followed by the statement: 'It is generally known that these kinds of noises were often heard in the Air in severall parts of England, not long before the unhappy breaking out of our Civil Wars.'[62] Another provocative parallel was drawn in relation to the invasion of Canterbury Cathedral, seat of the archbishop and symbolic centre of the power of the episcopal hierarchy of the Church of England, by two hogs. *Mirabilis Annus* claimed that the local inhabitants remembered the same thing happening before the downfall of the hierarchy in 1641.[63] Significantly, this incident supposedly took place on November 5, a particularly important Protestant holiday commemorating the deliverance of the nation from the Catholic Gunpowder Plot.

Parallels were not the only way to give an oppositional significance to prodigies and unusual events. Another was that of describing prodigies as visual representations of desired occurrences. For example, *Mirabilis Annus* claimed that a Surrey gentleman had a vision of a glorious cathedral in the sky beside a small church with a star inside it. The cathedral vanished, while the small church, whose star suggests the glory of God, was exalted.[64] This symbolically represented the hope of dissenters that the Church of England would be overthrown and that the small gathered churches of the dissenters would triumph over it. Even less subtle was the appearance of a black cloud dropping fire over Westminster Palace and the Parliament House.[65]

The credibility of these accounts of prodigies was a problem, particularly after the controversies surrounding the Fairford frogs story and *The Lord's Loud Call*.[66] The politically suspect nature of the compilation made one standard way of establishing the truth of prodigy accounts – appending lists and attestations of named witnesses – impracticable, as such witnesses could become targets of the government's wrath. In some cases where the magistracy had investigated a prodigy, its findings could be invoked as showing the prodigy's genuineness, but these cases were rare. Most of the prodigy accounts included do refer to witnesses, but they could not be named or too closely identified. Their qualifications could be stated only in general terms. This was compatible with the continued emphasis on witnesses' social respectability, as in the case of the Surrey man who had the vision of the cathedral and the church was identified as a gentleman 'of good Quality'.[67] Another strategy for lending veracity to a prodigy account was identifying the witness as predisposed to reject accounts of prodigies through a general scepticism or a lack of sympathy for the dissenters' cause.[68] This marked a fundamental shift in the idea of what constituted a veracious witness. Rather than the witnesses' godliness adding weight to their testimony, now ungodliness – conformity to the established Church, scepticism regarding the providential view of prodigies – did so. The necessity of self-described pious believers ceding to nonbelievers the authority to authenticate prodigies indicated the lessening of control over the prodigious exerted by the godly. The suspicion with which prodigies could be regarded also made the compiler reluctant to include foreign prodigies, on the grounds that he had no confirmation of them.[69]

In addition to guarding against accusations of fraud, the compiler of *Mirabilis Annus* was also concerned to establish the intellectual legitimacy of providential prodigy interpretation. One strategy for achieving both objectives was to associate prodigy interpretation with respected names such as Martin Luther, Thomas Jackson (particularly useful as an orthodox Anglican believer in providential prodigy), the Scottish clergyman James Weems and the Dutch Gomarist, or strict Calvinist, Gisbert Voetius (1589–1676), author of *De Signis*, all of whom were invoked in the Preface.[70] The compiler continued throughout to refer to the authority of 'learned men', presenting the work as following in the tradition of the sixteenth-century German humanist Conrad Lycosthenes's 1557 *Prodigiorum et Ostentorum Chronicon*.[71]

The second *Mirabilis Annus* tract, *Mirabilis Annus Secundus* (1662), covered the period from April 1661 to June 1662, and largely followed the pattern of the original *Mirabilis Annus*, keeping the fourfold categorization of prodigies. However, it also showed the effects of controversy over the first tract and the events it recounted in several ways. The most direct was the inclusion of the story of a man on a Thames boat discussing a 'Book of Prodigies' in a scoffing way who was immediately rebuked by the sudden appearance of a monster, reinforcing the idea that prodigies bore an immediate relation to the divine will.[72] The

Introduction attempted to shore up its truth-claims by acknowledging the presence of false information in the first tract, ascribing these errors to misleading informants or to misprints. The anonymous compiler also claimed that the first *Mirabilis Annus* had been produced by a different publisher.[73] The reader would have had to take this on faith, however, as *Mirabilis Annus Secundus*, like the first tract, carried no information as to the identity of its publisher.

The most important change in the textual matter was the elimination of historical parallels. This was presented as a response to the charges of sedition levelled at the original *Mirabilis Annus*, a charge the compiler unconvincingly professed to abhor.[74] By eliminating the recounting of prodigies that took place during 'weak' reigns like that of Henry VI or before civil wars, *Mirabilis Annus Secundus* masked its attack on the current government, but it did continue to oppose the Restoration order. The claims it made for prodigies were in some ways even greater than those of the previous tract, as the removal of prodigies from historical–annalistic time by eliminating parallels only strengthened their position in theological–apocalyptic time. For example, *Mirabilis Annus Secundus* claimed that the previous few years had seen 'more warnings by Signs and Prodigies than (so far as we have heard or read) since the dayes of Jesus Christ his being on Earth to this very day'.[75]

The dissenting experience characterized the form which some of the prodigies actually took, as in an East Sussex celestial apparition of armed men thrusting preachers from pulpits, a reference to the ejection of Nonconformist ministers following the Restoration.[76] The author frequently abused Church of England clergy. A monstrous birth in The Strand provoked adverse reflections on the Anglican establishment, as a timeserving Church of England minister was charged with being the monster's father.[77] Even an incident as minor as a chattering magpie disturbing an Anglican parson and a bishop was presented as prodigious.[78] Canterbury Cathedral was again the site of prodigies and omens, as poltergeist-type incidents there were carefully recounted, particularly those phenomena associated with the cathedral treasury, emphasizing the association of the restored Church of England with wealth and opulence.[79]

One of the most prominent attacks on the Restoration order

contained in *Mirabilis Annus Secundus* was not strictly a prodigy narrative, but a ghost story. It concerned a house near Reading, which had belonged to a regicide. As such it had been forfeit to the crown, and King Charles had given it to one of his supporters. A ghost appeared, telling the servants of the new owner to vacate and to leave the house to its rightful heirs.[80] This was a clear denial of the legitimacy of the government's attack on the regicides and their families. This was one of the rare instances in *Mirabilis Annus Secundus* of a direct attack on the royal government as distinct from the Restoration Church of England. The tract also trod very carefully in its recounting of a recent, specifically anti-government, prodigy originating with a Quaker weaver named Serles, at whose home a message predicting the poisoning of the king had appeared for a quarter of an hour on the edge of a kettle. *Mirabilis Annus Secundus*, 'fearing lest indiscreet persons, and ill-affected, should make an ill construction, and application of them', did not quote the inscription, but merely gave the story of its appearance.[81]

The final *Mirabilis Annus* pamphlet, *Mirabilis Annus Secundus, or the Second Part of the Second Year's Prodigies* (hereafter referred to as *Mirabilis Annus Secundus II*) covers the period from June to September 1662 and was even more militant and uncompromising, as well as cruder in appearance, than the first two. It put a greater emphasis on judgements of particular individuals, which took up half the text, than on prodigies *per se*. The recipients of these judgements were usually backsliders from the dissenters' cause into conformity or persecutors, reflecting the often justified paranoia of increasingly beleaguered dissenting communities in the Restoration era, and demonstrating which side God was really on. The Preface to the work showed an almost hysterical anticipation of some great divine deed to reverse the situation in which dissenters then found themselves: 'God's warnings we see do croud in very fast upon us, and the throws of Providence come extream thick: Certainly there is some great thing at the Birth, and the Lord is rising from his place to do his Work, even his strange Work.' The celestial prodigies included in *Mirabilis Annus Secundus II* reflected this anticipation of great, catastrophic, even apocalyptic change. Envisioning through prodigies a violent overthrow of the Restoration order, *Mirabilis Annus Secundus II* was much more dominated by apparitions of celestial battles than had been its two predecessors.[82] The drawing of parallels was resumed, although not in the systematic way, nor with the use of old chronicles and histories, characteristic of the first *Mirabilis Annus*. Most of the parallels in *Mirabilis Annus Secundus II* derived from immediate memories of the Civil War, as when the water in an Irish lake allegedly turned bloody, repeating an event which had taken place before the Irish rebellion of 1641. *Mirabilis Annus Secundus II* linked this with the return of many Irish Catholics following the Restoration, and stated that many Protestants had fled the area after the prodigy.[83] Given the place that alleged massacres of Irish Protestants by Irish Catholics during the civil unrest occupied in the English imagination, this amounted to the highly seditious allegation that the English government was conniving at their repetition.

Distribution and reception of the *Mirabilis Annus* tracts

The royalist bishop and fellow of the Royal Society Samuel Parker (1640–88) reflected on the popularity of these prodigy tracts among dissenters and political radicals in his *History of His Own Time*: 'I was a young man in those Days, but very well remember that they read those books as diligently as they did the Bible. There was not one of the Party, that had them not, they read them, they reverenced them.'[84] The tracts circulated throughout England as well as in other parts of the British Isles, the European continent and North America. Government investigations were able to trace networks of distribution to Bristol and Leicester. Their readership extended as far up the social scale as the nobility, and as far down as maidservants.[85]

Individuals sympathetic to the political positions endorsed in the tracts reacted to them with varying degrees of hope or scepticism. Edmund Ludlow, the republican and commonwealth revolutionary-on-the-run, found in the *Mirabilis Annus* tracts comforting evidence that his cause was still God's, and that 'the Lord witnesseth against this sort of men [royalists]' by 'his contynued prodigies'.[86] Ludlow's memoirs included two stories from the tracts, a phantom troop of horse observed in Montgomeryshire and a qualm experienced by the strongly royalist preacher Robert South when preaching before the king

on the advantage of the Restoration over the Interregnum.[87] Ralph
Josselin in Earl's Colne, Essex, a Puritan minister then with some
difficulty holding a living in the Church of England, wrote in his
diary of 'a booke of prodigies, the drift seems to encourage the
down cast part of men, they shall up, and the episcopall way
come to utter ruin . . .'. Josselin discreetly did not give his own
opinion on the veracity or import of the prodigies. The *Mirabilis
Annus* tracts, along with other prodigies and illustrious providences, were also a subject of the correspondence between the
Cambridge doctor John Worthington and Hartlib.[88]

Supporters as well as opponents of the regime took note of the
prodigy pamphlets. The Oxford antiquary Anthony Wood commented on *The Lord's Loud Call* and the *Mirabilis Annus* tracts,
regarding them largely as frauds 'purposely to breed in the vulgar
people an ill opinion of the change of Government and Religon',
and including in his *History of Oxford* a point-by-point refutation
of the story from *The Lord's Loud Call* of some Oxford people
struck dead for participating in a play.[89] He also noted a con-
forming minister falling into a swoon, giving the natural causes
thereof, 'in case the phanaticks may take advantage of it hereafter
to publish it as a speciall judgement of God'.[90] However, Wood
was not above giving credence to one of the *Mirabilis Annus* tracts
when it recounted the similar story of Robert South's qualm, as
South was one of his pet hates.[91]

Outside England, the dissenting minister in Flintshire, north
Wales, Philip Henry, thought enough of these accounts of prodigies to make in his diary extensive transcripts from *Mirabilis
Annus* and *Mirabilis Annus Secundus* as evidence of God's 'witnessing agt [against] Prophanes & Persecution'.[92] John Lesley,
bishop of Clogher in Ulster, claimed in a letter to Archbishop
Bramhall: 'All Ulster is affrighted out of their wits with the
current report of most fearful and portentous visions from
England. My Lord . . . the brain that forges such devices hath
treason in the heart.' The bishop went on to hope that the authorities would more actively suppress the prodigy tracts and to claim
that 'the ghost of the Covenant is sent back again from Hell to
trouble us once more'.[93] Both prodigy stories and the news of the
publication of the tracts made it to New England along the information networks of dissenting ministers and ex-commonwealth
men.[94] Outside the dominions of Charles II, the tracts circulated

to the Dutch Republic, where the Amsterdam millenarian visionary Petrus Serrarius referred to *Mirabilis Annus* as one example of
a Europe-wide increase in prodigies heralding the millenium.[95]

Baxter's reaction to the tracts shows how the attitude of
dissenting ministers could be more complex than either simple
acceptance or rejection. In his autobiography Baxter gave an
explanation of the *Mirabilis Annus* affair which differed from both
that of the Restoration government and its supporters and that of
the prodigy pamphleteers themselves. Baxter believed that some
of the prodigies, such as the drying up of the Derwent, were
genuine works of God, but that the compilers of the tracts,
through haste and Fifth-Monarchist fanaticism, had mixed false
prodigies in with the true. Rather than promoting repentance,
these false prodigies had actually caused men to harden their
hearts further against God's warnings, and led to the discrediting
both of the interpretation of prodigies as divine signs and of innocent godly ministers along with the fanatics. The whole affair was
a story of 'how God's strange Judgements . . . were turned by the
Devil to his own advantage'. The lesson Baxter drew from this
was not a denial that prodigies were revelatory of God's will, but
that it was dangerous and mistaken to mix them with current politics. Baxter was left with a notion of prodigies as moral warnings
to, or judgements of, individuals, but as devoid of public meaning. Another conservative Presbyterian minster, Oliver Heywood,
had a similar reaction, claiming that 'tho everything in those
books of prodigys be not to be believed, yet some things are most
ceartainly true, which . . . betoken strange judgments'.[96]

The government's response to this threat took many forms, and
involved both counterpropaganda and the arrest of the makers
of the tracts with the confiscation of their goods. Government-
controlled newspapers assaulted the factuality of specific prodigies recounted in the *Mirabilis Annus* tracts, as they had the
Fairford frogs story. The *Kingdom's Intelligencer* in 1661 showed
the government using its power to define reality by authority
against the prodigy tracts. After enumerating a variety of alleged
prodigies, and attacking the 'excellent certificates with names
subscribed, to make (were it possible) such Forgeries to pass for
probable' the newspaper claimed 'that we have sent to those severall places, and have it under the respective Magistrats hands
that there is not the least colour or pretence for any . . .'. The mag-

istrates were presented as a more reliable source of information
than the religious radicals who had produced the prodigy tracts.
The article closed with an even more explicit invocation of the
power of the state, an announcement that some of the publishers
and distributors were under arrest, and that through them the
government hoped to get at the original forgers of the prodigies.[97]

A different newspaper response followed *Mirabilis Annus
Secundus*. An advertisement in the second government newspaper, *Mercurius Publicus*, purported to be from the friends of a
Mr Martyn, an individual slandered in *Mirabilis Annus Secundus*.
The pamphlet claimed that Martyn had fallen sick immediately
after being assaulted by two ravens, and that while he was dying
the bell in the local church steeple tolled by itself, but stopped
when he died.[98] The advertisement denounced all this as a 'most
horrid untruth'. Like other anti-prodigious writings of the period,
it followed the format of earlier prodigy pamphlets. The adver-
tisers asserted their first-hand knowledge of Martyn's death, and
a list of their names was appended to the statement.[99] In October
1663 a proactive attempt was made to discredit a prodigy collection in advance with the publication of a report from Ipswich
claiming: 'The Phanatiques hereabouts are observ'd of late to be
very busy with their Prodigies and Prophesys.' The writer
claimed to have sent the editor of the newspaper true accounts of
the incidents the fanatics would be claiming to be prodigies, and
offered his services as an informer should the government desire
either to prosecute the organizers or hold them up to ridicule.[100]

More direct action against the seditious collectors of prodigy
stories themselves showed that the government took the tracts
very seriously. Even the rhetoric of the State authorities showed
their evaluation of the threat which these prodigy pamphlets
posed. A warrant for the reception into custody of Elizabeth
Calvert spoke of the first *Mirabilis Annus* as

> a forgery of false and feigned prodigies, prognosticating mischie-
> vous events to the King, and instilling into the hearts of subjects
> a superstitious belief thereof, and a dislike and hatred of his
> Majesty's person and government, and preparing them to effect
> a damnable design for his destruction, and a change of
> government.[101]

The government's actions matched its rhetoric, and included
raids on bookshops, questioning of buyers and sellers of the

tracts, and arrest and imprisonment without trial of those suspected of involvement in their production under the secretary
of state's power of detention.[102] One important aspect of the government's persecution was its concern over the circulation of
prodigy accounts by ministers and other religious radicals.
Francis Smith was asked: 'Did you not receive any . . . out of
divers Countries concerninge some late Prodigies, or wonderful
Accidents, and did you not communicate the same to some other
persons for the perfecting of the collection?' He denied having
done so.[103] Jessey also was asked about his prodigy collecting
activities, and, unlike Smith, freely admitted to them, although he
continued to deny actually being involved in the production of
the *Mirabilis Annus* tracts.[104]

The circulation of accounts of English prodigies and their connection to political subversion continued to concern the government and its supporters throughout the 1660s. The activities
of the Irish healer Valentine Greatrakes, a former Cromwellian
officer, were linked by one of his opponents, Davis Lloyd, to the
earlier books of prodigies:

> Besides that, since the true wonder of his Majesties Restauration,
> evidencing the presence of God with his Person and Government,
> the men of Mr. Greatrakes party have spent their time in venting
> and dispersing false Prodigies, to delude men into an Opinion of
> the displeasure of God against both: and those that look narrowly
> into things, are apt to suspect, that Mr. Greatrakes being concerned,
> that the reports of Miracles and Prodigies did not work upon us,
> imagined that he might promote the cause further, and perform
> miracles himself.[105]

Counterposing the truly wonderful and providential Restoration
with false prodigies was a common device of royalist writers.

The government's informers continued to treat prodigy gathering as of potential interest. In 1665 a spy reported that he was
desired by the fanatical ex-followers of the Fifth-Monarchist minister Christopher Feake to 'send as full a narrative as I can of the
last strange sights which have been seen by many people of
Honiton in Devon because there were now some ministers
writing a booke concerning such things'.[106] The spy hinted at a
possible revival of the *Mirabilis Annus* project. In 1670, a spy
named Wyndham, reporting on the detention of a suspected sedi-
tionary, Major Hume, enclosed a written description of a prodigy
found on the major's person. This prodigy was an apparition of

a large group of people and horses seen by some people in East Brandon. Wyndham, claiming 'I do not believe the paper of any great consequence', added: 'the apparition he mentions I think is an invention to make the people suspect some rebellion predicted by that prodigiye'.[107] The same year, a Coventry correspondent of Secretary and Spymaster Joseph Williamson, in a letter containing various news items, concluded: 'A Jay hath built her nest and now sitts in our new repaired cross, which being a very wild shy bird is by all lookt on as a very strang thing, and by some as ominous.'[108]

Prodigy tracts were among those subversive writings which prompted the government to issue its most devastating attack on the underground press, the Licensing Act, in 1662. This Act attempted to suppress subversive writings by requiring printers to be licensed, and forbade the issue of books without the name of the printer, as had been the case with the three *Mirabilis Annus* tracts. Roger L'Estrange, who had heard of the first tract while it was in press and had attempted to prevent it from appearing, frequently mentioned the prodigy tracts in his writings of the early 1660s campaigning for a more effective censorship. This campaign was succesful enough to culminate in his appointment as 'licenser of the press'.[109]

In addition to outright censorship, prodigies could be de-fanged through satire. Samuel Butler, whose burlesque epic *Hudibras* attained quasi-official status when it became known that Charles II was an avid reader of the work, mocked prodigy belief as characteristic of the Puritans and parliamentarians, the principal objects of his satire.[110] The astrologer Sidrophel, often identified with the parliamentarian astrologer William Lilly, saw a kite through a telescope and thought it a comet.

> Pray Heaven, divert the fatal omen
> For 'tis a Prodigie not common
> And can no less than the world's end
> Or Nature's funeral portend.[111]

The allegorical portrait of fame also mocked prodigy belief on a more popular level:

> About her neck a Pacquet Male
> Fraught with Advice, some fresh, some stale
> Of men that walked when they were dead

> And Cows of Monsters brought to bed
> Of Hailstones big as Pullet's egs
> And Puppies whelped with twice two legs
> A Blazing-Star seen in the West
> By six or seven mOen at least.[112]

In 1674, *A True and Perfect Account of the Miraculous Sea-Monster* would incorporate in a prodigy pamphlet similar satire against those who found religious and allegorical significance in monsters. The pamphlet described a strange sort of squid–jellyfish found washed up on the shore. As the writer acknowledged, a beast coming from the sea had apocalyptic relevance: 'We might now divert the Reader a little, and tell him, that some zealots hearing of a strange Creature, with several Heads, ten horns, and more than triple crowns, took it for the Apocaliptical Beast, and fancied the Pope was landed in Person . . .'.[113] Apocalyptic zealots now were not even given the respect of being considered socially dangerous, but were objects of ridicule, as was, by implication, the providential and apocalyptic approach to prodigies.

Besides ridiculing hypothetical apocalyptic interpreters, another strategy for defusing the possible political danger of a prodigy account, one with a long history, was to assert that, although prodigies were messages from God, they were not interpretable by humans. An example of this approach was a 1661 compilation of, mostly, German prodigies, *A Strange and True Relation of Several Wonderful and Miraculous Sights* (foreign prodigies were generally less dangerous than English ones):

> What the effect of these strange sights, wonderful signs, and prodigious births may be, I shall not attempt to give you an account of, many now living having already heard & seen the events of some strange apparitions that have bin visible in these latter Ages, yet not altogether so miraculous as these herein mentioned, which indeed are too hard for any mortal to dive into the Interpretation of, and the true meaning being known to none but God alone, who ordereth and decreeth all things in Heaven and Earth . . .[114]

'Adhere to the writings of astrologers': John Gadbury and the astrologers' response to the prodigies of the early Restoration

One important group of respondents to the *Mirabilis Annus* tracts were the astrologers who had risen into prominence with the relatively relaxed censorship of the Civil War and the Interregnum and were now, with some difficulty, trying to establish a position in the Restoration world. Some, like the best-known parliamentarian astrologers Lilly and John Booker, used their annual almanacs to disassociate themselves from the sedition of the prodigy tracts. The most elaborate response from an astrologer was from Lilly's rival John Gadbury, who had traversed the spectrum from religious radicalism in the early 1650s to staunch royalism by the Restoration – a path he would continue to the point of converting to Catholicism in the reign of James II. Gadbury's approach to the *Mirabilis Annus* controversy developed from his earlier writings on prodigies. Gadbury's 1660 *Natura Prodigiorum* was an attempt to set forth a theory of prodigy interpretation that kept prodigies as divine signs, but in a more secular way than the dominant providential approach.[115] Gadbury tried to save prodigies as political signs from the disrepute into which they had fallen through their use by all sides during the Civil War and the Interregnum. He accomplished this by relying heavily on classical, non-Christian, sources and insisting that, although prodigies were explicable through secondary causes, this did not vitiate their usefulness for divination. Gadbury's definition of a prodigy focused on unusualness rather than divine causation, or violation of the laws of nature: 'A Prodigie is a thing (generally) that comes to pass beyond the Attitude of a mans imagination, and begets in him a miraculous contemplation, yea oftentimes horror and amazement, and this by its coming to pass without his expectation or thought.'[116]

Although Gadbury believed that God was the ultimate source of prodigies, as indeed of everything else, he was at pains to emphasize that no prodigy, not even the Star of Bethlehem, was actually a violation of a law of nature.[117] God, as a constitutional sovereign, invariably worked through the established laws of nature rather than against them. 'God doth nothing contrary to the order of second causes, or the power of Nature; but doth rather act Nature in an extra-ordinary way, to shew that he hath by his overruling power a soveraignty sufficient to do what he pleaseth, and is not tied to one way or manner of working.'[118] Even the representation of complex visual images such as armies or animals in the sky, difficult to explain except as instances of divine intervention, Gadbury believed explicable by natural causes: they may be caused naturally, and are so for the most part, viz. when the temper and disposition of the air is sufficiently able to receive the impress or image of those things done on earth. And because the air is apt to receive divers images and shapes in divers parts or places thereof, these monstrous forms, and strange actions, and stories, and characters, &c. proceed from the joyning of divers forms and actions there.[119]

For Gadbury, in *Natura*, the laws of nature were not fully deterministic, but left room for divine intervention which did not violate nature's regularity.

Although Gadbury's interpretation was providentialist, he was completely uninterested in either repentance, as a proper response to a prodigy, or in the apocalypse, discredited for many royalists by its association with Fifth-Monarchist radicals. He did speak briefly, in the Address to the Reader of *Natura*, of the great changeableness of the times, and claimed that 'The order of Nature now . . . is obstructed by Monsters and Prodigies'. But these assertions were merely observations, connected with the obvious political instability of the period, and not integrated into a theory that either the last judgement was approaching or that the world was in an advanced state of decay. In fact, the greatest 'prodigy' of all for Gadbury was the Restoration, a very positive phenomenon.[120]

Gadbury argued for the meaningfulness of prodigies in basically secular and annalistic terms, claiming that the consensus of the learned supported the idea that prodigies are heralds of forthcoming disaster or great change,[121] and that observational evidence proved as much: 'if we consult History, we shall find, that there hath never been any notable Apparition or Prodigie seen in the Heavens, but it hath been attended in the sequel with some more than ordinary . . . change here on earth'.[122] The centerpiece of both *Natura* and Gadbury's *De Cometis* (1665) was a double-column table arranged chronologically, giving historical prodigies and comets in one column and the disasters which they had presaged in the other.

Since Gadbury believed that prodigies did have political relevance, the important question was who should have the right to interpret them. He fully shared the distrust, common among the Restoration elite, of authority in the hands of the uneducated or politically radical. Speaking of the three wise men who divined the meaning of the Star of Bethlehem, Gadbury explained the superiority of learned to unlearned analysis.

> Because that persons of meaner knowledge and parts are tied both by the Laws of Reason, Nature, and Nations, to give credence to those that do excel; and by this means Christ's coming would be noted the more, and believed the sooner, whereas, if any of meaner parts should have reported the same it is more than probable, it would have been the more slighted and the lesser believed.[123]

Gadbury was quite clear as to which group in society possessed the expertise to correctly interpret prodigies. This was, unsurprisingly, the group of which he himself, as well as the three magi, were members: astrologers.

The astrological orientation of Gadbury's approach to prodigies can be clearly seen in the disproportionate amount of space devoted to celestial, as opposed to terrestial, prodigies. The only non-celestial type of prodigy which Gadbury treated at length in *Natura* was the earthquake. His discussion of meteors, apparitions, and comets makes clear who the experts were:

> Those that would judge of, or be acquainted with the particular portents and significations of comets; may adhere to the writings of Astrologers; where according to the place, motion, duration, figure, and colour of all Comets, or blazing stars, they may meet with singular and experienced Aphorisms, which will be conveniently assisting to all necessary and industrious scrutinies pertaining thereunto.[124]

The relevant criteria for evaluating the significance of prodigies were also astrological, as when Gadbury discussed the significance of lunar and solar eclipses according to the astrological signs in which they occurred.[125]

Gadbury's subsequent writings on the subject of prodigies showed his position on providential interpretation of prodigies hardening in response to the *Mirabilis Annus* controversy. He became involved in the controversy in 1661, with the publication of his *A Brief Examination of that Nest of Sedition, and Phanatick Forgeries*, a rebuttal of *The Lord's Loud Call to England*. The *Brief Examination* was an attack on fraudulent prodigy claims placed in the political context of the defence of the royal government, going so far as to incorporate material likening the allegedly Anabaptist champions of the Fairford frogs story to the Pope, or 'man of sin', as perpetrators of 'lying wonders'.[126]

However, *A Brief Examination* was not a denunciation merely of fraud. It contained an argument about the nature of prodigies which differed somewhat from that of *Natura Prodigiorum*. The need to rebut *The Lord's Loud Call* led Gadbury to reject one of the key tenets of *Natura*, that of the compatibility of secondary causes with ultimate divine causation. Throughout *A Brief Examination* explanations based on secondary causes were considered sufficient for refuting arguments of divine causation. Clarke's argument, that the swampy terrain of Fairford was a sufficient explanation for the presence of the masses of frogs, was accepted as valid in a section of *A Brief Examination* actually prepared by Gadbury's friend, the heliocentrist astrologer, and by then Anglican clergyman, the Reverend Joshua Childrey.[127] Speaking of a minister who broke a vein while preaching, Gadbury stated: 'I esteem it no Judgement of God upon him, but an accident very common to men.'[128] Throughout, Gadbury, following Clarke's assumptions, asserted that only those incidents lacking *any* explanation based on secondary causes could be ascribed to divine action, thus narrowing the scope of providential activity.

A more original argument on Gadbury's part in *A Brief Examination* was to attack prodigies of judgement for their lack of universality. The death of the Oxford players could not have been a judgement upon them, as other actors in other plays had survived.[129] If those Anglicans who employed the *Book of Common Prayer* had been struck down by an angry God, why had the bookbinders who actually made the book not been also struck down?[130] If a man died after eating dinner, was this a judgement on him for dining?[131] These arguments, purposely or not, missed the entire point of providential prodigies of judgement, that they were warnings and examples. Gadbury assumed that the connection between judgement and sin should operate like a physical law, or like the law he elsewhere claimed associated comets with ensuing great changes on earth.

Gadbury's direct response to the *Mirabilis Annus* tracts was *Dies Novissimus, or Dooms-Day Not So Near as Dreaded* (1664). *Dies Novissimus* attacked apocalypticism, asserting that prodigy interpretation, astrological analyses of conjunctions and other attempts to predict the Apocalypse were both intellectually illegitimate and politically subversive. The section of *Dies Novissimus* dealing with prodigies followed *A Brief Examination* in offering explanations of such phenomena as *parelii* and the sudden drying up of rivers that did not involve direct supernatural intervention. Gadbury claimed that this refuted their claim to significance as divine prodigies.[132]

Gadbury was not alone among astrologers in his attack on prodigy interpreters as lacking specific expertise. Lilly and Booker were now desperately seeking royalist respectability. They included denunciations of the prodigy tracts in their 1662 almanacs. Booker denounced the authors of the tracts as ignorant of astronomy, and Lilly, offering his own interpretations of a recent earthquake and the drying up of the Derwent, spoke of 'imprudent judgements, being not warranted with the Authority or President of any Author who is considerable'.[133] Lilly's 1663 almanac continued the attack, presenting the authors of the tracts as divorced from any public knowledge whatsoever. 'Let us not be misled with pretended inspirations, or receive incouragement from the tempestuous fancyes of Dreams.'[134] His manuscript tract interpreting ancient prophecies as predicting Charles II's triumph over the French and the Dutch included material on how the astrological interpretation of prodigies and eclipses provided further testimomy of Charles's assured success.[135] These eminent astrologers, along with the learned royalist astrologer and spy Elias Ashmole, continued to believe in the relevance of prodigies to divination, and informal exchange of prodigy accounts among astrologers and their associates continued to take place throughout the Restoration period.[136] However, the astrologers' bid for control over prodigy interpretation ultimately failed, despite Gadbury's inclusion of prodigy interpretations in his highly politicized almanacs of the 1680s. Astrologers faced problems holding on to what they had during the Restoration era, and were unable to mount a takeover of the field of prodigies, in addition to having little expertise on terrestial prodigies. The future lay with another group of experts, the natural philosophers, and a much more radical denial of the providential tradition.

The *Mirabilis Annus* affair set the terms of the debate on the providential political import of prodigies for the rest of the seventeenth century. Providentialist prodigy interpretation was no longer inseparably united to religious orthodoxy. The compilation of accounts of prodigies in a providential context had become firmly identified with opposition to the Restoration State and the Church of England. Defenders of the regime, including astrologers, government censors and journalists, as well as its satirists had attacked *Mirabilis Annus* and related tracts themselves, and were mounting an assault on providential prodigy gathering as such. The defence of the Restoration order against providential prodigies did not stop with these groups and their fundamentally negative arguments. The *Mirabilis Annus* and subsequent controversies would also play a central, although largely hidden, role in the establishment of Restoration science.

Notes

1 Stuart Clark, *Thinking with Demons: The Idea of Witchcraft in Early Modern Europe* (Oxford: Clarendon Press, 1997), pp. 619–33, discusses the association of kings with miracles and wonders, emphasizing the Christian rather than the classical context.

2 *The Man in the Moon*, no. 39 (January 16–23, 1650); *Royall Diurnall*, no. 3 (March 4–11, 1650); Henry Townshend, *The Diary of Henry Townshend of Elmley Lovett. 1640–1663*, ed. J. Willis Bund (London: Worcester History Society, 1920), vol. 1: 26; and Isabella Twysden, 'The diary of Isabella Twysden', *Archaelogia Cantiniana*, 51 (1939): 129–30. For another royalist catalogue of prodigies demonstrating God's wrath against England following the execution, see C.H. Josten, ed., *Elias Ashmole (1617–1692): His Autobiographical and Historical Notes, his Correspondence, and Other Contemporary Sources Related to his Life and Work*, 5 vols (Oxford: Clarendon Press, 1966), 2: 485–6. For a parliamentarian attack on a royalist prodigy of the time, see *The Moderate Mercury*, no. 4 (June 21–28): 13–14.

3 *A Miracle of Miracles* (London, 1649) and *The Royall Legacies* (London, 1649), 3. Belief in the healing power of Charles's blood persisted into the eighteenth century; see Ralph Thoresby, *The Diary of Ralph Thoresby*, ed. Rev. Joseph Hunter (London, 1830), vol. 2: 237–8 and Hearne, *Remarks and Collections of Thomas Hearne*, vol. 3: 491.

4 'It is Credibly reported, that in the Castle yard where Sir Charls Lucas and Sir George Lisle were shot to death, not any grass doth since that time grow within 4 yards round the place: though all over the yard beside; a thing in my judgement very miraculous'. *The Man in the Moon*, no. 17 (August 8–15, 1649).

5 For Suetonian prodigies on the fate of both Charles I and Charles II,

see Abraham Cowley, *Poemata Latina* (London, 1668), pp. 316–17, and Jacob Allestry, 'Some Observations' (Clark Library MS), p. 234.

6 Stephen Batman, *The Doome, Warning All Men to the Judgement* (London, 1581), 'To the Gentle Reader'.

7 Flavius Josephus, *The Jewish War*, VI, Ch. 300, included references to a comet shaped like a broadsword, a cow giving birth to a lamb, and battles in the sky. Thomas Jackson claimed that Josephus's works were 'now more common in our English language than the records of Chronicles of our own nation.' Jackson, *A Treatise Concerning the Signes of the Times*, p. 42. For Josephus's popularity in early modern Europe, which exceeded that of all other ancient Greek language historians, particularly in vernacular translation, see Peter Burke, 'A survey of the popularity of ancient historians, 1450–1700', *History and Theory*, 5 (1966): 136–9. As well as editions and translations of the works of Josephus himself, English people also had available an extensive adaptation of his narrative, ascribed to 'Joseph Ben Gorion', *A Compendious and Most Marveilous History of the Jewes Commonwealth* (London, 1558), which went through twelve editions between 1558 and 1615.

8 *A Blazyng Starre seen in the West at Totneis in Devonshire, on the Fourteenth of this instant November, 1642. Wherin is Manifested how Master Ralph Ashley, a Deboyst Cavalier, Attemted to Ravish a Young Virgin, the Daughter of Mr. Adam Fisher, Inhabiting neare the said Towne. Also how at that Instant, a Fearful Comet Appeared, to the Terrour and Amazement of all the Country Thereabouts. Likewise Declaring how He Persisting in his Damnable Attemt, was Struck with a Flaming Sword, which Issued from the Comet, so that he Dyed a Fearfull Example to al his Fellow Cavaliers* (London, 1642), pp. 4–5. Friedman, *The Battle of Frogs and Fairfords Flies*, pp. 31–2, discusses this incident, but by omitting the political affiliations of the persons involved he misses the point.

9 *A Great Wonder in Heaven* (London, 1642), p. 6; *The New Yeares Wonder* (London, 1642), p. 8. See also John Green, 'The diary of John Green', ed. E.M. Symons, *English Historical Review*, 43 (1928): 391.

10 *A Declaration of a Strange and Wonderful Monster* (London, 1646), pp. 7–8.

11 *A Perfect Diurnall*, no. 34 (July 29–August 5, 1650). Prophetic infants were not new, see Walsham, *Providence in Early Modern England*, p. 207.

12 Francis Bacon, *Novum Organum*, ed. Thomas Fowler (Oxford: Clarendon Press, 1878), pp. 216–17 (Aphorism XLVI).

13 For an excellent examination of the authoritarian roots of Bacon-organized natural philosophy, see Julian Martin, *Francis Bacon, the*

State, and the Reform of Natural Philosophy (Cambridge: Cambridge University Press, 1992).

14 Katherine Park, 'Bacon's "Enchanted Glass" ', *Isis*, 75 (1984): 290–302.

15 The most exhaustive discussion of this aspect of the Interregnum is Charles Webster, *The Great Instauration: Science, Medicine, and Reform, 1626–1660* (London: Duckworth, 1975). For the Hartlib circle specifically, see Stephen Clucas, 'Samuel Hartlib's Ephemerides 1635–59, and the pursuit of scientific and philosophical manuscripts: the religious ethos of an intelligencer', *The Seventeenth Century*, 6 (1991): 33–55.

16 CUL Dd.III.64, no. 61. On the Poole project, see Thomas, *Religion and the Decline of Magic*, pp. 95–6; Winship, *Seers of God*, pp. 60–2, and William Lamont, *Richard Baxter and the Millenium: Protestant Imperialism and the English Revolution* (London: Croome Helm, 1979), pp. 30–1.

17 Letter from Matthew Poole to Richard Baxter, August 27, 1657, in DWL Richard Baxter Correspondence, 4: 248. For Baxter's own role in circulating supernatural and prodigious stories, see William E.A. Axon, 'Welsh folk-lore of the seventeenth century', *Y Cymmrodor*, 21 (1908): 113–31.

18 CUL MS Dd.III.64, no. 62: 'Of Mr. Poole's Design'. For Beale's interest in the Civil War prodigies, see Beale to Hartlib, June 8, 1657, Hartlib Papers 25/5/14A (Sheffield) and an extract from a previous letter preserved in the Royal Society Boyle Letters 7, no. 4.

19 Beale to Hartlib, August 24, 1657, Hartlib Papers 31/1/35A–B (Sheffield).

20 For Hartlib's awareness of Poole's project, see his *Ephemerides*. For references connecting Hartlib to the circulation of manuscript material on prodigies, see Hartlib Papers, 18/1/42–3; the Preface to Mather, *An Essay for Recording Illustrious Providences*, and Boyle, *Works*, vol. 6: 127.

21 Boyle, *Works*, vol. 6: 430.

22 CUL MS Oo.VI.115.

23 Hartlib Papers 52/16–17 (Sheffield) and Poole to Baxter, February 3, 1658/59 in DWL Baxter Correspondence 2: 305.

24 A letter dated after the Restoration found in two copies in the CUL and recounting two ghost stories may be related to the Poole project but it does not speak of recording the stories or making them public, and indicates that if it persisted after the Restoration the project had declined to a private exchange of anecdotes among like-minded individuals. 'Of Illustrious Providences from Bater-Sea, Nov. 14 1661', CUL Dd.III.64 fos 150–1 and Dd.III.63 fos 68–9.

25 Preface to Increase Mather, *An Essay for the Recording of Illustrious*

Providences (Boston, New England, 1684); and DWL Baxter Correspondence I:217. For discussion of Mather's work see Peter Lockwood Rumsey, *Acts of God and the People, 1620–1730*, Studies in
Religion no. 2 (Ann Arbor: UMI Research Press, 1984), pp. 32–3,
107–9; Robert Middlekauf, *The Mathers: Three Generations of Puritan
Intellectuals 1596–1728* (New York: Oxford University Press, 1971),
pp. 143–8; Hall, *Worlds of Wonder, Days of Judgement*, pp. 83–5, 88–90;
and Winship, *Seers of God*, pp. 65–9. Mather distributed his work in
England. See Anthony Wood, *The Life and Times of Anthony Wood.*,
ed. Andrew Clark, 5 vols (Oxford: Oxford Historical Society,
1891–1907), vol. 3: 349n. During the political crisis of Charles II's
reign, Mather would be associated with politically subversive providential prodigy belief by Sir Roger L'Estrange's Tory periodical the
Observator. For Turner, see chapter 4, below.

26 Edmund Ludlow, *A Voyce From the Watch Tower*, ed. A.B. Worden.
Camden Society Fourth Series, vol. 21 (London: Camden Society,
1978), p. 287. For efforts to interpret this favourably, see Henry Bold,
*On the Thunder Happening after the Solemnity of the Coronation of
Charles the II* (London, 1661), and Jacob Allestry, 'Some Observations'
(Clark Library MS), pp. 294–6. For a similar attempt to interpret positively a storm at a great royal event while mocking belief in omens,
see a letter to the future Archbishop of Canterbury William Sancroft
from Thomas Holdsworth, an English observer at the wedding of
Charles's sister Henrietta to the Duke of Orleans, Oxford, Bodeleian,
Tanner MS vol. 49, fo. 96. Even the simple news pamphlet *An Exact
and True Relation of the Wonderfull Whirle-Wind* (London, 1660) went
to great lengths to demonstrate that the destructive wind was actually a good sign for King Charles, blowing away 'Ayres of Division
and Contention', pp. 2–3.

27 These tracts, and the reaction they provoked, are briefly discussed
in Thomas, *Religion and the Decline of Magic*, pp. 95–6; W.T. Hart,
Index Expurgatorius Anglicanus (London, 1872–78), pp. 183–8; J.G.
Muddiman, *The King's Journalist 1659–1689: Studies in the Reign of
Charles II* (London: Bodley Head, 1923), pp. 132–3, 153–9; Bryan Ball,
*A Great Expectation: Eschatological Thought in English Protestantism to
1660* (Leiden: E.J. Brill, 1975), pp. 111–14; Richard Greaves, *Deliver
Us From Evil: The Radical Underground in Britain 1660–1663* (New
York: Oxford University Press, 1986), pp. 213–16; C.E. Whiting,
*Studies in English Puritanism from the Restoration to the Revolution
1660–1688*, Publications for the Church Historical Society New Series
no. 5 (London: Society for the Promotion of Christian Knowledge,
1931), pp. 546–51; John Leonard, 'To warn proud cities: a topical
reference in Milton's airy knights simile (*Paradise Lost* 2533–8)',

Renaissance and Reformation, 19 (1995): 63–71; and J. Walker, 'The censorship of the press during the reign of Charles II', *History*, 35 (1950): 232–3. Edward N. Hooker, 'The purpose of Dryden's *Annus Mirabilis*', *Huntington Library Quarterly*, 10 (1946): 49–67, and Michael McKeon, *Politics and Poetry in Restoration England* (Cambridge, MA: Harvard University Press, 1975), pp. 194–6, discuss the tracts as part of the context of John Dryden's poem *Annus Mirabilis*.

28 For analyses of the controversy over the Fairford frogs, see Friedman, *The Battle of Frogs and Fairford's Flies*, pp. 248–53, and Andrew Warmington, 'Frogs, toads, and the Restoration in a Gloucestershire village', *Midland History*, 14 (1989): 30–42. Warmington ascribes the incident to the tension between small, lower-class, gathered churches, on the one side, and Puritan magistrates making their peace with the Restoration, on the other. His extension of the story to claim widespread opposition to the Restoration order in the area seems questionable, given that the anti-sectarian mob initiated the events by rabbling the sectarian minority.

29 This was not Chapman's first venture into prodigy tract publishing. In the late 1650s he had published two short tracts entitled *A Monstrous Birth* (London, 1657) and *A True Relation of a Very Strange and Wonderfull Thing that was Heard in the Air, October the Twelfth* (London, 1658). For the radical 'Confederacy' press of this period see Greaves, *Deliver Us From Evil*, pp. 207–25; and Walker, 'Censorship of the press', pp. 230–1. Studies of individual 'Confederates' include that of Chapman in Leona Rostenberg, *Literary, Political, Scientific, Religious, and Legal Publishing, Printing and Bookselling in England 1551–1700: Twelve Studies* (New York: Burt Franklin, 1965), pp. 203–36; 'Giles Calvert's publishing career', *Journal of the Friends' Historical Society*, 35 (1938): 45–9; Maureen Bell, 'Elizabeth Calvert and the "confederates"', *Publishing History*, 32 (1994): 5–49; and T.J. Crist, Francis Smith and the opposition press in England, 1660–1688, unpublished Ph.D. dissertation, Cambridge University, 1977.

30 Danvers's career, including his involvement in the production of the *Mirabilis Annus* tracts, is recounted in Richard Greaves, *Saints and Rebels: Seven Nonconformists in Stuart England* (Macon: Mercer University Press, 1985), pp. 156–77; and for Jessey's, see B.R. White, 'Henry Jessey in the great rebellion', in R. Buick Knox, ed., *Reformation, Conformity, and Dissent: Essays in Honour of Geoffrey Nuttall* (London: Epworth Press, 1977), pp. 132–53.

31 For production of *The Lord's Loud Call*, see Crist, Francis Smith and the opposition press, pp. 12–15.

32 The royalists John Gadbury and Anthony Wood, in their denunciations of *The Lord's Loud Call*, assumed as general knowledge that

Jessey was the author. See Gadbury, *A Brief Examination of that Nest of Sedition and Phanatick Forgeries* (London, 1661), and Anthony Wood, *History and Antiquities of the University of Oxford*, ed. John Gutch (Oxford, 1792), pp. 703–8. The earliest biography of Jessey, Edward Whiston's *The Life and Death of Mr. Henry Jessey* (?London, 1671), did not explicitly mention the still-sensitive subject of the prodigy tracts, but did claim that Jessey 'ever took special notice of the outgoings of God in all his providences' including 'the signs and wonders which he works in heaven above and earth below' (p. 35). Another early pro-Baptist writer, Thomas Crosby, included *The Lord's Loud Call* in a list of Jessey's works in *The History of the English Baptists*, 4 vols (London, 1738), vol. 1: 322–3, although he did not discuss it in the body of the text. Modern scholars accepting Jessey's authorship include Whiting, *Studies in English Puritanism*, p. 546, Thomas, *Religion and the Decline of Magic*, p. 95, and Walsham, *Providence in Early Modern England*, p. 68.

33 See the examination of Jessey in SP 29/45/28.
34 *The Lord's Loud Call to England* (London, 1660), pp. 33–42, 13–29.
35 *Lord's Loud Call*, pp. 3–6.
36 *Lord's Loud Call*, p. 43.
37 *Lord's Loud Call*, 'Epistle Dedicatory'.
38 *Lord's Loud Call*, 'Epistle Dedicatory'.
39 *Lord's Loud Call*, p. 44, incorrectly paginated as 35.
40 *British Library*, Thomason Collection 669, fo. 25 (167).
41 *Mercurius Publicus*, no. 33 (August 9–16, 1660).
42 For Clarke, see Warmington, 'Frogs, toads, and the restoration in a Gloucestershire village', 36–7.
43 Robert Clarke, *The Lying Wonders, or Rather the Wonderful Lyes* (London, 1660), 'Epistle Dedicatory'.
44 Clarke, *Lying Wonders*, 'To the Reader'.
45 Clarke, *Lying Wonders*, pp. 13–17.
46 Clarke, *Lying Wonders*, p. 8.
47 Clarke, *Lying Wonders*, p. 8.
48 Clarke, *Lying Wonders*, p. 10.
49 Clarke, *Lying Wonders*, p. 4.
50 Clarke, *Lying Wonders*, p. 4.
51 SP 29/45/74; 29/45/117; and Francis Smith, *An Account of the Injurious Proceedings of Sir George Jeffreys Kt., Late Recorder of London, Against Francis Smith, Bookseller* (London, 1680), p. 9. The production and distribution of the *Mirabilis Annus* tracts and the prosecution of those involved is discussed in Crist, Francis Smith and the opposition press, pp. 19–33.
52 SP 29/45/28.

53 SP 29/43/130. Cokayne already had two printed works, both sermons unrelated to prodigies: *Flesh Expiring, and the Spirit Inspiring in the New Earth* (London, 1648) was printed by and for Giles Calvert; and *Divine Astrology* (London, 1658) for Brewster; both Calvert and Brewster were later involved in the *Mirabilis Annus* affair.

54 SP 29/45/28.

55 DWL MS 12.40 (Blackmore Papers), Item no. 5: 'A Brief Narrative of an Apparition of a great number of horsemen seen on a common called Kefen-y-cord near unto Montgomery upon the 20th day of December 1661'. This account appeared in very similar wording in *Mirabilis Annus Secundus*, pp. 48–9.

56 *Mirabilis Annus*, 'Preface'.

57 *Mirabilis Annus*, 'Preface'.

58 *Mirabilis Annus*, pp. 59–60.

59 *Mirabilis Annus*, pp. 1–2.

60 *Mirabilis Annus*, p. 52.

61 *Mirabilis Annus*, p. 44.

62 *Mirabilis Annus*, pp. 21–2.

63 *Mirabilis Annus*, p. 50.

64 *Mirabilis Annus*, p. 15.

65 *Mirabilis Annus*, pp. 24–5.

66 *Mirabilis Annus* did not repeat the Fairford frogs story, but it did include that of the Brookington clerk's daughter struck dead for mocking dissenters (pp. 62–3).

67 *Mirabilis Annus*, p. 15.

68 *Mirabilis Annus*, p. 15.

69 *Mirabilis Annus*, p. 36.

70 Frank Engehausen, 'Luther und die Wunderzeichen: Eine englische Übersetzung der Adventpostille im Jahr 1661', *Archiv für Reformationsgeschichte* (*Archive for Reformation History*), 84 (1993): 276–88, argues that a translated work of Martin Luther, *The Signs of Christ's Coming* (London, 1661), which appeared with no publisher or translator indicated, was associated with the *Mirabilis Annus* tracts. The work (pp. 4–5, 8–9) expounded the providential theory of prodigies and attacked those who would reduce them to natural phenomena.

71 *Mirabilis Annus*, 'Preface'.

72 *Mirabilis Annus Secundus*, pp. 71–2.

73 *Mirabilis Annus Secundus*, 'Preface'.

74 *Mirabilis Annus Secundus*, 'Preface'.

75 *Mirabilis Annus Secundus*, 'Preface'.

76 *Mirabilis Annus Secundus*, p. 9.

77 *Mirabilis Annus Secundus*, pp. 61–2.

78 *Mirabilis Annus Secundus*, p. 45.

79 *Mirabilis Annus Secundus*, pp. 52–3.

80 *Mirabilis Annus Secundus*, pp. 49–50.

81 *Mirabilis Annus Secundus*, p. 64 and William Hull, *Benjamin Furly and Quakerism in Rotterdam* (Swarthmore: Swarthmore College, 1941), pp. ??–4. For a transcription of the words, and a slightly different narrative of their appearance, see Gerard Croese, *The General History of the Quakers* (London, 1696), vol. 2: 30. Another account with a somewhat different transcription is in Ashmole MS 423, fo. 241 (Oxford, Bodeleian). Benjamin Furly, the Rotterdam Quaker and friend of John Locke, who owned copies of the *Mirabilis Annus* tracts, recalled this prophecy in 1689, and enquired of Locke concerning 'the *Mirabilis Annus* 1663'. This is the only reference I have found to a fourth *Mirabilis Annus* tract, and Furly was probably misremembering. See William Hull, *Benjamin Furly and Quakerism in Rotterdam*, p. 23; *The Correspondence of John Locke*, ed. E.S. DeBeere, 8 vols (Oxford: Clarendon Press, 1976–1989), vol. 3: 572; and *Bibliotheca Furleiana*. Croese was probably working from the copy of the prophecy written by the Quaker John Coughen and held in Furly's library, which would explain the differences between his account and that in *Mirabilis Annus Secundus*.

82 Fifteen of the 28 accounts of prodigies in the sky in *Mirabilis Annus Secundus II* involved armies, weapons or fighting, as compared to 8 out of the 54 in *Mirabilis Annus* and 19 out of the 63 in *Mirabilis Annus Secundus*. For another apocalyptic and military series of prodigies, see *Mather Papers*, pp. 175–6.

83 *Mirabilis Annus Secundus II*, p. 26. Another tract coming out at this time which used a prodigy to attack the government was Owen Lloyd's, *The Panther-Prophecy* (London, 1661), which combined an account of an army in the sky with an old prophecy. For a possible connection between the publishing of *The Panther-Prophecy* and the *Mirabilis Annus* tracts see SP 29/62/36.

84 Samuel Parker, *History of His Own Time* (London, 1730), p. 18.

85 SP 29/81/73 (CSPD incorrectly lists the 'Seven Years Prodigies', instead of *Second Part of the Second Years Prodigies*), 29/43/7,8,9, 29/41/41, 29/43/9. For a provincial, middle-class, dissenting owner of *The Lord's Loud Call* and the *Mirabilis Annus* tracts, see Samuel Jeake, *An Astrological Diary of the Seventeenth Century*, ed. Michael Hunter and Annabel Gregory (Oxford: Clarendon Press, 1988), p. 94. Jeake also verbally circulated apocalyptic prodigy stories among dissenters, p. 87.

86 Ludlow, *A Voyce from the Watch Tower*, pp. 292–4. Ludlow admired Jessey; see A.B. Worden's Introduction to *A Voyce*, p. 10.

87 *Mirabilis Annus Secundus*, p. 48 and *Mirabilis Annus Secundus II*, pp. 32–5. Ludlow, *A Voyce*, pp. 292, 306–7.

88 Ralph Josselin, *The Diary of Ralph Josselin*, ed. Alan Macfarlane, Records of Social and Economic History New Series no. 3 (London: Oxford University Press for the British Academy, 1976), p. 482; *The Diary and Correspondence of Dr. John Worthington*, ed. James Crossley (Chetham Society, 1847–1886), vol. 1: 280, 291; vol. 2: 66, 71. Some of the prodigies discussed were also related in the pamphlet *Strange News from the West* (London, 1661).

89 *Lord's Loud Call*, pp. 1–2; and Anthony Wood, *History and Antiquities of the University of Oxford*, ed. John Gutch (Oxford, 1792), pp. 703–8.

90 Wood, *Life and Times*, vol. 2: 379.

91 Wood, *Life and Times*, vol. 1: 437.

92 Philip Henry, *Diary of Philip Henry*, ed. Matthew Henry Lee (London: Kegan, Paul, Trench & Co., 1882), pp. 101, 104–7. For another case of a dissenting minister reading and discussing prodigy accounts, see Henry Newcome, *Diary of the Reverend Henry Newcome*, ed. Thomas Heywood, Chetham Society no. 18 (London: Chetham Society, 1849), pp. 136, 157.

93 San Marino, Huntington Library, Hastings MS 15179, calendared in HMC Hastings MSS, IV, 121.

94 *Mather Papers*, pp. 177–8, 185, 194–7, 198–9, 205–6, 494–5. For the continuation of concern over prodigies among New England ministers after the *Mirabilis Annus* affair, see *Mather Papers*, pp. 126–7.

95 Petrus Serrarius, *An Awakening Warning* (Amsterdam, 1662), p. 20. Serrarius maintained an interest in prodigies and the approaching millenium, eventually becoming one of the few Christian followers of the Jewish 'Messiah' Sabbatai Sevi. See Richard Popkin, 'Hartlib, Dury and the Jews', in Mark Greengrass, Michael Leslie, and Timothy Raylor, eds, *Samuel Hartlib and Universal Reformation: Studies in Intellectual Communication* (Cambridge: Cambridge University Press, 1994), p. 133. For the relationships between Serrarius, born and educated in England, and Jessey and the Hartlib circle, see Ernestine G.E. van der Wall, 'The Amsterdam millenarian Petrus Serrarius (1600–99) and the Anglo-Dutch circle of Philo-Judaists', in J. Van den Berg and Ernestine G.E. van der Wall, eds, *Jewish–Christian Relations in the Seventeenth Century: Studies and Documents*, International Archives of the History of Ideas no. 119 (Dordrecht: Kluwer Academic Publishers, 1988), pp. 73–95. Serrarius was also a regular correspondent of Henry Oldenburg, the coordinator of information for the Royal Society. *The Correspondence of Henry Oldenburg*, ed. A. Rupert Hall and Marie Boas Hall, 11 vols (Madison: University of Wisconsin Press; London: Mansell, 1965–77), vol. 3: 446–7.

96 Richard Baxter, *Reliquiae Baxterianae*, ed. Matthew Sylvester (London, 1696), pp. 432–3. See also Baxter, *The Certainty of the World of Spirits* (London, 1691), pp. 163–4; *Heywood Diary*, vol. 3: 20.

97 *Kingdom's Intelligencer* (October 14–21, 1661). *Mirabilis Annus Secundus* (p. 48) claimed that one of its prodigies had stood up to an investigation by JPs. See also Ludlow, *A Voyce*, p. 292.

98 *Mirabilis Annus Secundus*, p. 45.

99 *Mercurius Publicus*, no. 27 (July 2–9, 1663): 429. For evidence of a similar certificate concerning another case from *Mirabilis Annus* being circulated in manuscript form, see White Kennett, *A Register and Chronicle Ecclesiastical and Civil* (London, 1728), p. 453.

100 *The Intelligencer*, no. 7 (October 12, 1663): 7.

101 SP Entry Book 5, p. 39.

102 For these efforts, see Crist, Francis Smith and the opposition press, pp. 23–32, and SP 29/38 (56, 57, 58) 29/39 (132), 29/41 (40, 41, 42), 29/43 (7, 8, 9, 30, 31, 130), 29/45 (28, 74, 75), 29/47 (55), 29/56 (135), 29/75 (117), 29/81 (73, I, II, III, IV), and 44/51 (p. 39), as well as *Calendar of the Clarendon State Papers*, vol. 5: 64–5.

103 SP 29/45/74–5.

104 SP 29/45/28. Jessey was probably telling the truth, at least as regards *Mirabilis Annus Secundus*, which praised Presbyterians, but did not specifically mention Baptists. *Mirabilis Annus Secundus*, p. 87.

105 Davis Lloyd, *Wonders no Miracles* (London, 1666), pp. 11–12. Eamon Duffy, 'Valentine Greatrakes, the Irish stroker: miracle, science, and orthodoxy in Restoration England', in Keith Robbins, ed., *Religion and Humanism*, Studies in Church History no. 17 (Oxford: Basil Blackwell, 1981), pp. 251–73, gives an analysis of the Greatrakes case stressing the potential political danger of claiming a direct relation to God.

106 SP 29/120/24.

107 SP 29/277/27, 27i.

108 SP 29/275/154. For other prodigies deemed of interest to government, see SP 29/51/5 and 29/309/158.

109 Roger L'Estrange, *A Modest Plea both for the Caveat and the Author of It* (London, 1661), pp. 11–15; *Truth and Loyalty Vindicated* (London, 1662), pp. 58–9; and *Considerations and Proposals in Order to the Regulation of the Press* (London, 1663), p. 16.

110 There was some satire that employed ridicule of providential prodigy belief to attack the Restoration regime. For an example see the anonymous *On the Prorogation*, in *POAS*, vol. I: 84. The target was more the Cavalier Parliament, depicted as credulous concerning the prodigious import of commonplace events such as 'Moon shone at midnight and at noon the sun', than providential prodigy belief itself, however.

111 Samuel Butler, *Hudibras*, ed. John Wilders (Oxford, 1967), p. 165.

112 Butler, *Hudibras*, p. 102. It is unclear if this is a reference to the actual *A Blazyng Star Seene in the West*, which as a parliamentarian pamphlet would have been an appropriate satirical target.

113 *A True and Perfect Account of the Miraculous Sea Monster* (London, 1674), p. 8.

114 *A Strange and True Relation*, p. 5.

115 Gadbury claimed that his work on prodigies had been carried on for years, and much of it had previously appeared anonymously in *Miraculum Signum Coeleste: A Discourse of those Miraculous Prodigies, that have been Seen since the Birth of our Blessed Lord and Saviour Jesus Christ with a Chronological Note of such Eminent Accidents, Which have Immediately Ensued the Appearance of Every of Them* (np, 1658). Gadbury claimed that this work, much less royalist than *Natura Prodigiorum*, had been pirated. *Miraculum Signum* was more sceptical of the prodigies surrounding the execution of Charles I and, written before Gadbury's break with his teacher, Lilly, more friendly to the commonwealth astrologers Lilly and Booker. *Miraculum Signum Coeleste* (p. 23) refers to the 'the Learned Mr. Lilly' whereas the same passage in *Natura Prodigiorum* (p. 35), published after the beginning of Gadbury's extremely bitter feud with Lilly, refers to him simply as 'one'. On the headless body of Charles I hovering over Whitehall after his execution, compare *Miraculum Signum Coeleste* (p. 12) with the same passage in *Natural Prodigiorum*. However, the clean-up of passages that had become problematic after the Restoration was incomplete – a reference to bees as 'those monarchical and rarely wel-governed creatures' (*Miraculum Signum Coeleste*, p. 7) was left unchanged in *Natura Prodigiorum* (p. 10). Another edition of *Natura Prodigiorum* came out in 1665. The only change was an updating of the table of prodigies and associated events to cover the elapsed time since the first edition.

116 John Gadbury, *Natura Prodigiorum* (London, 1660), p. 4.

117 Gadbury, *Natura*, p. 27.

118 Gadbury, *Natura*, p. 27.

119 Gadbury, *Natura*, p. 158.

120 Gadbury, *Natura*, 'Dedication'. *Natura Prodigiorum* was dedicated to the royalist hero General George Monk, a leader in bringing about the Restoration.

121 Gadbury, *Natura*, p. 3.

122 Gadbury, *Natura*, p. 37.

123 Gadbury, *Natura*, pp. 29–30.

124 Gadbury, *Natura*, p. 101.

125 Gadbury, *Natura*, pp. 107–21.

126 John Gadbury, *A Brief Examination of that Nest of Sedition, and Pha-natick Forgeries* (London, 1661), p. 23.

127 Gadbury, *A Brief Examination*, pp. 22–4. Gadbury later paid tribute to his friend after Childrey's death in his almanac *Ephemeris, or a Diary Astronomical and Astrological, For the Year of Our Lord 1695* (London, 1695), 'August'. For Childrey's and Gadbury's earlier roles in a controversy over the providential interpretation of solar eclipses, see William E. Burns, ' "The terriblest eclipse that hath been seen in our days": Black Monday and the debate on astrology during the interregnum', in Margaret J. Osler, ed., *Rethinking the Scientific Revolution* (Cambridge: Cambridge University Press, 2000), pp. 137–52.

128 Gadbury, *Brief Examination*, p. 8.

129 Gadbury, *Brief Examination*, p. 7.

130 Gadbury, *Brief Examination*, pp. 4–5.

131 Gadbury, *Brief Examination*, p. 9.

132 John Gadbury, *Dies Novissimus, or Dooms-Day not so Near as Dreaded* (London, 1664), pp. 18–27. Gadbury alluded (p. 27) to Childrey's recently published *Britannia Baconica* in explaining the prodigy of the sudden drying up of the river Derwent by invoking a recent frost.

133 John Booker, *Telescopium Uranicum 1662* (London, 1662), 'Concern-ing Elections'; and William Lilly, *Merlini Anglici Ephemeris 1662* (London, 1662), 'To The Reader'.

134 Lilly, *Merlini Anglici Ephemeris 1663* 'To the Reader'.

135 Ashmole MS 371, section III (Oxford, Bodeleian).

136 For Ashmole's interest in prodigies and his collecting prodigy accounts during this period, see Ashmole MSS 242, nos 27 and 32, and 423, fo. 282 (Oxford, Bodeleian), and Josten, *Ashmole*, vol. 4: 1434, 1667, 1701, 1725, 1741–42, 1855–56.

2

'A kind of philosophy-office': Restoration science and the regulation of prodigies

An institutionalized culture of natural philosophy closely associated with the State and the 'gentlemanly' social elite emerged in the 1660s. Although there had been much important work done in natural philosophy in the previous decade, the Restoration saw the establishment of continuing institutions with a high cultural profile, most prominently the Royal Society and the periodicals associated with it, *Philosophical Transactions* and *Philosophical Collections*. Institutional natural philosophy became a permanent cultural presence, whether as a pastime for aristocratic and even royal virtuosos or as a target for satire, and began to include prodigies under its jurisdiction. In this chapter I examine the activities of the Royal Society and its fellows from the establishment of the Society in 1661 through to the early eighteenth century, as well as of the societies corresponding with the Royal Society, the Oxford Philosophical Society and the Dublin Philosophical Society. Beyond the membership of these organizations, I examine some English natural philosophers who corresponded with the Society, identified themselves with its mission and were published in its journals, but were not fellows, such as Joshua Childrey and Samuel Colepresse.

Much recent – and controversial – scholarly work on late seventeenth-century science in England has treated the founding of the Royal Society as part of the creation of new forms of authority following the shocking, albeit temporary, overthrow of Church, aristocracy and king in the Civil War and the Interregnum. Peter Dear and Brian Vickers have examined this through the rhetorical analysis of natural philosophical experimental and programmatic texts, Simon Schaffer and Steven Shapin have approached the issue on the level of scientific practice, and James Jacob and Margaret Jacob on the level of the political and religious ideology of leading figures.[1] None of these scholars has looked specifically at the treatment of prodigies by the organized natural philosophers of the Restoration, yet it was in this area that the issue of the authority of natural philosophers and its relation to political authority was most explicit.

Natural philosophy and the anti-providential programme: John Spencer's *Discourse Concerning Prodigies*

During and after the *Mirabilis Annus* controversy, natural philosophers not only attacked politically destabilizing providential prodigy interpretation but went further to claim that they themselves were the proper arbiters of the meaning of prodigies. The strongest statement of this claim, however, was not made by a natural philosopher, but by a Cambridge scholar of biblical antiquity, John Spencer (1630–93). Spencer articulated both the claim of natural philosophers and of institutions of natural philosophy in his 1663 *Discourse Concerning Prodigies*.[2] At that time, he was a fellow of Corpus Christi College, one of the few scholars able to make a successful career at early Restoration Cambridge without a record of support for the monarchy during the Civil War and the Interregnum.[3] In the zealously Anglican environment of Restoration Cambridge, Spencer was noted for charity to Nonconformist ministers and had some acquaintance with Latitudinarian clergy, particularly the future Archbishop of Canterbury Thomas Tenison, also a fellow of Corpus Christi, who he made his executor.[4]

Spencer's was the only response to the *Mirabilis Annus* material to compare with Gadbury's in length and complexity of argument, but, unlike Gadbury, Spencer did not engage the *Mirabilis Annus* prodigies directly, keeping to the highly theoretical level. However, he did place his work firmly in the context of recent controversies. Explaining his reasons for writing on the subject, Spencer claimed:

That which further engaged my thoughts upon this argument, was a consideration of the seasonableness thereof. We have been so late perswayded by three or four several impressions of Books (as there never wanted those which would farme the weaknesse and easiness of the multitude) that England is grown Africa, and presents us every year (since the return of his Majesty) with a new scene of monstrous and strange sights, and that our lot is fallen into an Age of Wonders; and all held forth to the People (like black clouds before a storm) the harbingers of some strange and unusual plagues approaching in the State.[5]

Prodigy writers, in pursuit of their own political and economic ends, and with the support of popular credulity, had made Restoration England into a monstrous state. Spencer wanted to dispel this credulity. However, he was not primarily concerned with denying the reality of specific prodigies, a task accomplished by others such as Clarke, but with the more radical project of entirely denying the relevance of prodigies to religious and political issues.

Spencer used several strategies to discredit providential prodigy belief. One obvious one was to generalize the royalist–Anglican interpretation of the *Mirabilis Annus* affair into an assertion that providential prodigy belief contributed to social discord and resistance to rightly constituted authority. Although Spencer claimed that rulers in ancient pagan societies used diviners to uphold their rule by manufacturing oracles, he saw the prodigy writers of his own time as opponents, not supporters, of authority.[6] Those offering prodigious evidence were therefore shown to belong to politically rebellious groups, and as such they were contrasted with the ruling and authoritative group.

How mean a value and regard shall the issues of the severest debates, and the Commands of Authority find, if every pitifull Prodigy-monger have credit enough with the People, to blast them, by telling them that heaven frowns upon them, and that God writes his displeasure against them, in black and visible characters, when some sad Accident befalls the complyers with them?[7]

The political context of Spencer's critique of prodigy belief was particularly evident when he linked prodigy belief to melancholy, apocalypticism and 'new and impracticable Ideas of government'.[8] He endorsed the censorship of writings on prodigies, along with astrological predictions and old prophecies, such materials being illusionary lights leading people astray, 'ignes fatui leading to the boggs of sedition'.[9]

Given the Christian context of Restoration thought, however, merely showing that the providential interpretation of prodigies was socially disruptive was insufficient. Spencer needed to go beyond this pragmatic argument to demonstrate the theological error made by believers in prodigies. Like Clarke and Gadbury, Spencer did this by eliminating the middle ground between ordinary events and miracles which prodigies had formerly occupied. He kept the traditional threefold distinction between natural, preternatural and supernatural wonders, but put it to different use.[10] Natural prodigies, such as earthquakes and *parelii*, could be traced back to a particular cause. Supernatural prodigies were miracles, and, following a standard (although not universal) Protestant line, Spencer asserted that miracles had ceased after the first few centuries of Christianity. For Spencer, preternatural events, such as monstrous fish and battles in the sky, were not, as they had been for earlier writers, above and beyond the ordinary course of nature, but natural or diabolical events the causes of which were not known. By claiming that prodigies were the result of God's direct action, therefore, prodigy-mongers were claiming that they were miracles, and, thus, aligning themselves with Roman Catholicism.[11] Using the common and controversial Anglican device of linking extreme Protestants with Catholics, Spencer spoke of 'my two Adversaries in this Argument, the Papist and the Enthusiast'.[12]

Historically, Spencer traced prodigy belief to the ancient Chaldeans, Egyptians and Romans, pre-Christian religion being an area in which he had special expertise. The invocation of pagan Rome enabled Spencer to link his attack on prodigy belief to the revered name of the Roman philosopher Marcus Tullius Cicero, referring to Cicero's attack on diviners, *De Divinatione*. Spencer ascribed the prodigies of Josephus to the influence which Greek and Latin historians, about whom Spencer was much more sceptical than was Gadbury, had on the Jewish historian.[13] The association with paganism furthered Spencer's project of dissolving the link between providential prodigy belief and Christian piety.

One propensity of the soul which encouraged a false belief in prodigies as divine signs was the excessive fear with which people approached God. In rejecting fear of God as an appropriate religious emotion, Spencer was part of the movement, largely emanating from his own university, Cambridge, and associated with the Cambridge Platonists and the latitudinarians, toward rational religion. God's reasonableness and aimiability was one of his constant themes. Spencer argued that prodigy belief

> detains men under a constant Paedagogy to many base and servile fears. Whence Religion is easily concluded a great adversary to (what it mainly designes to bring on upon the world) a true generousness, and universal freedom of spirit, and that its whole business is to subdue the spirits of men to some cold and little observances, pale and feminine fears . . . Religion can never be aimiable, till it appears designed not to increase the fears of men, but truly to cure and remove them.[14]

Spencer's belief in God's benevolence also led him to charge providential prodigy believers with exaggerating God's wrath and minimizing his glory. God's true nature was seen not in monstrous or prodigious events, but in the magnificent regularities of nature. Prodigies served only the role of throwing the regularities of nature into sharper relief by the contrast they provided. Those who viewed every untoward event as a sign of God's wrath actually wronged God, in that God was primarily benevolent. Comets, for example, were for Spencer 'these wonderfull appearances in heaven, not so much the monitours of his anger, as of his glory'.[15] Like Cicero, Spencer claimed that speaking through prodigies was beneath the dignity of a powerful and majestic God. 'Now then what man, that hath any great thoughts of the Majestie of heaven, can once imagine he ever intended any base or deformed monsters, the interpreters of any of his great counsels or purposes?'[16] Elsewhere, Spencer mocked as ludicrous the idea of looking for the 'Jewel' of divine wisdom on the 'dunghill of obscene and monstrous births, apparitions of lying spirits, strange voices in the air, mighty winds, alterations in the face of heaven, &c.'.[17] Discussing Josephus's fall-of-Jerusalem prodigies, which included a cow that gave birth to a lamb, Spencer asked rhetorically: 'Can any man think God would ever work so ludicrous, so cheap, so insignificant a miracle?'[18]

Prodigies were not truly beyond nature; nor could they be correlated with ensuing events in the manner of Gadbury's tables.

Spencer attacked astrologers and almanac-makers for fabricating a connection between comets and disasters, and went so far as to assert that the most remarkable political event of recent years, the Restoration, had not been preceded by prodigies.[19] The uncertainty about how a given prodigy should be interpreted was another argument against the generally practised approach to prodigies. God always spoke clearly and directly, as he did by sending the plagues of Egypt, and eschewed 'such winding and squint-ey'd oracles as the Old Serpent made use of'.[20] Insofar as prodigies had a spiritual cause, that cause was not God but rather the Devil, the 'Old Serpent'.[21] Spencer believed in an active Devil, although he suspected that the Devil had been permitted a larger field of activity in pagan antiquity.[22] The Devil was ultimately responsible for belief in prodigies as divine signs, having promoted this belief among the ancient pagans by employing his limited foreknowledge to arrange that prodigious signs should precede great events. As Spencer linked nature's regularities to God, so he associated its irregularities with the Devil.

Prodigy believers were also wrong to believe that their present time was particularly fertile in monsters and prodigies. The *Mirabilis Annus* material had continued the tradition of prodigy writers, claiming that the present time was unparalleled in the number of prodigies occurring. Spencer substituted a vision of a decreasingly prodigious universe for theirs of an increasingly prodigious one. He claimed that the universe had been steadily gaining in regularity and uniformity since the time of Christ and the ancient pagans, in accord with his view of Christianity as fundamentally rational.

> But they which talk of and look for any such vehement expressions of Divinity now, mistake the temper & condition of that Oeconomy which the appearance of our Saviour hath now put us under; wherein all things are to be managed in a more sedate, cool, and silent manner, in a way suited to, and expressive of the temper our Saviour discover'd in the world, who caused not his voice to be heard in the streets, and to the condition of a Reasonable Being made to be manag'd by steady and calm arguments . . .[23]

The belief that prodigies increased in times of discord was an illusion created by the fact that prodigies were simply more likely to be noted in troubled times than in peaceful ones.[24]

As a theological error, therefore, belief in prodigies as divine signs was not, as prodigy writers claimed, conducive to repentance and the strengthening of faith. Rather, by bringing religion into contempt by associating it with monstrosities, deformities, and trivialities, it led finally to Epicureanism and atheism.[25]

After having ruled prodigies out of politics and religion, Spencer asserted that they properly fell under the jurisdiction of natural philosophers. However, it was important that these philosophers hold to a particular kind of natural philosophy, Baconian as opposed to occultist. The *Discourse Concerning Prodigies* is full of Baconian echoes. Spencer's call for an authoritative body for the collection of accounts of prodigies recalls Bacon's earlier plea for a new collection of such accounts based on new principles. The emotion that this work would elicit from its readers would be neither repentance nor wonder, but an increased understanding of nature. Like Spencer, Bacon had rejected existing collections of prodigies and other unusual phenomena as useless for this purpose.

> For I find no sufficient or competent collection of the works of nature which have a digression and deflection from the ordinary course of generations, productions, and motions; whether they be singularities of place and regions, or the strange events of time and chance, or the effects of yet unknown proprieties, or the instances of exceptions to general kinds. It is true, I find a number of books of fabulous experiments and secrets, and frivolous impostures for pleasure and strangeness. But a substantial and severe collection of the Heteroclites and Irregularities of nature, well examined and described, I find not, specially not with due rejection of fables and popular errors, for as things now are, if an untruth in nature be once on foot, what by reason of the neglect of examination and countenance of antiquity, and what by reason of the use of the opinion in similitudes and ornaments of speech, it is never called down.[26]

An undisciplined natural philosophy was vulnerable to prodigy belief for reasons innate to human psychology, that is the susceptibility of imagination. The human soul was vulnerable to prodigy belief due to its propensity to be impressed by the strange and bizarre, which both Bacon and Spencer saw as intellectually dangerous. Spencer asserted: 'For things rare and unusual . . . call forth the soul to a very quick and gratefull attendance, whilst matters of greater worth and moment, of more familiar occurrence, (like things often handled and blown upon) lose their value and lustre in its eye'.[27] In natural philosophy as in religion, an excessive attention to irregularities was harmful if it led to an undervaluing of the regularities.

Spencer's psychologizing of prodigy belief extended to a critique of that way of thinking which Michel Foucault labels 'Renaissance' and William Ashworth has characterized as the 'emblematic world view' – based on an idea of the universe as a web of resemblances and connections.[28] This world view was particularly characteristic of the occult sciences. Indeed, the persistence of prodigy literature into the Restoration indicates that this style of thinking did endure past the mid-seventeenth century – which both Ashworth and Foucault, looking primarily at natural history, claim to have been the moment when it was replaced by the new view associated with the Scientific Revolution. Certainly, Spencer saw this habit of thinking in terms of parallels and similarities to be still common, and both as innate to the soul and as a fertile source of error.

> It is the Nature of the Soul to be greatly impressive to a perswaysion of parallels, equalities, similitudes, in the frame and government of the world: and that (indeed) so far, as to make them (by the poetry of phancy) where it cannot really discover them; that it so may please and solace itselfin some supposed lines and figures of its own uniform and harmonious nature pourtrayed upon the world; and 'twere easy to shew how this temper hath betray'd it to a great many pretty dreams, both in science and common life.[29]

Employing classic anti-occultist arguments, Spencer used some of the most common types of prodigy to illustrate how an inappropriate use of metaphoric thinking led people to misconstrue phenomena explicable in natural terms as divine signs of impending catastrophe.

> Thus, (as it is called) the raining of bloud (which is but water tinctur'd by the condition of the soyl whence it ariseth, or, rather, where it falls) shall strongly sollicite the fear of some great effusion of bloud in the state; the appearence of two Suns at once (which is but the figure and glory of the Sun drawn by its own beams upon a disposed cloud) doth greatly encourage the phancy of two competitours for Royalty in a Nation; some great Eclypse seems (to a soft imagination) to hang the world with black against the approaching funeralls of some Great Person; the Casual parting of

the River Ouse in Bedfordshire, seem'd (after the event) a presage
of the succeeding division between the house of York and
Lancaster.[30]

Spencer asserted that God's true miracles 'carried no similitudes
of the things whereof they were signs (as the apparitions of armies
in the air seem to do of some succeeding battel) that so none might
be encouraged to regard them as omens'.[31] Prodigies could be
metaphors, but only purely linguistic metaphors, as rebellion
could be described as the 'eclipse' of right authority in Church
and State.[32] Prodigies were metaphors for Spencer only within
the human mind; they did not constitute natural metaphors. The
actual physical order did not mirror the human order as the
macrocosm the microcosm, and actually occurring eclipses had
no connection with rebellions. Those who thought so exaggerated
the importance of humans in the universe.[33]

In *A Discourse Concerning Vulgar Prophecies* (1665), a work
immediately following the *Discourse Concerning Prodigies*, Spencer
brought together his historical and psychological arguments by
linking the emblematic or 'Renaissance' world view to the religion and the divinatory systems of the ancient heathens. 'They
regarded the whole world, and all the parts thereof, but as so
many . . . oracles: not a Star or Comet in the Firmament, not a
monster on Earth, not a Staff in the Wood, not a Gut in the Sacri-
fice, not a Line in the Hand, but was thought prophetical'.[34]

The best cure for these ignorant and socially disruptive applications of metaphoric thinking was an increase in natural knowledge. Prodigy belief characterized times of ignorance in religion
and philosophy, as well as times of public turbulence.[35] Greater
knowledge of natural philosophy, by leading people to know the
natural causes of things, would lead to the socially and religiously
beneficial weakening of prodigy belief. In the meantime, however, the enduring belief in prodigies as divine signs hindered
the advance of natural knowledge. 'For when once Superstition
hath advanced these Prodigies into the repute of divine messen-
gers, it will easily be inferr'd a necessary respect towards them to
keep some distance, and not to approach them too nearly by too
busy and curious an enquiry into their natural and immediate
causes.'[36] Spencer hoped, therefore, to contribute to the increase
of natural knowledge through his collapsing of prodigies into the
category of natural events. 'For as Nature is but a constant and

durable Prodigy, so a Prodigy but a more rare and unusual Nature.'[37]

Spencer approached current affairs optimistically. He did not refer directly to the newly institutionalized science of the Royal Society, but he did share the Royal Society's propagandists' belief in the rapid progress of natural knowledge. Gunpowder, for example, showed that what was considered miraculous in one age could be commonplace in another.[38]

> Now while Wisdom seems thus to have hewn out her seven pillars and her house is going up so fast, it is a duty to assist her work by removing all the rubbish of Prodigies, Vulgar Prophecies, and what ever doctrine makes the minds of men soft and easy (by teaching men to believe without evidence) and so, unfit to make a due judgement of things.[39]

Spencer followed Bacon in calling for a history of prodigies, and, also like Bacon, rejected those extant accounts as marred by an unsystematic seeking after wonder.

> And therefore if we had a more faithfull History of the Anomals in Nature, (the want whereof is owing not a little to the superstition of men, which stains all it toucheth) we might be soon able to see beyond the surface of these things, which as yet seem plac'd in the world, but to confound and pose us. But the evil is, that as the History of Times, is usually drawn up, so as it may minister not to truth but to faction, the History of Nature so as to gratifie either interest or curiosity, so the History of Praeternaturall occurrences, so as it may serve, wonder or superstition, not in so judicious and faithfull a relation of the criticall circumstances of accidents, as to make a square basis whereupon to erect the steady principles of Philosophy.[40]

The subject of unusual events in nature, therefore, should be taken out of the hands of 'prodigy-mongers' and placed in those of a group of experts, natural philosophers in Spencer's case, rather than Gadbury's astrologers. In discussing the use which natural philosophers would make of prodigies Spencer was at his most Baconian. Prodigies

> serve to lead us into a more distinct knowedge of the works of Nature. Nature is the best Interpreter of it self; now (like tortur'd men) she then discovers her secrets, either when vex'd by art in lesser bodies, or disturb'd by accident in greater. Comets, new

stars, monstrous Eclipses, Earthquakes, Meteors, &c. all serve the knowledge of one mystery in Nature or other.[41]

Spencer used the notion of *mountebankery* to link the interpretation of prodigies to a variety of other intellectual approaches that he hoped to see marginalized. Just as astrologers were mountebanks in astronomy, and alchemists and physiognomists in natural philosophy, and pansophists in science, so were prodigy-mongers, cabalists and those claiming to have received revelations from God in divinity.[42] He elsewhere linked 'critical observers of omens and prodigies' to intellectually stigmatized groups such as madmen, fortune-tellers and women. True prophecy worked quite differently: 'But we shall find God in Scripture so far securing the honour of true Divination, as to confer the gift thereof (generally) upon men, and those of a pious and learned education'.[43] Spencer consistently gendered providential prodigy belief as feminine, as in his reference to prodigy belief encouraging 'pale and feminine fears'. He expounded the figure of Tiresias, the sexually ambiguous prophet of Greek mythology, to signify that prophecy was feminine as 'credulous, talkative, and impotent', masculine as guided and expounded by wisdom and prudence.[44] This derogatory identification of views he opposed as feminine, although certainly not restricted to Baconians, also linked Spencer to Bacon.

Spencer spoke admiringly of the ancient Roman practice of strictly examining those who alleged having been witnesses to prodigious events (something Poole might also have admired), and concluded his book by calling for the establishment of an institution entrusted with overseeing and validating prodigies, a body uninfluenced either by a belief in prodigies as divine signs or by a love of wonder.

> It is to be wisht that there was a kind of Philosophy office; wherein all such unusual occurrences were registered; not in such fabulous and antick circumstances wherein they stand recorded in the writers of Natural Magick (designing nothing but wonder in their Readers) nor with a superstitious observation of any such dreadfull events which such relations are usually stain'd, in the writers which intend a service to religion in them: But in such faithfull noticies of their severall circumstances, as might assist the understanding to make a true judgement of their Natures and Occasions.[45]

This call, reminiscent of Bacon, for a transfer of jurisdiction over prodigies from unlearned diviners and religious polemicists to gentlemen learned in natural philosophy should be read in light of the development of new scientific practices and institutions in Restoration England, most importantly the Royal Society. Spencer offered a picture of a universe that was primarily regular in its operation, non-allegorical in its meaning, ruled by a benevolent and somewhat distant God, and comprehensible principally by an educated elite of male natural philosophers. In this rational universe, divinatory prodigies had no legitimate place, appealing only to the uneducated, women, and religious and political malcontents.

Moderate Spencerianism: the Royal Society propagandists Joseph Glanvill and Thomas Sprat

Spencer's influence on the debate over prodigies outlasted the immediate controversy. Nearly twenty years later the English dissenter Jonathan Tuckney claimed in a letter to Increase Mather concerning Mather's *An Essay on Recording Illustrious Providences*, that 'your peece of Prodigies may possibly have been prevented from efficacy by some we call here Latitudinarians, by a treatise of a Cambridgemans (Spencer by name)'.[46] Although Spencer's critique of *enthusiasm* was very congenial to the Latitudinarians and other defenders of organized natural philosophy, his extreme position also presented dangers. His denial of any supernatural causation or meaning to prodigies was uncomfortably close to Hobbesian materialism, and opened the door to a denial of any providential relationship between God and the world. Spencer himself would also become intellectually dangerous, as his subsequent work argued for the derivation of the rituals of the ancient Hebrews from those of the Egyptians, a position considered to be an attack on the authority of the Bible. Spencer would also be suspected of Socinianism.

The latitudinarian clergyman and Royal Society propagandist Joseph Glanvill, a leading foe of both enthusiasm and superstition, accepted Spencer's anti-providential position with some reservations in his 1671 *Philosophia Pia; or a Discourse of the Religious Temper, and Tendencies of the Experimental Philosophy, Which is profest by the Royal Society* (1671). In arguing that natural philosophy, far from being atheistic, actually served religious ends, Glanvill followed closely Spencer's discussion of prodigies, crediting 'a late very elegant Discourse about Prodigies' with showing how natural philosophic knowledge removed superstitious terror of the import of prodigies.[47] He qualified this positive use, though, by suggesting that Spencer had gone too far. In a later work in which he upheld the validity of witchcraft belief by attacking those who would deny the interaction of the spiritual and material worlds, Glanvill argued that prodigies of warning, such as those preceding the fall of Jerusalem, were the actions of good spirits. Although Glanvill proclaimed 'I scorn the Ordinary Tales of Prodigies, which proceed from superstitious fears, and unacquaintance with nature', he also attacked Spencer's arguments as 'short and inconsequent, and built upon too narrow hypothesis'.[48]

Although it made no reference to Spencer, the foremost manifesto of the new philosophy, Thomas Sprat's *History of the Royal Society* (1667), also referred to the possibility of defusing prodigies as public signs as part of the attack on enthusiasm that was one of the principal tasks of the Royal Society. Like Glanvill, Sprat was less radical than Spencer in his denial of God's direct action in the world. Like Spencer, to whom he did not directly refer, Sprat identified belief in prodigies as divine messages with England's recent political turbulence: 'This wild amuzing mens minds, with Prodigies and conceits of Providences, has been one of the most considerable causes of those spiritual distractions, of which our Country has long bin the Theater. This is a vanity, to which the English seem to have bin always subject above others.'[49] Part of the problem was 'that every fantastical Humorist ... though he be never so ignorant of the very common works of Nature' could expound the will of God by interpreting prodigies.[50] Like Spencer, Sprat believed that natural philosophers were the proper people to interpret prodigies, and he suggested that a proper set of canons for evaluating prodigies could be created by their collaborative efforts. 'We are guilty of false interpretations of Providences and Wonders, when we either make those to be Miracles that are none, or when we put a false sense on those that are real, when we make general effects to have a privat aspect, or particular aspects to have some universal signification.'[51] Also like

Spencer, Sprat believed that the knowledge of natural philosophy made belief in God's direct intervention in the world superfluous, and that God's glory lay principally in the regularities of nature.[52] The danger of the study of prodigies by the ignorant is that it 'withdraws our obedience, from the true Image of God the right-full Sovereign, and makes us dependent on vain Images of his power, which are fram'd by our own imaginations'. Sprat contrasted the subjectivity and irrational emotionalism of those who interpreted prodigies providentially with the public rationality of both experimental natural philosophy and royal authority.[53] Both Sprat and Spencer worked to discredit providential interpretation of prodigies as excessively democratic and to set up natural philosophers as the appropriate intellectual authority for the evaluation of prodigies.

'Vain apprehensions, of what they call prodigies': prodigies and the Royal Society

In practice, the Royal Society, its members, and particularly its secretaries such as Henry Oldenburg, actively produced and circulated accounts of prodigies and monsters.[54] Not only were the natural philosophers carrying out the same sort of activity as the dissenting circles that had produced the *Mirabilis Annus* tracts; they were in direct competition, asserting a rival jurisdiction over these phenomena. The degree to which dissenting or 'fanatic' clerics and laymen were thought of as contesting the territory of the prodigious with natural philosophers can be seen in a number of early Restoration texts, such as the anonymous verse satire *The Character of a Coffee-House* (1665), which treated this conflict as common knowledge. This short piece presented and ridiculed various habitués of an imaginary coffeehouse. A 'Phanatick' enquired:

> . . . did you not hear
> What Prodigies did late appear
> At Norwich, Ipswich, Grantham, Gothum
> And though prophane ones do not not'em
> Yet we – Here th'Virtuoso stops
> The current of his speech, with hopes
> Quoth he you will not tak't amiss

> I say all's lies that's news like this
> For I have Factors all about
> The Realm, so that no Stars peep out
> That are unusual, much less these
> Strange and unheard-of Prodigies
> You would relate, but they are tost
> To me in letters by first post.[55]

The satire portrayed the communication network of religious dissidents and that of natural philosophers as directly competing over the same set of phenomena, and tilted towards the virtuoso's claim of jurisdiction. Although both the phanatick and the virtuoso were satirical targets, the virtuoso's claim to superior sources of knowledge was the one that went uncontradicted.

As with other areas of knowledge during the Scientific Revolution, prodigies were increasingly evaluated by probabilistic standards.[56] Rather than absolute truth or falsity, the questions both of the occurrence or non-occurrence of a given prodigy and of choosing among the range of possible explanations were framed as choices between varying probabilities. Probabilism meant that it was not always necessary to assert God's absolute policy of non-intervention in the world in order to discredit the providential explanation of a prodigy. Instead, divine causation could be assigned the lowest position on the scale of explanations ranked on the basis of probability. Of course, the attack on the providential interpretation of prodigies did not mean complete opposition to providential explanation on the part either of natural philosophers or of the culture at large which continued to accept the idea of God's guidance of the universe and of humanity in particular. However, natural philosophers increasingly restricted providentialism to the 'big picture', leaving intact a non-providential realm of individual instances.[57]

When prodigies and monsters were discussed in *Philosophical Transactions* or other published material identified with the Royal Society, either a non-supernatural explanation or a choice between non-supernatural explanations was offered; alternatively, an unknown natural cause was assumed to be operating. The similarity between prodigy accounts and the experimental accounts produced by Royal Society science facilitated this shift.[58] Both prodigy accounts and experimental accounts emphasized the temporal situation of a unique event and placed authority for validating the event in eyewitnesses. In both, the weight to be assigned to eyewitnesses increased with their social standing, although other criteria of witness reliability changed in significant ways, from piety to natural-philosophical expertise. Prodigies now had to conform to the same standards of proof as other scientific phenomena.[59]

The eminent natural philosopher and paradigmatic 'Christian Virtuoso' Robert Boyle specifically cited prodigy literature to make a point about the contribution of witnesses' testimony to the veracity of their accounts of a phenomenon in discussing evidence for Christianity in *Some Considerations about the Reconcilableness of Reason and Religion* (1657). Speaking of earthquakes and volcanoes, along with 'other prodigies of too unquestionable truth', Boyle claimed that 'if they were attested but by slight and ordinary witness, they would be judged incredible, but we scruple not to believe them, when the relations are attested with such circumstances, as to make the testimony as strong, as the things attested are strange'.[60] Indeed, some of the techniques employed in the creation of the experimental account – such as specificity, appending the names of witnesses, and description of the experimental phenomenon in such detail as to induce in the reader the condition of 'virtual witnessing' – have precursors in the prodigy account.[61]

Following the lead of Spencer and Sprat, Royal Society writings consistently ascribed belief in direct divine causation of prodigies to lack of knowledge of natural causes and located it in groups separated from the natural-philosophical elite. This separation could be based on religion, gender, class, or level of education. Separation based on religion in natural-philosophic writings, consciously irenic at least among Protestants, differed from that expressed in the Royalist writings of the *Mirabilis Annus* controversy in that it linked providential prodigy belief not with 'fanatical' Protestant dissent but with ignorance or religions farther removed from Anglicanism. The Reverend Thomas Smith, in his report on Constantinople published in *Philosophical Transactions*, showed how belief in prodigies as divine signs was located both in the unlearned and in non-Christians. 'The Turks look upon Earthquakes as ominous, as the Vulgar do upon Eclipses, not understanding the Philosophy of Them.'[62] Roman Catholics, and particularly the Catholic clergy, were another group that could be accused of excessive credulity (although many Catholics were respected natural philosophers and even members of the Royal Society, such as Sir Kenelm Digby). In speaking of the eminent Jesuit scientist Athanasius Kircher, the leading English naturalist John Ray stated: 'As for Father Kircher, I account him a credulous person, possessed with the vanity of most of the Religious of his church who delight to tell strange and miraculous stories to amuse and delude the Vulgar.'[63] The professedly non-sectarian Society could also be used to attack Catholicism by proffering natural explanations for incidents Catholics claimed as miracles, as when the Society's secretary Henry Oldenburg planned to distribute a French translation of an account from *Philosophical Transactions* of the artificial projection of images in order to reveal as a fraud the alleged appearance of Christ at the altar of the church in a small French village.[64] Like Spencer, practitioners of the new science could stigmatize pagans as well as Catholics or Muslims as believers in the divine significance of prodigies; Ray also spoke of a swarm of locusts as something an 'Ethnick', or ancient pagan, 'Would be apt to think portentuous'.[65]

The conflict between sceptical natural philosophers, preferring a 'natural' explanation for the phenomena recounted, and ignorant crowds crying up a prodigy was often embedded in the prodigy narratives printed in *Philosophical Transactions* or appearing elsewhere. This made concrete the contrast between natural-philosophical expertise and 'superstition', strengthening the former's claim to particular knowledge and presenting belief in the divine causation of prodigies as a hindrance to the advance of natural philosophy. This was sometimes a literal hindrance, as the physician, collector, and natural philosopher Hans Sloane, a future president of the Royal Society, ascribed his incomplete observation of a meteor to the 'Noise of the People calling to one another to observe what they never had observed in their days, and thought to be prodigious'.[66] A correspondent of Oldenburg referred to ignorant local people killing a monstrous chick, out of fear it would prove an 'ill omen', and John Beale claimed to have been denied the sight of the head of a monster a woman had voided because the family had feared 'it was so ugly, as might raise ill fame'.[67]

Not only popular fear of the ominous nature of monstrosities and prodigies hindered natural philosophers. The mob's love of wonder also promoted its interest in prodigies, though this was an interest different from, and inferior to, that of the virtuosi. A discussion of planetary conjunctions made this point clear:

> Whilst the common people have admired to see the two superior planets Saturn and Jupiter continue so near this whole year, and our Astrologers have affrighted them with fearful Predictions of direful events to succeed this appearance, the more Judicious are desirous to know how often and at what time their conjunctions happen, that by compareing their Tables of those Planets motions with their observed appearance, they may be the better able to correct them . . .[68]

Mobs admiring without understanding the conjunction and astrologers prognosticating dire consequences were each contrasted with natural philosophers making use of the occasion to improve their astronomical tables. Edmond Halley's discussion of an unusual rainbow drew a similar contrast between the natural philosopher and the ancients: 'The Ancients who believed Iris the Messenger of the Gods, would have been apt to have thought she had some peculiar Message, when she placed her self so near me, as to be almost within reach: I understood her to invite me to inquire further into the Nature of her Production.'[69] The metaphorical language here replaces a communicative relationship of the ancients, the rainbow and the gods, where the prodigy was a self-contained message, with a sexualized relationship between Halley and nature, in which the prodigy figures merely as the invitation and the investigator as the (willingly) seduced.

A rain of wheat in Norwich provided the Royal Society with one of its earliest opportunities to normalize a strange event, and juxtapose its own explanations to providential ones. At the meeting of the Society on June 5, 1661, even before it received its royal charter, a Colonel Tuke brought some seeds that had allegedly rained on Norwich recently. Boyle and John Evelyn were designated to sow them. At the June 13 meeting, Tuke brought in some more seeds, and some ivy berries for comparison. When the husks were removed from the ivy berries they were revealed to be identical with the grains that had fallen on Norwich, and it was theorized that these seeds had been excreted by starlings after they had digested the husks. A certificate recording this 'official' explanation was placed in the Society's Register Book, juxtaposed to an outside narrative produced by a Norwich witness which spoke of a 'marvel' and of giving thanks to God for his bounty.[70]

Natural philosophers continued to exploit natural philosophy's usefulness in the political attack on lower-class credulity characteristic of royalist participants in the *Mirabilis Annnus* controversy. In 1716, describing the recent daylight appearance of Venus, Halley spoke of 'one of the principal uses of the Mathematicall Sciences' as delivering 'the Unskilful Vulgar . . . from the vain apprehensions of what they call Prodigies, which sometimes, by the artifices of designing Men, have been made use of to very Evil Purposes'.[71]

As natural philosophers' claims to authoritatively interpret prodigies grew stronger, excessive credulity regarding prodigies was often ascribed not to a particular group such as Roman Catholics or the vulgar but to all those not learned in natural philosophy. The naturalist John Ray, advising John Aubrey on his projected natural history of Surrey, claimed: 'I have found men that are not skilful in the History of Nature very credulous, and apt to impose upon themselves and others, and therefore dare not give a firm Assent to any thing they report upon their own authority . . .'.[72]

This approach to evaluating witnesses of prodigious events marked the break from the earlier tradition of prodigy accounts, in which a witness's key qualifications had been social status, veracity and piety. Now the most important criterion was an orthodox knowledge of nature, although social standing also maintained some importance, in opposition to 'vulgar' credulity. The emphasis on 'vulgar errors', or the credulity of people not skilled in natural philosophy, characteristic of many natural-philosophical accounts of prodigies, must be looked upon as a legitimating strategy for predominantly upper-class natural philosophers, and did not necessarily reflect the actual beliefs of the lower classes or those unskilled in natural philosophy. But by distancing themselves from uneducated people, natural philosophers hoped to establish the authority of their own form of knowledge.

In addition to offering non-supernatural explanations for prodigies, the members of the Royal Society also worked to rob them of a political significance by eschewing imagistic descriptive language. Although the Royal Society's natural philosophers did not altogether abandon the use of images in their writings, they did denounce this practice.[73] This was particularly true in descriptions of strange celestial events, in which imagistic language, such as the description of a comet as a sword, was replaced largely by mathematical language, a language in which it was much more difficult to derive a terrestrial meaning from celestial events. Robert Hooke, in his *Discourse of Comets* inspired by the great comet of 1680, denounced specifically the use of images of war and violence in comet descriptions as connected with belief in their divinatory significance, and linked both to outmoded and erroneous natural philosophy:

> So that for all the time that the Peripatetick Philosophy and the Ptolemaic Astronomy prevailed, all the Accounts concerning them [comets] are idle and insignificant to this purpose, and seem only suited to the use which they designed for them, which was to make them only as Messengers, to foretel, by the help of their own Chimeras and Fancies joined with them, what Alterations were like to happen in human Affairs, and thence I doubt not, proceeded the strange Shapes they have painted out to us of Targets, Shields, Spears, and Daggers, with Hands, &c. of Dragons and Serpents, and such like. A great variety of which kind of Figures you may find in Authors that have written concerning them; and you may see a great many of them together in Hevelius's Cometagraphy, most of which, I confess, I look on only as the Products of a prejudicate and prepossest Poetick Fancy in the Historians . . .[74]

A similar move away from imagistic language occurred in the study of monsters, where quantification, dissection, and precise illustration became more important than metaphorical physical description. Robert Boyle's 'Observables upon a monstrous Head', printed in *Philosophical Transactions*, is the classic example of this approach to monsters. In a style akin to that of medical descriptions, Boyle described the characteristics of the head of a monstrous colt and the circumstances of its birth.[75] Boyle refused to use colourful figurative and metaphorical language, and although he claimed the head was 'monstrous', he did not actually describe it as a whole, but merely part by part. The illustration accompanying the account is not particularly or exaggeratedly grotesque. It is recognizably an attempt to render a particular, three-dimensional physical object through the use of perspective and chiaroscuro, rather than a flat, stylized sign of something else, as can be seen by comparison with the illustrations of prodigy tracts. Boyle's verbal description of the monstrous head deconstructed its 'monstrosity' into a set of aberrant characteristics, such as the deep depression, or bag, over the eyes. The description reflected a decreasing tendency to describe monsters as mélanges of various animals, and a greater tendency towards precise anatomical descriptions.

The millenarian or apocalyptic version of the providential interpretation was also increasingly marginalized within natural philosophy. Although some natural philosophers, the most prominent example being Newton, were apocalyptic or millenarian in their thinking, they did not look to prodigies as 'signs of the times' – a habit discredited by its association with millenarian radicals. Ray, like most late seventeenth-century natural philosophers, did not accept the idea of the decay of nature, but did believe that the destruction of the world would be preceded by strange and unnatural events.[76] However he argued that these events would not be physical, as physical events such as meteors and comets would be too obvious, violating God's promise not to reveal the day or hour. Instead, Ray asserted that these strange events would be political, drawing a separation between the natural, the political and the apocalyptic realms which would have made little sense to previous apocalyptically minded prodigy writers.[77]

Not all members of the Royal Society held fast to the anti-providential line. A man such as Evelyn, intellectually formed in the 1630s and 1640s, did not simply abandon belief in prodigies as divine signs on becoming a fellow of the Royal Society. In reflecting on the comet of 1680, Evelyn, who believed the comet of 1618 to have been the source of all Europe's subsequent woes, asserted of comets in general: 'I cannot despise them; they may be warnings from God, as they commonly are for-runners of his Annimadversions'.[78] Evelyn was far from the most providence-oriented natural philosopher of his time: Dr Peter Nelson wrote to Oldenburg of a well-attested case in Liege of a man 'transpeciated into a Dog' with a human head as a punishment for blasphemy, and requested that Oldenburg make enquiry; and Oldenburg's equivalent in the Oxford Philosophical Society,

William Musgrave, received an account of how a 'fellow very active against the King' in the recent Civil War had had a shower of blood fall upon his property.[79]

Despite these instances of natural philosophers accepting providential causation, anti-providentialism remained dominant, particularly in statements made in public as opposed to correspondence. The caution that the orthodox Anglican Evelyn found it necessary to display in dealing with the miraculous or the prodigious was apparent from a 1670 case recounted in his *Diary*.[80] A servant to a friend of one of Evelyn's neighbours had developed a pattern of red crosses on her skin. The case was referred to Evelyn, who unfortunately does not explain in the *Diary* why he was viewed as an appropriate authority. It could have been due to his reputation as a natural philosopher or simply his social standing as a gentleman. Evelyn's primary concern with the case was religious. He assured himself that the maid was 'no Phanatic' and 'had never any commerce with the Popish Priests' but was 'well disposd to the Church established'. He did consider the possibility of fraud, referring to the case of the possessed nuns of Loudun in the early part of the century, but the willingness of the maid to let him scrape at the crosses made him think it no fraud. Having no idea of a natural explanation, Evelyn yet did not dare to pronounce the phenomenon supernatural. He did believe that any supernatural significance the marks did have would be favourable to the Church of England, arguing with a logic reminiscent of the teratology of the Civil War that God was endorsing the practice of 'the Church of England, who have respect to the crosse, & beare it on their fore-heads as soone as made Christians', and rebuking heretics, sects and atheists. However, he seems to have made no effort to publicize the miracle. The use of contemporary as opposed to biblical, prodigious and miraculous evidence had become so identified with sectarians and Catholics that the Anglican, but highly cautious, Evelyn, did not consider it.

Providential and apocalyptic interpretations of prodigies and strange events did occasionally appear in the pages of *Philosophical Transactions*, particularly in the 1690s and 1700s – the heyday of the attempt to deploy natural philosophy as a weapon against atheism – in the form of 'natural theology'. While many members of the Royal Society were active in the natural theology movement, natural-theological interpretations of prodigies were usually not associated with actual active members of the Royal Society, but instead with correspondents.[81] Even when putting forward a providential interpretation, the Leeds antiquary and natural philosopher Ralph Thoresby prefaced his claim regarding an earthquake in December 1703, that 'Famines, Pestilences, and Earthquakes, are joyn'd by our Blessed Saviour, as portending future calamities, and particularly the destruction of Jerusalem and the Jewish State, if not the end of the world, St. Math. 24. 7', with the disclaimer: 'I hope you will not think it unbecoming my character to make this reflection upon it'.[82] Thoresby's dissenting background may have made his thinking more susceptible to providential interpretations of prodigies. The most consistent source of providential musings on prodigies and wonders were the Society's New England correspondents, intellectual and religious allies of the English dissenters. John Winthrop invoked God's power in connection with a moving hill and was uncertain whether a mass death of fish had natural or supernatural causes.[83]

One of the few examples of uncritical acceptance of a providential explanation for a prodigious phenomenon occurred at a Royal Society meeting in 1686, where those present accepted 'preternatural' explanations of the Glastonbury Thorn and the New Forest Oak, both of which bloomed or brought forth leaves only on Christmas Day. It may be significant that this discussion occurred during the reign of a Catholic monarch who was perhaps assumed to be sympathetic to manifestations of the miraculous.[84]

The monster with the most explicit theological meaning to be considered in Royal Society writings of the early eighteenth century was the Friesland boy who had the words *DEUS MEUS* around the pupils of his eyes, Latin in the left eye and Hebrew in the right. The religious significance of this prodigy would appear to be undeniable, but it is interesting to note the extreme reluctance of English natural philosophers, many of them clergymen or else otherwise identified with the defence of religion, to admit to it. It was still possible to deny that the remarkable appearance of the boy's eyes was a prodigy at all. The Reverend Charles Ellis, on close examination, claimed that the cracks in the boy's iris did not actually form letters but the ambience of 'superstition' in the surrounding country led people to believe that they saw letters there. (Although Friesland was part of the Protestant Dutch Republic, Ellis saw the boy in Brussels, capital of the Catholic Spanish Netherlands, presumed to be an abode of 'superstition'.) He claimed: 'But it was like to have been of danger to me to have discovered this matter in those superstitious countreys; for acquainting a Gentleman in English of this Cheat, one of the Mob happen'd to understand it, and I was forced to make the best of my way.'[85] Evelyn once again hesitated to commit himself on the issue of the cause of a prodigy with religious meaning, stating that some thought the phenomenon artificial, and others found it 'almost supernatural', although he gave no indication of the means by which such a phenomenon could be artificially induced.[86]

In all these ways, the science of the Royal Society continued the project inaugurated in the royalist response to the *Mirabilis Annus* controversy, in severing the connection between prodigies and divine providence. However, prodigies also had positive value in the struggle to understand nature.

'Some things hitherto reckoned Prodigies': prodigies in local natural histories

In addition to the accumulation of specific instances of the prodigious and monstrous in scientific correspondence or the pages of *Philosophical Transactions*, prodigies also played a significant role in the national or local natural histories which appeared with increasing frequency in the last few decades of the seventeenth century.[87] These studies differed from previous works, for instance Lambarde's *Perambulation of Kent*, in being primarily devoted to natural history rather than antiquities. They were often presented to the public as exemplars of the new natural philosophy and Baconian fact gathering. (One early example, Childrey's *Britannia Baconica*, even incorporated a reference to Bacon into its title.) They frequently relied on information voluntarily supplied by non-scientists. These natural histories offer a good case study of how information regarding prodigies was acquired and presented in natural-history writing aimed at a relatively broad audience.

Childrey's *Britannia Baconica* incorporated prodigies and

marvels as part of the Baconian tripartite division of natural knowledge the author claimed to be following.[88] His attitude on the relation of prodigies to nature as a whole was decidedly non-providential. Like other royalist writers of the Restoration, Childrey wanted to draw a firm distinction between God's direct actions and mere unusual occurrences in nature. God's direct actions were to be restricted to the biblical past: 'Give unto Nature, the works that are Natures: and unto God, those that are Gods. There being a great difference between the dividing of the Red Sea, by Moses and Joshua, and the dividing of the River Ouse in Bedfordshire, related in this Book.'[89] This mission of offering non-supernatural explanations for prodigies was prominently announced on the title page of *Britannia Baconica*, which claimed that within its pages 'some things hitherto reckoned Prodigies, are fain to confess the cause, whence they proceed'.

Childrey wavered between the position that popular credulity was a problem in evaluating claims made for the operation of wonders and the belief that the populace was too apt to scoff at wonders. On the one hand, he expressed the hope that 'Vulgar' readers of his work would derive from it the benefit of being more accepting of the marvels found in traveller's accounts and else-where.[90] On the other, he consistently ascribed credulity to the common people, describing the belief that the husband or wife who drinks first from Saint Kaine's well 'gets the mastery' of the other as a 'fit fable for the Vulgar to believe',[91] and claiming that 'the simple and the most vulgar sort of men' were 'the most superstitious'.[92]

In the body of the text, arranged by counties, Childrey carried out this mission of offering natural or secondary causes for prodi-gious phenomena, explaining such classic past prodigies as the invasion of Essex by fieldmice in 1580 by changes in the weather.[93] He discussed at some length the parting of the Ouse before the outbreak of the Wars of the Roses, a classic case of the relation of discord in Nature to discord in the state previously invoked in *Mirabilis Annus*, and tentatively explained it by his favorite device of the sudden frost. For Childrey, the influence of the stars ranked among secondary causes, and he attempted to explain the con-nection between eclipses of the sun and disasters to the town of Oswestry astrologically by considering the position of the heavens at its founding.[94] Those predictive prodigies which

Childrey was unable to explain using natural causes he often dismissed with formulae such as 'And the relator doth in some sort believe it, and so may any one else if he please', disassociating himself from providential beliefs even when unable to offer a natural-philosophical explanation of a prodigy.[95]

Prodigies were also an important element in the late seventeenth-century natural histories of specific English counties and localities produced. The best known of the local natural historians, Dr Robert Plot, both a fellow of the Royal Society and a leading figure in the Oxford Philosophical Society, had an interest in prodigious phenomena. He included questions on the appearance of multiple suns and strange fountains 'such as are reputed to break forth but now and then, as against a dearth of Corn, war, Plague, &c.', in a list of questions he hoped could be given to inhabitants of every county in England to produce a series of local natural histories.[96] He followed this practice in his own county histories, those of Oxfordshire and Staffordshire.

The opening of Plot's *The Natural History of Oxfordshire* closely followed Bacon's tripartite division of natural knowledge in setting forth the programme of the work.

> And therefore I shall consider, first, Natural Things, such as either she hath retained the same from the beginning, or freely produces in her ordinary course; as Animals, Plants, and the universal furniture of the world. Secondly, her extravagancies and defects, occasioned either by the exuberancy of matter, or obstinacy of impediments, as in Monsters. And lastly, as she is restrained, forced, fashioned, or determined, by Artificial Operations.[97]

Plot's wonders included parhelia, triplets, an infant crying in the womb, a tree with the figure of a chalice, alb and stole, and the curious case of the bees of Christ Church College, which declined and died at the 'turning out of the Fellows' in 1648 'as if the feminine sympathised with the masculine Monarchy'.[98] Although Plot was unquestionably fond of marvels, he generally shunned providential and divinatory interpretations of prodigies.[99] In an extended passage on the idea, ascribed to astrologers, that a triple sun presaged a political triumvirate, he used the Bible to assail the idea of divinatory prodigies, echoing Isaiah in invoking 'He that frustrates the tokens of the Lyars, and makes the Diviners mad'.[100]

Although Plot took a consistent line against the divinatory use of prodigies for public purposes, he was somewhat less certain on the question of direct divine causation of prodigies in general. In some cases he was willing to acknowledge the possibility of direct divine causation of a prodigy as one of a group of possible explanations. After adducing a range of natural and theological explanations for the Glastonbury Thorn, Plot did not indicate his own choice, but left it to the reader. 'Whether of these is most probable, I shall not determin, but leave every reader best to please himself.'[101] Plot also employed probabilistic criteria where the choice between natural philosophy's explanations was unclear, as when he presented Aristotle's, Réné Descartes's and Christiaan Huygens's explanations of parhelia.[102] Plot did not treat providential explanations differently from natural ones, but placed them among the choices presented by the natural philosopher to the reader.

However, there were a few cases, mostly involving remarkable judgements on individuals, where Plot positively asserted direct divine causation. One involved a Duncalf man whose hands rotted after stealing a Bible, a case which attracted a great deal of interest in the late seventeenth and early eighteenth centuries.[103] Another was the miraculous revival of Anne Greene after being hanged. Even though Plot thought that this event had its source 'in the Justice of God', he hastily added: 'it must also be allowed, that God himself makes use of natural means in production of the most wonderful, most amazing effect'.[104] He also attempted to explain relations between prodigies and subsequent disasters by naturalistic means, arguing that there were many pools in England which were held to prognosticate dearths through overflowing, and that this was explained by 'our dearths here in England being most frequently the consequents of great rains'.[105]

Both Childrey and Plot disseminated a basically secular approach to prodigies through works identified as products of Baconian science, reinforcing the claim of natural philosophers to be the judges of prodigies, and of the explicability of most prodigies in natural-philosophical terms. However, subsequent local natural historians would take an even more critical, even hostile, attitude to prodigies. One of the most aggressive of the local natural historians of the early eighteenth century in his approach to prodigies was the Reverend John Morton, FRS, author of an impressive volume, *The Natural History of Northamptonshire*

(1712).[106] Morton used his work to deny not merely the theological and political import of prodigies but the actual occurrence of some of the most common types of prodigious event. For example, Morton denied that rains of frogs actually occurred, asking why the frogs which were supposed to have fallen from heaven showed no signs of injury, and why all of them were on the ground, and not on rooftops. He also asserted that although many saw the frogs on the ground, no one claimed to have actually seen them fall from heaven. 'My design in taking notice of these things, is only to show what a slender foundation there is for them', wrote Morton in giving an alternative explanation for the sudden appearance of large numbers of small frogs based on the propensity of frogs to leave rivers and ponds *en masse* shortly after having metamorphosed from tadpoles.[107] This was essentially the same explanation Clarke had given for the Fairford frogs' incident, but Morton put it forward more aggressively as an explanation of all gatherings of frogs and toads rather than of a specific incident.

Even more than Plot or Childrey, Morton was a consistent critic of the 'vulgar' and their allegedly credulous attitude to nature, ascribing to them 'the Easiness of the Vulgar, and their proneness to believe any strange thing'.[108] The ease with which Morton was able to use the notion of vulgar credulity to explain away prodigious phenomena is particularly apparent in his discussion of 'strange Appearances of Military Skirmishes in the Air'. Morton was concerned that these relations had of late 'impos'd upon some of better Rank than the Vulgar'. He believed that these stories traced back to 'a great many small clouds of uncouth shapes, from which there flash'd out Lightning, and now and then they heard a Thunder-crack'. The elaborate descriptions of armies and manoeuvres characteristic of the pamphlets of the Civil War and the Interregnum or the *Mirabilis Annus* tracts were 'a product of their own superstitious imaginations'.[109]

'For the reader's diversion': prodigies and natural theology in the Boyle Lectures

Monsters and prodigies also played important roles in the emerging field of natural theology. Natural theology had a long history in Christian apologetics, as an attempt to demonstrate the being and attributes of God from sources outside of the specifically Christian revelation. In its late seventeenth- and eighteenth-century form, natural theology arose in response to the perceived threats of atheism and of deism, and it sought to prove the existence of God through philosophical and scientific reasoning, employing the evidence of nature itself. Natural theologians usually sought to avoid taking positions on disagreements between sects of Christians. The most important continuing forum for natural theology, the Boyle Lectures founded in the will of Robert Boyle, forbade lecturers from taking sides in disputes among Christians, bidding them concentrate on refuting the positions of atheists, deists, Jews and Muslims.[110] Since neither Judaism nor Islam were gaining converts in significant numbers in late seventeenth-century England, Boyle lecturers concentrated their fire on the deists and particularly the atheists. By focusing on the idea of a law-governed universe and a rational God, natural theologians hoped to confute atheistic materialism, while avoiding a hylozoistic pantheism which identified a vitalistic nature with God. In a version of the argument from design, informed by the rapidly expanding body of natural knowledge, they aimed to demonstrate that the intricate but inanimate fabric of nature proved the presence of a divine creator.

Monsters and prodigies constituted a standing challenge to this law-governed universe and its rational God, and were thus excluded from a central role in the apologetics of natural theology, but they could be used within natural theology's debates, and could even be turned, in specific cases, to the service of demonstrating the truth of natural theology. For example, the question of why, if God made nothing in vain, men had nipples, could be answered by invoking prodigy cases where men actually had suckled children.[111]

The assumed incompatibility between a rationally ordered universe subordinated to a rational God and the existence of monsters and prodigies could also be inverted, and the alleged scarcity of monsters and prodigies presented as evidence of God's existence. This argument was used both by the Cambridge Platonist Ralph Cudworth and by Richard Bentley in his 1692 Boyle Lectures, published as *The Folly and Unreasonableness of Atheism*. Cudworth and Bentley argued that atheism, identified as a random atomism, implied a monstrous universe rather than the regulated one presumed to exist:

> But from the Atheists supposition, that among the infinite Diversity of the first terrestial Productions, there were Animals of all imaginable shapes and structures of Body, all of which survived and multiplied, that by reason of their make and fabric could possibly have done so; it necessarily follows, that we should now have some nations without Nails on their Fingers; others with one Eye only, as the Poets describe the Cyclopes in Sicily, and the Arimaspi in Scythia; others with one Ear, or one Nostril, or indeed without any Organ of Smelling, because that Sense is not necessary to Man's subsistence, others destitute of the use of Language, since mutes may also live; one people would have the Feet of Goats, as the feigned Satyrs and Panisci, another would resemble the Head of Jupiter Ammon, or the horned Statues of Bacchus. The Sciopodes, and Eutocoetae, and other monstrous Nations would no longer be Fables, but real instances in Nature: and, in a word, all the ridiculous and extravagant shapes that can be imagined, all the fancies and whimzies of Poets and Painters and Aegyptian Idolaters, if so they be consistent with Life and Propagation, would now actually be in Being, if our Atheist's Notion were true, which therefore may deservedly pass for a mere dream and an Error: till they please to make new Discoveries in Terra Incognita, and bring along with them some savages of all these fabulous and monstrous continuations.[112]

Not only had no monsters of these types been found, but now the absence of monstrous races was assumed to extend to all those areas not yet explored by Europeans. This shift from an unknown assumed to be monstrous to an unknown assumed to be non-monstrous marked a growing confidence in the universal regularity of nature. The presupposition in favour of a regular universe now meant that even 'Terra Incognita' was assumed to be free of monsters, and their absence was evidence against atheism and in favour of God's existence.

The most thoroughgoing and influential effort to put natural philosophy to theological use was the Reverend William Derham's 1711–12 Boyle Lectures, published in an expanded version as *Physico-Theology: Or, a Demonstration of the Being and Attributes of God, from his Works of Creation*, and reprinted innumerable times throughout the eighteenth century. Reflecting a shift in natural philosophy's apologetics from physics to natural

history, Derham, a fellow of the Royal Society, sought to demonstrate through an exhaustive catalogue of the plant and animal
worlds that everything in nature was designed so as to minister
to the good either of man or of other creatures.[113] The organs of
vision, of the other senses, of respiration, ingestion and genera-
tion were all so good of their kind that they could not have been
bettered. 'We find those works of GOD abundantly to deserve the
Psalmist's Character of being Great and Noble; inasmuch as they
are made with the most exquisite Art . . . contrived with the
utmost Sagacity, and ordered with plain wise Design, and minis-
tering to admirable Ends'.[114]

Derham's emphasis on cosmic regularity and the perfection of
God's design, which as he pointed out several times was superior to that of the best human artisan, meant that he had little
interest in prodigies and monsters as evidence of God's work-
manship. However, *Physico-Theology* did contain material on the
prodigious. Some of it was introduced specifically for the purpose
of amusing the reader, often with a half-apologetic phrase clearly
setting it off from the rest of Derham's work. Phrases such as 'for
the Reader's Satisfaction' and 'for the Reader's Diversion', used
to introduce the topics of bloody rains and bellowing caves
respectively, placed the onus for the inclusion of prodigy material not on Derham himself but on the hypothetical reader with
a presumed taste for marvels.[115] Segregating the prodigious from
the main argument in this way served to emphasize its irrele-
vance to the theological questions Derham sought to address,
while acknowledging its continuing fascination.

Derham did introduce some prodigious material to serve his
arguments, as well as to amuse the reader. One example of this is
material on extraordinary height, longevity and strength among
humans, used not to display the marvellousness of these individuals, but rather to show the invariance of these characteristics
over time, thus refuting the thesis of the decay of nature, which
Derham seems to have thought still had some support in his own
time. Derham denied changes in primary human or natural characteristics over time, at least since the re-peopling of the earth
after the Flood. Odd and exceptional giants and long-livers in
Derham's own era corresponded to odd and exceptional giants
and long-livers in biblical and classical times, but Derham
claimed that the averages of height and length of life among

people had not altered in the intervening time. These regularly occurring irregularities demonstrated the overall unchangingness of the universe.

Following the tradition established by the polemical opponents of the *Mirabilis Annus* tracts during the 1660s, natural philoso phers of the late seventeenth and early eighteenth centuries had deprived prodigies of all particular significance, whether provi- dential or otherwise, as prodigies, and had reduced them to merely unusual natural phenomena.[116] In doing so, they asserted both their claim to primary intellectual authority over a particu- lar class of natural phenomena, and the social usefulness of their philosophy in combating potentially revolutionary prodigy inter- pretation. The success of their efforts, and the growing intellec- tual authority of natural philosophy, however, did not eliminate the tradition of prodigies as divine signs or objects of wonder- ment. It continued to thrive for the rest of the seventeenth century.

Notes

1 See Peter Dear, ' "Totius in verba": rhetoric and authority in the early Royal Society', *Isis*, 76 (1985): 145–61; Brian Vickers, 'The Royal Society and English prose style: a reassessment', in *Rhetoric and the Pursuit of Truth: Language Change in the Seventeenth and Eighteenth Centuries* (Los Angeles: William Andrews Clark Memorial Library, 1985), pp. 1–76; Simon Schaffer and Steven Shapin, *Leviathan and the Air-Pump: Hobbes, Boyle, and the Experimental Life* (Princeton: Princeton University Press, 1985); Steven Shapin, *A Social History of Truth: Civility and Science in Seventeenth-Century England* (Chicago and London: University of Chicago Press, 1994); James Jacob and Margaret Jacob, 'The Anglican origins of modern science: the metaphysical foundations of the Whig constitution', *Isis*, 71 (1980): 251–67; James Jacob, *Robert Boyle and the English Revolution* (New York: Burt Franklin, 1977); and Margaret Jacob, *The Newtonians and the English Revolution 1689–1720* (Ithaca: Cornell University Press, 1976).

2 Spencer's *Discourse Concerning Prodigies* appeared in two editions, a 1663 quarto and a 1665 octavo, with only minor textual variance. The 1665 edition was bound with the *Discourse on Vulgar Prophecies*. The following references to the *Discourse Concerning Prodigies* will be to the 1663 edition. Spencer's *Discourse Concerning Prodigies* is dis-

cussed in Daston and Park, *Wonders and the Order of Nature*, pp. 321, 329; John Gascoigne, ' "The wisdom of the Egyptians" and the secularization of history in the age of Newton', in Stephen Gaukroger, ed., *The Uses of Antiquity: The Scientific Revolution and the Classical Tradition* (Dordrecht: Kluwer Academic Publishers, 1991), pp. 176–8; Hooker, Purpose of Dryden's *Annus Mirabilis*', pp. 128–31; Victor Harris, *All Coherence Gone* (Chicago: University of Chicago Press, 1949), pp. 166–8; and Winship, *Seers of God*, pp. 38–9.

3 Spencer did preach a sermon of thanksgiving for the Restoration, published as *The Righteous Ruler* (Cambridge, 1660). Interestingly, in light of his later views, in this sermon Spencer accepted the Suetonian royalist prodigy theory of the Civil War. 'A King doth not fall like common men, a prodigie in nature commonly gives us notice of his death' (*ibid*), p. 7. Spencer eventually became master of Corpus Christi in 1667.

4 Biographical information on Spencer is from the *DNB* and R. Masters, *Master's History of the College of Corpus Christi and the Blessed Virgin Mary in the University of Cambridge with additional Matter and a continuation to the Present Time by John Lamb D.D. Master of the College* (Cambridge: Cambridge University Press, 1831), pp. 193–201. For Isaac Newton's regard for Spencer, to whom he referred in a letter as 'Spencerus Noster', see *The Correspondence of Isaac Newton*, ed. H.W. Turnbull (Cambridge: Cambridge University Press for the Royal Society, 1961), vol. 3: 185, 291. Another future president of the Royal Society, Samuel Pepys, was also an admirer. In his *Diary* he referred to 'reading Mr. Spencer's book of Prodigys, which is most ingeniously writ, both for matter and style', and later of 'discoursing and admiring of the learning of Dr. Spencer'. See Pepys, *The Diary of Samuel Pepys*, 11 vols, ed. R. C. Latham and W. Matthews (Berkeley and Los Angeles: University of California Press, 1970–83), vol. 5: 165; vol. 7: 133. The royalist poet and clergyman Henry Oxenden excerpted *Discourse Concerning Prodigies* in his *Commonplace Book* (Folger Library MS V.b.110), pp. 485–9.

5 John Spencer, *A Discourse Concerning Prodigies* (Cambridge, 1663), 'Preface'. Since classical antiquity, Africa had been associated for Europeans with the monstrous and strange. See Eldred Jones, *The Elizabethan Image of Africa* (Charlottesville: University Press of Virginia for the Folger Shakespeare Library, 1971), pp. 2–5.

6 Spencer, *Discourse Concerning Prodigies*, 'Preface'.

7 Spencer, *Discourse Concerning Prodigies*, 'Preface'.

8 Spencer, *Discourse Concerning Prodigies*, pp. 73–4. The embarassing case of Thomas Jackson, now a minor hero of the establishment, Spencer handled by asserting that Jackson suffered from melancholia (p. 32). When Jackson's works were reprinted in 1673, the editor,

the Anglican clergyman Barnabas Oley, attempted to position Jackson's views on prodigies between the extremes represented by the *Mirabilis Annus* tracts and Spencer. Thomas Jackson, Preface to *The Works of the Reverend and Learned Divine, Thomas Jackson*, 3 vols (London, 1673).

9 Spencer, *Discourse Concerning Prodigies*, p. 84
10 Spencer, *Discourse Concerning Prodigies*, pp. 2–3.
11 Gascoigne links Spencer's biblical scholarship, which claimed that the ancient Israelites did not receive their religion all at once from God but derived much of it from the Egyptians, with the *Discourse Concerning Prodigies* as demonstrations of how God works through secondary causes. See Gascoigne, 'Wisdom', pp. 175–8.
12 Spencer, *Vulgar Prophecies*, p. 20.
13 Spencer, *Discourse Concerning Prodigies*, p. 60.
14 Spencer, *Discourse Concerning Prodigies*, 'Preface'.
15 Spencer, *Discourse Concerning Prodigies*, p. 17.
16 Spencer, *Discourse Concerning Prodigies*, p. 34.
17 Spencer, *Discourse Concerning Prodigies*, p. 10.
18 Spencer, *Discourse Concerning Prodigies*, p. 60.
19 Spencer, *Discourse Concerning Prodigies*, pp. 17–18, 80.
20 Spencer, *Discourse Concerning Prodigies*, p. 7.
21 Spencer continued to uphold this line in a later conversation with Increase Mather. See Mather, *Angelographia* (Boston, New England, 1696), 'To the Reader'. Despite Spencer's belief that the Devil could cause prodigies, his only reference to witchcraft belief in either the *Discourse Concerning Prodigies* or *Vulgar Prophecies* was sceptical; See *Discourse Concerning Prodigies*, p. 21.
22 Spencer, *Discourse Concerning Prodigies*, pp. 61–2.
23 Spencer, *Discourse Concerning Prodigies*, p. 11.
24 Spencer, *Discourse Concerning Prodigies*, p. 9.
25 Spencer, *Discourse Concerning Prodigies*, 'Preface'.
26 Francis Bacon, *The Two Bookes of Francis Bacon*, II: 8: verso.
27 Spencer, *Discourse Concerning Prodigies*, 'Preface'.
28 Michel Foucault, *The Order of Things* (New York: Vintage Press, 1979); and William Ashworth, 'Natural history and the emblematic world view', in David Lindberg and Robert Westman, eds, *Reappraisals of the Scientific Revolution* (Cambridge: Cambridge University Press, 1990), pp. 303–32.
29 Spencer, *Discourse Concerning Prodigies*, p. 26. Spencer's opposition to this kind of thinking was not consistent. He accepted the doctrine of signatures in discussing the case of medicinal herbs which resemble the parts of the body whose ills they cure. *Discourse Concerning Prodigies*, p. 91.

30 Spencer, *Discourse Concerning Prodigies*, p. 27.
31 Spencer, *Discourse Concerning Prodigies*, p. 61.
32 Spencer, *Discourse Concerning Prodigies*, pp. 40–1.
33 Spencer, *Discourse Concerning Prodigies*, p. 37.
34 Spencer, *Vulgar Prophecies*, pp. 31–2.
35 Spencer, *Discourse Concerning Prodigies*, pp. 8–9.
36 Spencer, *Discourse Concerning Prodigies*, 'Preface'.
37 Spencer, *Discourse Concerning Prodigies*, p. 10.
38 Spencer, *Discourse Concerning Prodigies*, pp. 66–7.
39 Spencer, *Vulgar Prophecies*, pp. 5–6.
40 Spencer, *Discourse Concerning Prodigies*, p. 45.
41 Spencer, *Discourse Concerning Prodigies*, p. 44.
42 Spencer, *Discourse Concerning Prodigies*, p. 103.
43 Spencer, *Discourse Concerning Prodigies*, pp. 83–4. See also *Vulgar Prophecies*, p. 36, where Spencer claimed that 'knowledg [*sic*] of the works of Nature' was one qualification of an Old Testament prophet.
44 Spencer, *Vulgar Prophecies*, pp. 11–12.
45 Spencer, *Discourse Concerning Prodigies*, p. 104.
46 *Mather Papers*, p. 354.
47 Joseph Glanvill, *Philosophia Pia; or a Discourse of the Religious Temper, and Tendencies of the Experimental Philosophy, Which is profest by the Royal Society* (London, 1671), pp. 48–52. Glanvill kept the Spencer material when *Philosophia Pia* was incorporated into *Essays upon Several Important Subjects in Philosophy and Religion* (London, 1676), vol. IV: 15–16.
48 Joseph Glanvill, *Some Philosophical Considerations Touching the Being of Witches and Witchcraft* (London, 1667), pp. 48–9.
49 Thomas Sprat, *History of the Royal Society*, facsimile reprint of London 1667 edition with Introduction and notes by Jackson Cope and Harold Whitmore Jones (St Louis: Washington University Studies, 1959), p. 362.
50 Sprat, *History*, p. 364.
51 Sprat, *History*, p. 358.
52 Sprat, *History*, p. 350.
53 Unlike Spencer, however, Sprat was willing to preserve an occasional intervention by God to punish notorious sin. Sprat, *History*, p. 363.
54 See Royal Society, Register Book Copy (RBC) 8, p. 79, for an account of *parelii* and an upside-down rainbow, and British Library, MS 15948 (Evelyn Correspondence), fos 138–9.
55 *A Character of a Coffee-House* (London, 1665), p. 5.
56 See Barbara Shapiro, *Probability and Certainty in Seventeenth-Century England* (Princeton: Princeton University Press, 1983).

57 For natural-philosophical providentialism, see, *inter alia*, Margaret Jacob, *The Newtonians*; and Larry Stewart, *The Rise of Public Science: Rhetoric, Technology, and Natural Science in Newtonian Britain, 1660–1750* (Cambridge: Cambridge University Press, 1992), pp. 31–59.

58 For rhetorical analysis of Royal Society experimental accounts see Dear, ' "Totius in verba" ', and 'Narratives, anecdotes, and experiments: turning experience into science in the seventeenth century', in Peter Dear, ed., *The Literary Structure of Scientific Argument: Historical Studies* (Philadelphia: University of Pennsylvania Press, 1991), pp. 135–63; and Charles Bazerman, *Shaping Written Knowledge: The Genre and Activity of the Experimental Article in Science* (Madison: University of Wisconsin Press, 1988), pp. 59–150. Dear does not deal with accounts of events outside of the laboratory, however, and neither Dear nor Bazerman spends much time on predecessors to the experimental account.

59 For a struggle between supernatural and medical explanations of a prodigy during the Restoration, see the story of the prolonged fasting of Martha Taylour in Joan Jacobs Brumberg, *Fasting Girls: The History of Anorexia Nervosa* (Cambridge: Harvard University Press, 1988), pp. 50–4; see also *Memoirs for the Ingenious* (October, 1693): 311–24.

60 In Boyle, *Works*, vol. 4: 171.

61 Steven Shapin, 'Pump and circumstance: Robert Boyle's literary technology', *Social Studies of Science*, 14 (1984): 481–520.

62 *Philosophical Transactions*, 14, no. 155 (January 20, 1683/84): 442. Credulity could be located in Russians as well as Turks; see Boyle, *Works*, vol. 6: 642.

63 John Ray, *Further Correspondence of John Ray*, ed. R.T. Gunther (London: Ray Society, 1928), pp. 209–12, Ray to Edward Lhwyd, November 7, 1690. This belief in the light-mindedness of continentals could be put in a national as well as a religious context. Edmond Halley had his doubts about a story from France of a hermaphrodite, although the problem with the French he identified was not credulity or superstition, but 'the bantring ridiculing humour of that light nation'. *Correspondence and Papers of Edmond Halley*, ed. Eugene Fairfield MacPike (Oxford: Clarendon Press, 1932), pp. 81–2. Shapin, *A Social History of Truth*, pp. 97–8, discusses the widespread belief in the general untrustworthiness of the French and the Italians among English natural philosophers.

64 *Correspondence of Henry Oldenburg*, 5: 60–1, and *Philosophical Transactions*, 3, no. 38 (August 17, 1668): 741–43. For another incidence of the Society's activities being put into an anti-Catholic context, see Evelyn, *Diary*, vol. 4: 251–2. This general approach to Catholic

credulity did not preclude the use of Catholic and other foreign writings which argued against the providential view of prodigies. See *Philosophical Collections*, 4 (January 10, 1682): 116–17; and 7 (April 1682): 196–9.

65 John Ray, *Further Correspondence*, pp. 240–2, Ray to Lhwyd, October 26, 1693.

66 *Philosophical Transactions*, 30, no. 360 (March–May 1719): 980.

67 *Correspondence of Henry Oldenburg*, vol. 3: 457–60; and Boyle, *Works*, vol. 6: 386.

68 *Philosophical Transactions*, 13, no. 14 (July 10, 1683): 244–5. Robert Boyle drew a similar contrast between the uses made of eclipses by the 'superstitious vulgar' and those of 'knowing men' who used them for chronology and navigation. See Boyle, *Works*, vol. 5: 418.

69 *Philosophical Transactions*, 20, no. 240 (May, 1698): 193–6.

70 Birch, *History*, vol. 1: 25, 29. For subsequent applications of this theory to rains of wheat see Birch, *History*, vol. 4: 531–2. Rains of wheat could be linked to the Biblical story of manna: see CUL MS Mm.VI.50, fo. 1*.

71 *Philosophical Transactions*, 29, no. 349 (July–September 1716): 466.

72 John Ray in John Aubrey, *The Natural History and Antiquities of the County of Surrey* (London, 1719), p. 408.

73 See Vickers, 'The Royal Society and English prose style'; and Lotte Mulligan, 'Robert Boyle, "right reason", and the meaning of metaphor', *Journal of the History of Ideas*, 55 (1994): 235–57.

74 Robert Hooke, *A Discourse of Comets*, in *Posthumous Works*, ed. Richard Waller (London, 1705), pp. 151–2.

75 *Philosophical Transactions*, 1, no. 5 (July 3, 1665): 85.

76 John Ray, *Miscellaneous Discourses Concerning the Dissolution and Changes of the World* (London, 1692), pp. 41–2.

77 Ray, *Miscellaneous Discourses*, pp. 178–80.

78 Evelyn, *Diary*, vol. 2: 7; vol. 4: 235.

79 Thomas Creech to William Musgrave, September 4, 1684, in Gunther, *Dr. Plot and the Correspondence of the Philosophical Society of Oxford*, Early Science in Oxford no. 12 (Oxford: For the Subscribers, 1939), p. 225.

80 John Evelyn, *The Diary of John Evelyn*, ed. E.S. DeBeer, 6 vols (Oxford: Clarendon Press, 1955), vol. 3: 556–8.

81 *Philosophical Transactions*, 19, no. 215 (January–February 1694/95): 28–31. An interesting example of the transmission of material between the providential realm and that of natural philosophy was the story of some strange lightning which a correspondent of the secretary of the Oxford Philosophical Society, the eminent mathematician and divine Dr John Wallis, relayed to him from Mather's *Essay*

for the Recording of Illustrious Providences. This material had originally appeared in *Philosophical Transactions*, 14, no. 521, from which Mather had taken it. See Gunther, *Dr. Plot*, 221.

82 *Philosophical Transactions*, 24, no. 289 (January–February 1704): 1555. For another theological remark in this issue, see p. 1558. For Thoresby's reading of such classics in the Puritan tradition of providential interpretation as the mid-century Puritan divine Samuel Clarke's *A Mirror or Looking Glass for Saints and Sinners* and Mather's *Essay on Illustrious Providences*, see his *Diary*, vol. 1: 3 and vol. 3: 325.

83 Birch, *History*, vol. 2: 473–4 and Boyle, *Works*, vol. 6: 581–2. The ambivalent relationship of Cotton Mather, a fellow of the Royal Society, to contemporary science was in large part the result of Mather's hostility to what he saw as its denial of providentialism. See Winship, *Seers of God*.

84 Birch, *History*, vol. 4: 483. King James II and VII regarded himself as sceptical of miracles; see Evelyn, *Diary*, vol. 4: 469. However, given English stereotypes about Catholics, this may not have mattered. For Elias Ashmole's non-providential view of the Glastonbury Thorn, see Josten, *Ashmole*, vol. 3: 1286.

85 *Philosophical Transactions*, 33, no. 286 (July–August 1703), 1418. For a more accepting view of the supernatural origin of this prodigy, that of a Scottish Presbyterian minister, see Robert Wodrow, *Analecta, or Materials for a History of Remarkable Providences mostly relating to Scotch Ministers and Christians*, Maitland Club no. 60 ([Edinburgh] Maitland Club, 1842–43), vol. 1: 3. Like the New Englanders, the Scotsman Wodrow, highly educated and also interested in the new natural philosophy, continued to interpret prodigies providentially. He provides an interesting contrast with his English contemporaries. For a view of wonders as a rebuke to atheists, see M. Marsin, *An Answer to Dr. Whitby* (London, 1701), pp. 46–7.

86 Evelyn, *Diary*, vol. 5: 453.

87 A recent study of these is Stan A.E. Mendyk, *'Speculum Britanniae': Regional Study, Antiquarianism, and Science in Britain to 1700* (Toronto, Buffalo, and London: University of Toronto Press, 1989).

88 *Britannia Baconica* is discussed in R. Balfour Daniels, *Some Seventeenth-Century Worthies in a Twentieth-Century Mirror* (Chapel Hill: University of North Carolina Press, 1940), pp. 13–17; and Mendyk, *'Speculum Britanniae'*, pp. 166–9. For Childrey's influence on Robert Plot and subsequent natural historians see Ken Arnold, Cabinets for the curious: practicing science in early modern English museums, Ph.D. dissertation, Princeton University, 1991, pp. 96–7.

89 Joshua Childrey, *Britannia Baconica* (London, 1660), 'Epistle Dedicatory'.

90 Childrey, *Britannia Baconica*, 'Preface'.

91 Childrey, *Britannia Baconica*, p. 24.

92 Childrey, *Britannia Baconica*, 'Epistle Dedicatory'.

93 Childrey, *Britannia Baconica*, p. 14.

94 Childrey, *Britannia Baconica*, pp. 126–7.

95 Childrey, *Britannia Baconica*, p. 128. For a rare example of a prodigy which Childrey neither explained by secondary causes nor dismissed, see *Britannia Baconica*, p. 157.

96 Robert Plot, *Enquiries to be propounded to the most Ingenious of each County in my Travels through England and Wales, in order to their History of Nature and Arts* (np, nd), section I. For recent discussions of Plot's work as a local natural historian and its influence, see Mendyk, *'Speculum Britanniae'*, pp. 193–205; and Arnold, 'Cabinets for the curious', pp. 89–133. For an abortive attempt to create a natural history for the entire British Isles, on a scheme very similar to Plot's and including similar questions on prodigies, see *Athenian Mercury*, 7, no. 3 (April 5, 1692): v.

97 Robert Plot, *The Natural History of Oxfordshire* (Oxford, 1677), p. 1.

98 Plot, *The Natural History of Oxfordshire*, pp. 1–3, 194, 192–93, 171, 181.

99 The notice of *The Natural History of Oxfordshire* in *Philosophical Transactions* referred to it as containing many 'marvels'. *Philosophical Transactions*, 12, no. 138 (May 26, 1677): 875–9.

100 Plot, *Oxfordshire*, p. 3, quoting Isiah 44: 24–5.

101 Plot, *Oxfordshire*, p. 157.

102 Plot, *Oxfordshire*, pp. 2–3.

103 Robert Plot, *The Natural History of Staffordshire* (Oxford, 1686), pp. 304–5.

104 Plot, *Oxfordshire*, p. 197.

105 Plot, *Staffordshire*, pp. 46–7.

106 For Morton and *The Natural History of Northamptonshire*, see Mendyk, *'Speculum Britanniae'*, pp. 223–7.

107 John Morton, *The Natural History of Northamptonshire* (London, 1712), p. 338.

108 Morton, *Northamptonshire*, p. 340.

109 Morton, *Northamptonshire*, p. 351.

110 For the Boyle Lectures, see John Redwood, *Reason, Ridicule, and Religion: The Age of the Enlightenment in England* (London: Harvard University Press, 1976), pp. 103–8; Stewart, *Rise of Public Science*, pp. 64–7; and Margaret Jacob, *The Newtonians*, pp. 143–201. Jacob lists the Boyle Lectures and lecturers to 1714 on pp. 273–4.

111 John Ray, *The Wisdom of God Manifested in the Works of Creation* (London, 1691), p. 156.

112 Richard Bentley, *The Folly and Unreasonableness of Atheism*, 4th edition, corrected (London, 1699), pp. 150–1. Bentley credits this argument to Cudworth, *The True Intellectual System of the Universe*, p. 673.

113 For the rise of 'physico-theology' as opposed to Newtonian apologetic based on astronomy and mathematics, see Neal Gillespie, 'Natural history and the social order: John Ray and the "Newtonian ideology" ', *Journal of the History of Biology*, 20 (1987): 37–8. Gillespie discusses Derham specifically on pp. 47–9. Derham's Boyle Lectures are also discussed in Stewart, *Rise of Public Science*, 52–6.

114 William Derham, *Physico-Theology: or, a Demonstration of the Being and Attributes of God, from his Works of Creation*, 3rd edition (London, 1714), p. 2.

115 Derham, *Physico-Theology*, pp. 23n, 131n.

116 There was a parallel development in the contemporary debate on miracles, which elaborated stricter criteria for what could count as a direct divine intervention in earthly affairs. Thus the category of the preternatural was under increasing pressure both from theology and from natural philosophy. The Whig Bishop William Fleetwood defined a miracle as 'An Extraordinary Operation of God, against the known Course, and settled Laws of Nature, appealing to the senses'. William Fleetwood, *An Essay upon Miracles. In Two Discourses* (London, 1701), p. 2.

3

'A noise of fictitious prodigies': comets and other prodigies in later Restoration politics

Even after the *Mirabilis Annus* affair many prodigies, particularly comets, continued to be interpreted politically and providentially. One of the last major efflorescences of political prodigy writing in England occurred during the Popish Plot and the Exclusion Crisis from 1678 to 1682. However, politically and religiously oppositional prodigy writing also became increasingly defensive, and the long-term trend was clearly towards the political marginalization of prodigies.

One striking aspect of Restoration providential prodigy writing after the *Mirabilis Annus* affair is the prominence of comets, or 'blazing stars', as paradigmatic providential signs, rather than as one of a number of prodigious phenomena.[1] There were several reasons for this. Providential interpretation of comets was somewhat easier to defend against detractors like Spencer than were such interpretations of other prodigies. Unlike the apparitions of battles in the sky, the sighting of a comet was not dependent on the testimony of a small body of witnesses, as it would have been apparent to a wide range of observers throughout the British kingdoms and abroad. A comet's sighting, therefore, unlike that of a rain of blood, could not be attacked. Only its status as the bearer of providential meaning was vulnerable. Comets had another advantage over monstrous births, grotesque squid–jellyfish washed up on the seashore, or other prodigies marked by an undeniable physical object, in that a splendid comet was much easier to associate with a transcendent God than was an ugly or deformed monster. In the increasingly civil world of Restoration England it was difficult to associate the ugly and grotesque with the divine majesty, a point Spencer had made with great effectiveness. The dominant strains of Restoration Anglicanism, whether neo-Laudian or Latitudinarian, associated God with rationality and glory, not monstrosity.

Finally, a number of splendid comets did actually appear during the reign of Charles II. The comets of 1664, 1675, 1677, 1680 and 1682 were often linked with the political and other changes and disasters of the period. Comets which appeared in 1664 and 1665 were linked, as portents, to the great Plague, the Dutch War and the Fire of London. These were particularly strong connections, memorialized iconically in a medal as well as in print and manuscript.[2] Comets were also discussed in the intellectual and natural-philosophical worlds outside of Britain, with the Huguenot Pierre Bayle being inspired by the comet of 1682 to produce his famous tract denouncing belief in the connection of comets to earthly disasters. Bayle's *Pensées sur la comète* was not translated into English until 1708, and its innovative argument that a society of atheists could exhibit moral behaviour had more impact in England than did that part of the book specifically arguing against the divine import of comets and other prodigies, much of the thinking of which had been anticipated by Spencer and others.[3]

Not everyone accepted the providential interpretation of these comets, and one observer thought them generally 'laught at . . . by the Gallants of the Towne'.[4] Pepys, in his correspondence with the Earl of Sandwich who was making important astronomical observations of the 1682 comet, was unsure as to the comet's divine significance, saying: 'God avert its ill bodings (if it have any) and preserve your Lordship.'[5]

This scepticism about the divine meaning of comets and other prodigies had always been present in English culture, but the specific impact of the *Mirabilis Annus* controversy in discrediting providential prodigy interpretation as politically radical and intellectually disreputable was apparent in comet writings, which sometimes explicitly disassociated themselves from providential interpretations. An example of a prodigy pamphlet that, consciously or unconsciously following Spencer and the Royal Society propagandists, disavowed a providential and divinatory line was *The Blazing-Star, or, a Discourse of Comets* (1664).[6] This pro-government work, inspired by the comet of 1664, emphasized natural causes and denied even the possibility of using comets and other prodigies to interpret God's will. It asserted that knowledge of nature took from prodigies not only their divinatory import but even their power to provoke wonder:

> For indeed, it is only our ignorance of things that makes them seem prodigious and miraculous to us, whereas if we knew the true cause, the wonder would soon decline, and seem less, so that what at first seem'd monstrous and miraculous, would then become common, if not altogether slighted.[7]

The Blazing-Star followed the Restoration strategy of identifying providential prodigy interpretation with the lower classes and religious dissenters. 'These Meteors and Commets very rare (scarce one in an age) are by the vulgar people beheld with great admiration, as betokening the destruction of some Nation or Countrey, and thereupon they fancy to themselves strange whimzies and chimeras . . .'.[8] The pamphlet was overtly positioned against a revival of the *Mirabilis Annus* tracts: 'In vain therefore let the Phanaticks hope to reap a golden harvest to themselves, and think to gain Proselytes thereby, which may perhaps produce a new book of Prodigies.'[9]

Gadbury followed his contributions to the *Mirabilis Annus* controversy with a comet tract. *De Cometis* (1665), inspired by the comet of 1664, showed the greater suspicion of prodigies that the astrologer had acquired thanks to the *Mirabilis Annus* affair. His narrative of his initial reaction to reports of the comet was shaped by royalist analysis of subversive prodigy stories: 'The reporters of this Coelestial Prodigie unto me, at the first, were such as I esteemed Discontents, and might therefore reasonably be supposed to raise, spread and promote stories of a strange tendencie, on set purpose to amaze and amuse our late distracted, and not yet well quieted Kingdom.'[10] However, Gadbury claimed to have been eventually convinced of the comet's existence by the writings of astrological friends and a fellow of the Royal Society – people with expertise in the area of astronomical phenomena.[11]

Gadbury's position that comets and other celestial and terrestrial prodigies could be used, with appropriate caution, for the purpose of foreseeing the future had not changed, however: 'Comets, as often as they appear in the world, denounce unto the earth (or persons rather dwelling thereon) heavie tribulations, sorrows, and afflictions; even as earth-quakes, or some prodigious terrene births, or fishes to foresake their elements, birds theirs, or the like.'[12] He retained the idea that this interpretation was the purview of those with specific expertise, most definitely including astrologers.

The comets of 1675 and 1677 became in retrospect heralds of the Popish Plot, and were linked to the 1664 comet as a series of disastrous omens.[13] Subsequent highly noticeable comets followed in 1680 and 1682 during the crisis itself and were merged into its discourse.[14] The surveyor John Holwell published a number of astrological and millenarian tracts drawing on the comet and the conjunction of Saturn and Jupiter.[15] Both supporters and opponents of the providential meaning of prodigies focused on comets, as did the Irish cleric Edward Wetenhall in his tract attacking those who derived meaning from the 1680 comet, *A Judgement of the Comet* (1682), and the Church of England Calvinist John Edwards in his defense of that position in *Cometomantia, or A Discourse of Comets* (1684).[16] Wetenhall set his work within the context of strange consternations and fear of plots occasioned by the comet, an appropriate one for the early 1680s. Edwards, by contrast, writing in favour of providential interpretations of comets, at the height of the Tory reaction following the defeat of the Whigs, avoided current politics entirely. In an echo of old Interregnum and early Restoration battles between astrological and providential interpreters of strange celestial phenomena, Gadbury attacked Edwards for denying that regular and predictable celestial events could be predictive of the future, employing the work of natural philosophers such as the French astronomer Adrien Auzout to argue that comets as much as any other celestial phenomena followed ascertainable laws.[17]

Prodigies and the press in the Popish Plot and Exclusion Crises

Unlike the English Civil War, the crisis of the Stuart state extending from 1678 to 1683 has been viewed by historians in a largely rational and secular light. This period was marked by a return to sharp political polarization, now defined as between 'Whig' and

'Tory' positions, as these terms were first introduced into English politics. The existence of organized Whig and Tory parties in the 1670s and 1680s has been asserted in previous works on the crisis, such as J.R. Jones's *The First Whigs: The Politics of the Exclusion Crisis 1678–1683* (1961) and K.H.D. Haley's *The First Earl of Shaftesbury* (1968). The usefulness of treating the Whigs and the Tories as parties, or even of talking about the existence at the time of Whigs and Tories, has been questioned in more recent scholarship, most notably by Jonathan Scott in *Algernon Sidney and the Restoration Crisis* (1991). Certainly many members of the political nation did not identify with either position, or else moved between the two. However, there were certainly distinct Whig and Tory discursive and ideological positions, and even Scott acknowledges the existence of a hard core on either side. Neither traditionalists nor revisionists have had much to say about prodigies.

The crisis began with false allegations of a Catholic plot to assassinate the king and to enthrone his Catholic brother James, Duke of York – the 'Popish Plot'. Subsequently, Whigs attempted to pass a law through Parliament excluding James, and other Catholics, from the hereditary succession, or, alternatively, to limit royal power – the so-called 'Exclusion Crisis'.[18] Although anti-Catholicism has been given, rightly, much weight in examining the roots of the crisis, it has often been viewed either as an unthinking xenophobic prejudice on the part of the common folk or as a justified fear of absolutism or French domination on the part of the ruling classes and intellectuals, such as John Locke or Algernon Sidney. Scholarly analysis of the 'Restoration Crisis' as a whole has portrayed politics, particularly Whig politics, in a cool and secular, 'Lockean', light in which the belief in prodigies as apocalyptic signs could find no place. Even studies specifically devoted to Whig ideology and propaganda, such as Melinda Zook's study of radical Whigs or Richard Ashcraft's work on Locke, have not, in my opinion, fully plumbed those aspects of Whig politics, particularly the religious motivations, that in the twentieth century seemed less rational.[19] Historians have used less than the full range of sources, ignoring in particular prodigy tracts and accounts, almanacs, prognostications, and astrological and millenarian works. This has impoverished our picture of the controversy, leading to an exaggeration of Whig modernity.

An examination of the prodigy and other supernatural literature surrounding the crisis, however, reveals that many Whigs were still radical and apocalyptic anti-Catholics, occupying much the same mental universe as the writers of the *Mirabilis Annus* tracts and other radical dissenters and Puritans of the Civil War and the early Restoration. Many Whigs expected great political events to be accompanied by signs and wonders. This expectation can be traced to the very roots of the crisis. Ezerel Tonge, Oates's somewhat unbalanced promoter and collaborator in setting forth the initial plot story, published in 1680 a collection of old prophecies and eccentric apocalyptic interpretation, *The Northern Star the British Monarchy*, urging an aggressively anti-Catholic policy. This collection also included providential analysis of prodigies such as comets and new stars.[20]

Prodigy writing was also well suited to the constraints imposed on discourse during the crisis. The type of reading associated with opposition during the Restoration, one based on decoding references and the insertion into what appeared to be 'harmless' works of opinions that could not be openly espoused, was easily adaptable to decoding prodigies.[21] The *Mirabilis Annus* tracts had already employed this device, for example in the case of the Surrey gentleman who saw the large cathedral in the sky destroyed and the small church exalted.

The necessary condition for the emergence of prodigy tracts and other printed propaganda in the crises was the lapsing of the Licensing Act with the dissolution of Parliament in 1678. This led to the outpouring of oppositional material from the presses, including the first non-governmental newspapers to appear since the Restoration, in a situation reminiscent of the collapse of censorship during the Civil War. These newspapers and other tracts included a great deal of prodigy and other supernatural material.[22] One of the most indefatigable prodigy compilers and interpreters of the late seventeenth century, the London Independent minister Christopher Ness (1621–1705), also published works related to the crises.

The central event of the early phase of the Popish Plot Crisis was the finding of the murdered body of the London magistrate Sir Edmundbury Godfrey on October 17, 1678. His murder was ascribed to Catholics. Fittingly then, the image of Godfrey, a Protestant hero, was connected with some of the earliest prodigy material surrounding the crisis. One of these early prodigies was a mysterious darkness over London for about half-an-hour, during which an image of Godfrey allegedly appeared in the chapel of Queen Catherine of Braganza, a Catholic and the target of much xenophobic and anti-Catholic resentment.[23] Gadbury, who would later be imprisoned as a suspected Catholic plotter, found this story of sufficient importance to attack it two years later in a discussion of recent prodigies in his almanac for 1681, claiming that the darkness had natural causes and the appearance of Godfrey was mythical.[24]

Although not exactly a prodigy, the story of the maid of Hatfield, Elizabeth Freeman, who received a vision ordering her to warn the king not to dissolve Parliament, shows the pervasiveness of supernatural and divine intervention in the minds of some Whigs, and was often discussed in the context of prodigies.[25] However, the Whig press and some Whig individuals treated the woman and her vision with some scepticism, showing a growing reluctance to admit the possibility of direct divine communication, especially with women, even when the communication supported Whig political goals.[26] The Tory press treated the Maid as a 'melancholic' and the fact that her warning to the king went unheeded was seen as discrediting the Whig cause.[27]

The comet of 1680 was connected to a more complex political prodigy, harder to decode, but clearly confrontational. The broadside *The Wonderful Blazing Star, With the Dreadful Apparition of Two Armies in the Air* (1681) has the fullest account of this battle in the sky, reminiscent of the prodigy accounts of the Civil War. The broadside began by asserting that comets were providential signs. It then gave a description of the event, credited to an anonymous witness who had been out with a group of others to view the comet. Suddenly they beheld two armies appear, one from the north, one from the south. The leader of the northern army was described as coroneted, a coronet being associated with nobles of princely or ducal rank. The north was the location both of York, of which James was duke, and Scotland, where he was residing as high commissioner while England was too politically dangerous for him. The north of England had a larger Catholic population than did the south, and it was in the north that the sixteenth-century Catholic revolts of the Pilgrimage of Grace and the Northern Earls had emerged. The narrative went on to describe the defeat of the northern by the southern army, implicitly expressing hope for the ultimate defeat of James and Catholicism.[28]

The most bizarre Whig prodigy presented during the crisis was undoubtedly the Protestant Elm Board. This piece of elm appeared in 1682, during the defeat of the Whigs, and would purportedly utter Protestant slogans when touched with a hot iron. Elm boards toured the country, and one newspaper claimed the 'Groaning-Board' had been shown before the king.[29] Groaning boards quickly became targets of Tory ridicule, focused on the 'Giddy Vulgar'.[30] Groaning elm boards could be severed from Protestant propaganda – Anthony Wood mentioned a groaning board which was exhibited at Oxford in November of 1682, but did not treat it as having political meaning. However, in the Tory stronghold of Oxford, the vice-chancellor of the university quickly shut down the exhibit.[31] At least one natural philosopher filled the role envisioned by Spencer and Sprat in combating providential explanation. In his 1682 *The Anatomy of Plants*, the botanist and fellow of the Royal Society Nehemiah Grew presented a natural-philosophical explanation for 'Groaning-Boards, lately exposed, as a kind of Prodigy, to the view and hearing of many People' based on the expansion of air and water within the veins of the wood.[32]

Whig newspapers presented a variety of prodigy stories, with and without providential contexts. Some of the Whig newspaper printers also printed or published prodigy tracts – Langley Curtiss printed Ness's *Signes of the Times* for the author, subsequently advertising it in his newspaper, the *True Protestant Mercury*.[33] Not all Whigs by any means used or approved of the use of prodigy accounts to advance Whig political goals. Whig newspapers, perhaps mindful of the discrediting of the *Mirabilis Annus* tracts, were often sceptical of prodigies and providential interpretation.[34] They sometimes cast doubt on prodigy stories, explicitly disassociating themselves from the veracity of the accounts, and disclaiming 'any intent to disturb people with a noise of fictitious Prodigies'.[35] Some, usually those more inclined to a relatively secular than an apocalyptic political analysis, ascribed providential prodigy belief to 'ignorant people'.[36] This Whig scepticism points to changes in the relation of prodigy beliefs to social divisions which would accelerate in the ensuing decades. Social rank and gender rather than religious and political affiliations would be seen as dividing believers and non-believers in providential interpretation.

The first important Whig journalist was Henry Care, whose periodical, taking different names but most commonly that of the *Weekly Pacquet of Advice from Rome*, combined tendentiously anti-Catholic recountings of the history of the Catholic Church or satirical expositions of Catholic doctrine with a satirical 'Popish Courant', often in dialogue form. Care took one of the most consistently anti-providential and anti-astrological attitudes toward prodigies of any Whig journalist, although, any stick being good enough to beat Rome with, he was not above attacks on popes for failing to take note of prodigies.[37]

Tory defenders of the royal family and the Church of England continued to attack their Whig opponents as the heirs of the rebels of the 1640s. Part of their counteroffensive was to allege both credulity and cynical manipulation of false prodigies on the part of the Whigs. The principal printed vehicles for Tory propaganda were two quasi-official periodicals, the veteran propagandist and censor Roger L'Estrange's *Observator* and Edward Rawlins's *Heraclitus Ridens*.[38] These were less newspapers than presentations of the Tory position in dialogue form. Nathaniel ('Popish Nat') Thompson's *The Loyal Protestant, and True Domestick Intelligence*, along with the official *London Gazette*, were the newspapers most closely identified with the Tories.

Attacks on Whig newspapers were a specialty of L'Estrange. In an attack on the Whig newspapermen Richard Janeway and Richard Baldwin, L'Estrange accused them of fabricating prodigies and judgements to benefit the Whig cause:

> Some Prodigy is found out perhaps, to foretell a Change of Government; and not so much as a Glow-worm, for the Foundation of it. They'l tell you of a man that was strangely visited with an ulcer under his Tongue, as a just Judgement upon him, for whistling Greensleeves upon the Lord's Day. But you hear nothing of their own popular minion that was eaten up with lice.[39]

Sincere or pretended belief in the providential interpretation of prodigies was generally ascribed to Whigs as one aspect of their dissenting fanaticism and hatred of the king and the Church. Conversely, 'Trimmer', the butt of the later *Observator*, accused 'Observator', L'Estrange's mouthpiece, of excessive scepticism.

Quoting 'Mr. Mather of New England' as an authority on comets, Trimmer declared: 'You have no more opinion of Providence, then if the world were Govern'd at Hap-Hazzard: Blazing Stars, Prodigies, Comets, Portents, and Signs in the Heavens, go for Nothing with you.'[40] It was not a charge which troubled L'Estrange.

In addition to direct attacks on Whig prodigy material, the *Observator* attacked the providential and astrological intellectual systems which supported prodigy-belief. L'Estrange consistently attacked astrologers, including even the royalist Gadbury, as politically subversive, claiming that the ambiguity and generality of astrological predictions were ruses to mask an anti-governmental intent.[41] What L'Estrange claimed was the dissenting and Whig habit of calling for God's judgements on their opponents he condemned for being no better than cursing, as both involved the invocation of divine power to settle a personal score.[42]

The anonymously published and satirical *Heraclitus Ridens* printed the more jocose attacks on Whig prodigy stories. Its first issue included an parodic 'advertisement' that satirized Benjamin Harris, the Whig editor of the *Domestick Intelligence*, as a prodigy-monger.

> If any person out of Natural Curiosity desire to be furnished with Ships or Castles in the Air, or any sorts of Prodigies, Apparitions, or strange Sights, the better to fright People out of their Senses, and by persuading them there are strange Judgements, Changes, and Revolutions hanging over their heads, thereby to persuade them to pull them down by Discontents, Fears, Jealousies, and Seditions, let them repair to Ben. Harris at his Shop near the Royal Exchange, where they may be furnished with all Sorts and Sizes of them, at very cheap and easie Rates.[43]

In a subsequent issue, *Heraclitus Ridens* described the allegorical marriage of 'Popular Fears' and 'Jealousy'. This marriage, for which the Maid of Hatfield would be a maid of honour, 'will beget Apparitions with White Hands and Red Hands, Visions, Revelations, true Protestant Intelligences, Mercuries, Speeches, and so on to the End of the Chapter'.[44] In a story about people vomiting pins and needles, *Heraclitus Ridens* exclaimed: 'Bless us all! I wonder the prodigy-makers never got this by the end; with good Husbandry they might have made a world of Mercuries and Intelligences out of it.[45] These satirical Tory attacks linked three different critiques of the prodigious. Prodigies were attacked, not only as politically subversive, but as the product of popular superstition, and as sensations fabricated and exhibited for commercial profit.

As both *Heraclitus Ridens* and *The Observator* were attempting to win over the middle ground of those undecided on the Popish Plot, their use of the charge of credulity concerning prodigies as a way of discrediting the Whig press indicates their editors' view that their audiences were coming to be suspicious of providential prodigy interpretation.

Attacks on the Whigs as spreaders of prodigy tales continued in the period of Whig defeat. In late 1682, as the Whig cause was collapsing, an anonymous satirist attributed to the Whig leader Shaftesbury a plan to spread prodigy tales such as those of speaking newborn children and multiple suns to encourage rebellion. Significantly, 'good wives', a very marginalized group in terms of intellectual authority, were to be the spreaders of the fictitious prodigies, continuing the feminine gendering of providential prodigy belief.[46]

In addition to journalistic and satirical writings, other vehicles of Tory propaganda, such as the Anglican pulpit, attacked Whig's and dissenters' prodigy belief. Ralph Thoresby, himself sympathetic to dissent, attended a Church of England sermon preached on November 12, 1682 in which the vicar 'showed prettily how apt we are to fear such things as are seldom observed, or that appear in an extraordinary manner, as eclipses, lightnings, thunders, &c. and yet how few make them arguments to fear the Lord, who made the heavens and the earth, and then for comets, apparitions, whales, what strange effects they have on vulgar apprehensions; and then gave a lash or two at the poor Dissenters . . .'.[47] Another Church of England pulpiteer attacked groaning boards, preaching 'that an Enthusiast was so infatuated, that he would take a rotten post for a prophet'.[48] By posing as deniers of the providential meaning of prodigies, Tories hoped to appeal to the undecided, painting Whigs as superstitious and unscrupulous peddlers of ridiculous lies.

Not all Tory propaganda was sceptical of prodigies, however.

As might be expected, Tories used prodigy stories in the Suetonian tradition to indicate the peculiar supernatural status of the royal house. The herald John Gibbon made something of a specialty of demonstrating providence's marking out of James as a future king.[49] The principal employment for Suetonian biographical prodigies, however, was not as journalistic or topical propaganda but as poetic conventions, as in the omens recounted in John Dryden's *Threnodia Augustalis* on the death of Charles II in 1685. Interestingly, however, the equally Tory Aphra Behn rhetorically complained that Charles's death was *not* heralded by prodigies in her poem on the subject, *A Pindarick on the Death of our Late Sovereign, with an Ancient Prophecy on his Present Majesty* (lines 19–34) Behn had previously worked within the Suetonian tradition, making use of a great deal of royalist prodigy material in her English translation of the sixth book of Abraham Cowley's poem on plants, published as *Of Plants*, including Charles II's star.[50] This discrepancy indicates more than Dryden's and Behn's differing poetic choices. The fact that such diametrically opposed positions could be taken on the announcement of a king's death by Suetonian prodigies, one of the most common ways that prodigies appeared in both history and poetry, shows that by the end of Charles's reign royalist conventions about the poetic connection of prodigies to monarchs had become unsettled.

Both Whig and Tory satire, as well as works not immediately related to political controversy, contributed to the marginalization of the providential interpretation of prodigies by adopting the form and characteristics of prodigy accounts as vehicles for messages having little to do with prodigies. This began to be a widely used device during the Exclusion Crisis, when either side described the other as monsters, in writings whose titles and contents closely paralleled pamphlets describing monstrous births, such as *New News of a Strange Monster found in Stow Woods near Buckingham of Human Shape, with a Double Heart, and no Hands; a Head with Two Tongues, and no Brains* (1679); or the satirical denunciation of Oates as a sodomite, which took the form of a description of the wonder of a male giving birth, in *Strange and Wonderful News from Southwark* (1684). By the early eighteenth century, the use of such titles had become quite common. Such transparently fictional allegories may have contributed to a diminished belief in actual prodigies.

The last stand of radical Protestant prodigy interpretation: the Reverend Christopher Ness

Dissenting ministers such as Oliver Heywood continued to be the leading interpreters of prodigies as 'moral tokens of a lying spirit prevailing in the world', and possible evidence of the return of popery to England.[51] The most prolific of these ministerial interpreters of the Popish Plot and the Exclusion Crises in prodigious and apocalyptic terms was the London Independent minister, astrologer and Shaftesbury Whig Christopher Ness (or Nesse).[52] Although he published a great deal, and his Independent congregation allegedly included 'some people of quality', Ness is an almost entirely forgotten figure.[53] Historians of astrology such as Curry have focused, in studies of the late seventeenth century, on the rational reformers of astrology like Gadbury, and have completely ignored Ness's prophetic and religious astrology. Historians of the Popish Plot have generally ignored its apocalyptic dimension, which was central for Ness. Even historians of the dissenting opposition to Charles II and James II, Richard Greaves for example, have not written about Ness.

Although Ness, a Yorkshireman by birth, was already an old man by the time of the Popish Plot, I have not been able to find evidence of his involvement in prodigy gathering or prodigy writing before the 1670s. One clue as to Ness's attitude to prodigies before the crisis is in the notes for a sermon he preached on Daniel 3:28, probably sometime between 1669 and 1672. These note are in the Hall Sermon Notebook in the British Library. Ness contrasted at length the behaviour of the king in spreading the story of the miraculous survival in the fiery furnace of Meshach, Shadrach and Abednego with that of the Jews in suppressing the story of Lazarus.[54] Given the strongly anti-government and anti-established Church tenor of the sermon as a whole, this was probably a veiled reference to the suppression of the *Mirabilis Annus* tracts and other prodigy stories by the Restoration government.

During the Popish Plot Crisis, Ness was a zealous Whig and supporter of Shaftesbury, to whom he fulsomely dedicated his anti-Catholic and apocalyptic *A Discovery of the Person and Period of Antichrist* (1679). His principal prodigy writing concerning the Popish Plot was *The Signes of the Times* (1681), printed for the author by Langley Curtiss, and advertised in Curtiss's news paper *True Protestant Mercury*.[55] This work was the last of the important prodigy compilations designed to promote a particular oppositional politico-religious stance on current issues to be produced in England. It followed in the general tradition stemming from Lycosthenes, Batman and the Elizabethan Protestant prodigy writers in drawing a distinction between prodigies and miracles, the latter having ceased in the early ages of the Church. Throughout Ness's prodigious and astrological writings, contemporary miracles were presented as papist frauds.[56] Ness continued to use the distinction between supernatural and preternatural wonders to distinguish between prodigies and miracles.[57] Like many providential astrologers and interpreters of celestial prodigies, Ness also tried to distinguish himself from the practitioners of judicial astrology, which he identified with pagan star-worship.[58]

Signes of the Times was presented as a continuation of the *Mirabilis Annus* tracts. Like the first of them, it covered a single year, referring to 1680 on the title page as 'another Annus Mirabilis'. The comparison between 1680 and 1660 was made explicit later in the body of the text.[59] Although a much more diffuse and rambling text than any of the *Mirabilis Annus* tracts, and containing a much smaller number of prodigies, *Signes* was also divided into sections on air, earth and water. In the last section, the recent drying up of the River Wye was compared to the drying up of the Derwent in 1660, an event discussed in the *Mirabilis Annus* tracts.[60] Like the first *Mirabilis Annus* tract, Ness also connected contemporary prodigies to those marking previous unsuccessful reigns.[61] *The Signes of the Times* was also recommended as a discussion of the present 'Age of Wonders' in the influential pseudonymous Whig tract *Multum in Parvo*, which traced parallels between the Parliaments of Charles I and the Parliaments of the crisis itself.[62]

The response to the *Mirabilis Annus* affair shaped Ness's text at a deeper level. Ness presented himself as learning from the mistakes of his predecessors:

> Many strange Meteors which I designedly omit, untill I get better prooff (which I truly desire from all good Hands) well knowing my Brethren that went before me in this work 20 years ago, some do blame for credulity: Alterius perditio mea fit cautio. The censure passed upon my Predecessors (in the like work) for being over

Credulous, hath been cogent to make me a little the more cautelous.[63]

Ness also attempted to extenuate the failed apocalypticism of the *Mirabilis Annus* tracts, suggesting that the prodigies of 1660 and 1661 were portents of the Plague and the Fire of London rather than the apocalypse.[64] He did not exclude the coming of the millenium from the range of possible significations of prodigies, however. He argued that a contemporary comet could possibly presage the Fifth Monarchy, but did not commit himself in this tract on the imminence of the apocalypse.[65] (Some of his other writings during the crisis were much more apocalyptic in orientation.)

Ness discussed a much smaller number of prodigies than had his predecessors in the *Mirabilis Annus* tracts, possibly reflecting more caution and also a smaller or non-existent network of people to gather prodigy accounts. Unlike the producers of the *Mirabilis Annus* tracts, Ness does not seem to have attracted the attention of the government. This might reflect a weakening of censorship in the time following the expiration of the Licensing Act or indicate that Ness's work was simply less well circulated and influential than the preceding prodigy tracts.

The politics of Ness's tracts was not entirely religious and apocalyptic. He was also capable of using secular Whig or 'commonwealth' arguments, as when he made an analogy between a serpent becoming a dragon by devouring other serpents and Royal Prerogative becoming monstrous by devouring 'Privilege of Parliament', 'Liberty' and 'Property'.[66] Nor did his Exclusionist politics determine completely his attitude to particular prodigies – like the newspaper writers he was highly sceptical of the Maid of Hatfield, finding it difficult to accept the idea of direct spiritual contacts with mortals in the current era.[67]

The challenge to the providential interpretation of prodigies posed by the natural philosophy of the seventeenth century posed a specific problem for Ness's work. The dedicatory epistle in *Signes* attempted to identify the reduction of prodigies to natural events as atheism: 'There be too many Atheists, who do extenuate, and undervalue all Prodigies, Heathenishly ascribing them to Dame Nature only, whereby they do dangerously Darken the Power and Providence of Almighty God.' This passage is of particular interest in that it shows that Ness, like others in this period, drew no clear distinction between atheists on the one hand and heathens worshipping a fecund nature on the other. Both denied the essentially providential causation of prodigies. Ness's opposition to ascribing prodigies to a personified Nature, whose inferior gender he emphasized by the term 'Dame Nature', was in fact shared by natural philosophers, for instance Boyle. Ness was not opposed to finding some role for natural philosophy in collecting observations of prodigies, however, and he employed material from 'Foreign mathematicians' in describing a comet.[68]

Ness's other prodigy writings, mostly following *Signes*, placed the crisis in an eschatological and astrological framework focusing on a recent series of significant astrological events including a Jupiter–Saturn conjunction and the many comets. Such works as *A Philosophical and Divine Discourse Blazoning upon this Blazing Star* (1681), *An Astrological and Theological Discourse upon this Present Great Conjunction* (1682), *A True Account of this Present Blasing-Star* (1682), and *A Strange and Wonderful Trinity; or, a Triplicity of Stupendious Prodigies, consisting of a Wonderful Eclipse, as well as of a Wonderful Comet, and of a Wonderful Conjunction* (1683), all of which were published by Langley Curtiss, attempted to keep the banner of apocalyptic astrology and prodigy interpretation aloft, in a milieu in which it they were increasingly marginalized, by providing a systematic body of interpretations.[69] In a more general context, Ness claimed that 'if so many prodigys attended Christs' passion, surely many more may attend his Return in Glory and the end of the World, many strange conjunctions in Heaven, Earth and Sea'.[70]

Although Ness published a great deal of prodigy- and prophecy-related material during the crises, the frequency with which his works were advertised in the newspapers indicates that they were not best sellers, and the evidence for them having been read at all is much sparser than for the *Mirabilis Annus* tracts. His work never attained a high public profile, and his failure indicates the growing marginalization of radical Protestant prodigy interpretation. Ness was also the last radical Protestant prodigy interpreter to treat prodigies at length as directly related to current political issues. After the Exclusion Crisis, during the Tory reaction when a more effective censorship was back in place, prodigy stories with political implications would be circulated orally and in private letters among dissenters, but not published. Even after the freeing of the press in 1695, radical Protestant apocalyptic prodigy interpretation would be published mainly by self-consciously marginal radical millenarians such as the dissenting minister Thomas Beverley and the pseudonymous prophetess M. Marsin whose predictions of impending doom were politically irrelevant.[71]

Prodigies and politics after the Exclusion Crisis

Whig defeat in the Exclusion Crisis was followed by Tory and Anglican dominance, the period of 'Tory reaction'. This culminated in the peaceful and uncontested accession of the openly Catholic James II in 1685. Although no spectacular prodigies marked these events, Whigs could console themselves by circulating stories concerning the bad omens at James's coronation such as the collapse of the canopy over him and the loss of pearls from his crown.[72] Whigs and dissenters could also console themselves with the terrible storms which followed the execution of the Whig martyr Lord Russell or the beating of the invisible drum at Oundle, known to be always succeeded by 'some great revolution', such as the death of Charles I or of Charles II.[73] However, prodigies played little role in the Whig-backed duke of Monmouth's disastrous rebellion against James in 1685, possibly reflecting the regime's tight control of the press.

Official discourse continued to scorn prodigies and providential interpretation. Henry Care had turned his coat early in 1688 to write *Publick Occurences Truly Stated*, a newspaper propagandizing for James's attempt to install tolerance by royal authority, which was strongly opposed by the leadership of the Church of England. One position that Care retained from his days as an Exclusionist Whig was a contempt for prodigy-mongering, and in his new role as a supporter of James he continued to scoff at 'foolish omens' of 'idle heads'.[74] Ironically, when Care died shortly after the inauguration of his new paper, he himself became a subject of exactly the kind of story he would have detested, and his successor as writer of *Publick Occurences* had to dispel a rumour that Care's death had been precipitated by his hand rotting off as 'a Judgement upon him for Writing against the Church of England'.[75]

The bad omens at James's coronation were more than fulfilled in the Revolution of 1688, which worked a seachange in English politics, replacing James II with his Dutch nephew and son-in-law William of Orange and his wife and James's daughter Mary, ending what some English Protestants regarded as the threat of a Catholic monarch. This revolution was preceded and accompanied by far fewer and widely publicized prodigies than had been the Popish Plot.[76]

One panegyrist of William exploited this lack of prodigies by reversing the usual relation of Suetonian prodigies to monarchical glory, claiming that a particular mark of heaven's favour was that William's invasion was not preceded by 'Prophetick Stars', although this was not quite true.[77] The old Exclusionist Richard Janeway, more politically consistent than Care, included a prodigy account in the first issue of his publication *A Collection of Papers Relating to the Present Juncture of Affairs in England*. Janeway claimed that on May 6, 1665, when William had first taken possession of the Principality of Orange, a 'Crown of Light' had appeared over the chair of state, and that a similar crown had appeared the same day in 1688.[78] The purpose of this story was clear – to indicate the divine favour William enjoyed, and to show him as not merely a Dutch *statholder*, but a possessor of some of the aura of kingship associated with Suetonian prodigies. However, the story never assumed a great deal of prominence, nor was it supplemented with other prodigy stories about William.[79] One possible reason for this silence is that neither supporters nor opponents of the revolution knew any longer how to work prodigies into their propaganda. As can be seen in the ambivalence of the Whig press toward prodigies during the Exclusion Crisis, prodigies had become increasingly problematic for dissenters and oppositionists, but supporters of the Stuarts were also still leary of them.

The revolution's settlement and the assumption of the throne by William and Mary meant that radical opposition to the dominant order was no longer identified with the dissenters, but with the extreme high-church faction of the Church of England, 'non-jurors' who refused to swear the new oaths to William and Mary, claiming that this act would violate their obedience to their rightful monarch. These 'Jacobites', upholding the right of the exiled King James and later of his descendants, were now the principal domestic targets of the state's ideological mobilization, while the dissenters, enjoying the benefits of tolerance and identifying William's war against Louis XIV as an anti-Catholic crusade, were rapidly becoming pillars of the established order. No longer was it necessary or desirable for dissenting ministers to compile accounts of prodigies to demonstrate God's displeasure with England. Although occasional pamphlets and ballads appeared using prodigies to demonstrate God's love for the regime, Whigs and other supporters of the post-revolution order tended to eschew the presentation of prodigies, as had the victorious royalists of the Restoration period.[80] In both cases, the association of prodigies with social disruption and civil unrest limited the use that governments and their supporters could make of them.

Not all Whigs were to accept the monarchy, whether of William and Mary or of King George, as the fulfilment of their dreams, but even radical republican or 'commonwealth' Whigs repudiated the political use of prodigies, as can be seen from the edition of Ludlow's *Memoirs* appearing in 1698. This edition was edited and expurgated by the deist and republican John Toland, who secularized Ludlow's originally religious and apocalyptic work. In doing so, Toland removed all reference to the *Mirabilis Annus* tracts, along with much other providential and millenarian material.[81] As the religious basis of radical Whig opposition shifted from trinitarian Calvinism of the style of Christopher Ness to deism, Socinianism or Arianism, radical Whigs began to think of divine action as remote from the day-to-day operations of the world. This way of thinking usually precluded the religio-political use of prodigies. However, the Jacobites did not pick up the fallen banner. No non-juring Jessey or Ness compiled and publicized prodigies to show God's anger at William, Anne or the Hanoverians, despite the somewhat more favourable conditions for expression created by the lapse of the Licensing Act in 1695. So ingrained had become the anti-providential way of thinking about prodigies and the association between political prodigy interpretation and radical dissenters among royalist Tories in the reigns of Charles II and James II that it persisted into the period of Jacobite opposition.

Although the period from the Restoration to the revolution did not end the political use of providential prodigies in England, it clearly identified such use as intellectually and culturally suspect. Now such uses had to be defended not only from charges of being potentially revolutionary, but from charges of being superstitious, fraudulent or simply vulgar. Conversely, the mere charge of employing providential prodigies in politics, whatever the prodigies or their interpretation, was now something discrediting. However, prodigies remained too useful to be simply abandoned. They could still be interpreted in providential, if not politically partisan, ways. This type of interpretation would be the hallmark of the prodigy literature of the reign of William III.

Notes

1 For English reaction to comets in this period, see Sara Schechner Genuth, *Comets, Popular Culture, and the Birth of Modern Cosmology* (Princeton: Princeton University Press, 1997), pp. 66–88; and G.S. Rousseau, ' "Wicked Whiston" and the Scriblerians: another ancients–modern controversy', *Studies in Eighteenth Century Culture*, 17 (1987): 17–44.

2 For an account in a letter of the comet, or 'blazing star', of 1664 explicitly linking it to other recent apparitions and 'a strange monster', see Trevelyan and Trevelyan, eds, *Trevelyan Papers*, part III, 293–4. For other interpretations by contemporaries of comets and blazing stars of the 1660s as providential signs, see Thomas Rugge, 'Mercurius Politicus Reviv'd, or Diurnall', BL Add. MSS 10116–17, II: fos 125r, 126v; Ralph Josselin, *The Diary of Ralph Josselin*, 515, 541; Adam Martindale, *The Life of Adam Martindale written by Himself*, ed. Reverend Richard Parkinson, Chetham Society no. 4 (Manchester: Chetham Society, 1845), p. 179; Pepys, *Diary*, vol. 9: 208; Josten, *Ashmole*, vol. 4: 1511; *Heywood Diary*, vol. 3: 92–3; and Wood, *Life and Times*, vol. 2: 53–4. Englishmen did not only link comets to political changes in England and Europe: see Robert Knox, *An Historical Relation of the Island of Ceylon in the East-Indies* (London, 1681), p. 58, for a connection of the 'fearful Blazing-star' with a Ceylonese rebellion. For a sampling of the connections made between the comet and the Plague and Fire, see Edward Terrill's *The Record of a Church of Christ in Bristol*, ed. Roger Haydon, Bristol Record Society's Publications no. 27 (Bristol: Bristol Records Society, 1974); p. 121; Wood, *Life and Times*, vol. 2: 24; John Pinney, *Letters of John Pinney 1679–1699* (London:

Oxford University Press, 1939), p. 127; and James Yonge, *The Journal of James Yonge [1647–1721], Plymouth Surgeon*, ed. F.N.L. Poynter (London: Longmans, 1963), p. 71. The medal is reproduced in Augustus Franks and Herbert Gruber, eds, with Edward Hawkins, compiler, *Medallic Illustrations of the History of Great Britain and Ireland to the Death of George II* (London: Trustees of the British Museum, 1885), vol. 2: medal no. 173.

3 For evidence of the seventeenth-century reception of Bayle in England, see the note by the earl of Dartmouth in Gilbert Burnet, *Bishop Burnet's History of His Own Time*, 2nd edition, enlarged, 6 vols (Oxford: At the University Press, 1833), vol. 6: 54–5. Although Bayle, who did not read English, could not have read Spencer's *Discourse Concerning Prodigies*, he was familiar with Spencer's Latin works on the ancient Israelites: see Leo Pierre Courtines, *Bayle's Relations with England and the English* (New York: Columbia University Press, 1938), pp. 169, 226. The Independent minister Christopher Ness believed that the comet, as a sign of impending doom, had frightened the pope: see Christopher Ness, *The Devil's Patriark, or a Full and Impartial Account of the Notorious Life of this Present Pope of Rome Innocent the 11th* (London, 1683), p. 133.

4 Letter of Thomas Salusbury to the earl of Huntingdon, January 9, 1664/65, Huntington Library, Hastings MS 10663; Calendared in Historical Manuscripts Commission (HMC) Hastings MSS 2: 148.

5 *Further Correspondence of Samuel Pepys 1662–1679* (London: G. Bell & Sons, 1929), p. 33. For another uncertain but sceptical reaction, see *Correspondence of John Locke*, vol. 2: 323.

6 In a letter to Ashmole concerning the comet, Lilly claimed: 'I had sent mee an idle peece writ uppon the blasing starr', but gives no further clues as to the nature of the tract. Josten, *Ashmole*, vol. 3: 995. For Ashmole's interest in reports of comet sightings, see Bodleian Ashmole MS 242, nos 27 and 32, 423 fos 244 and 266–70, and 546.

7 *The Blazing-Star, or, a Discourse of Comets* (London, 1664), pp. 6–7.

8 *The Blazing-Star*, p. 4.

9 *The Blazing-Star*, p. 7.

10 John Gadbury, *De Cometis* (London, 1665), p. 2.

11 Gadbury, *De Cometis*, pp. 2–3.

12 Gadbury, *De Cometis*, p. 21.

13 John Gadbury, 'Astrological Observations', in *Ephemeris, or, a Diary Astronomical and Astrological, for the Year of Our Lord 1680* (London, 1680); and W(illiam).G(reene). *Memento's to the World* (London, 1680), p. 23. *Memento's to the World* is an example of how comets subsumed other prodigies during this period. Primarily a chronology of comets along the lines of Gadbury's *De Cometis*, *Memento's* included other

prodigies as well. Although dedicated to Patience Ward, the Whig lord mayor of London, *Memento's* did not make a political argument. Greene's mode of interpretation of comets resembled Gadbury's, relying on the colour and shape of the comet and the sign in which it originally appeared rather than the drawing of a astrological figure for the time of the comet's appearance; see Greene, *Memento's*, pp. 27–30. Other prodigies were also put in the providential context of the earlier comets or 'blazing stars' in *Strange News from Barkshire of an Apparition of Several Ships and Men in the Air, which Seemed to the Beholders to be Fighting. They were Seen by the Carrier of Cirencester and his Company, as they were upon the Road coming for London, near Abingdon, on Tuesday the 26th of August, 1679* (np, nd); Oliver Heywood linked the 1675 comet to the recent suspension of Nonconformist ministers' licences to preach: *Heywood Diary*, vol. 1: 303.

14 *Merlin Reviv'd: or, an Old Prophecy Found in a Manuscript in Pontefract Castle in York-Shire* (London, 1681), Benjamin Keach, *Sion in Distress: or the Groans of the Protestant Chruch* (sic) (London, 1681), p. 19; *The Wonderful Blazing Star: with the Dreadful Apparition of two Armies in the Air* (London, 1681), broadsheet; *A True Relation and Description of the Strange and Prodigious Blazing Comett Seen in the Heavens* (London, 1680), printed by the notorious Whig printer Benjamin Harris; *Pepys Ballads* (Additional Ballads), p. 34: 'The English-Mans Advice'; 'Democritus', *The Petitioning-Comet: or a Brief Chronology of all the Famous Comets, and their Events, that happen'd from the Birth of Christ, to this very day. Together with a Modest Enquiry into this Present Comet* (London, 1681) – the comet was 'petitioning' for a new Parliament; and *Strange and Wonderful Prophecies and Predictions Taken from the Apparition of the late Dreadful Comet, The Last Wonderful Ecclips, and the Great and Signal Conjunction of Jupiter and Saturn in the Fiery Trigon* (London, 1682). For other providential reactions to the 1682 comet, see *Mather Papers*, pp. 494–5 and *Heywood Diary*, vol. 2: 91.

15 *A New Prophecy: or a Prophetical Discourse of the Blazing Star, that Appeared, April the 23d, 1677* (London, 1679); *Remarkable Observations on the Comet, in the Year 1680. As Also on the Blazing Star, Now Seen this present Month of August, 1682* (London, nd) and *Catastrophe Mundi: or Europe's Many Mutations until the Year 1701. Being an Astrological Treatise of the Effects of the Tripple Conjunction of Saturn and Jupiter 1682, and 1683, and of the Comets 1680 and 1682, and other Configurations Concomitant* (London, 1682).

16 Edward Wetenhall, 'To The Reader', *A Judgement of the Comet* (Dublin, 1682). Edwards's theory of comets as signs is summarized in Sara Schecner Genuth, From monstrous signs to natural causes: the assimilation of comet lore into natural philosophy, unpublished Ph.D.

thesis, Harvard University, 1988, pp. 240–51. Another Calvinist Church of England divine who defended comets as prodigies, although he disavowed human ability to know 'what they (in particular) portend', was Bishop Thomas Barlow. See his letter to Boyle on the 1682 comet in Boyle, *Works*, vol. 6: 305. For an explicitly astrological defence of the status of comets as signs of impending changes, see Henry Coley, *Merlini Anglici Ephemeris 1684* (London, 1684).

17 Gadbury, *Ephemeris 1685* (London, 1685), 'Astrological Observations'. Gadbury's quondam teacher and bitter rival Lilly included a defence of the providential meaning of prodigies in his last almanac, *Merlini Anglici Ephemeris 1680* (London, 1680), 'Astrological Observations'.

18 Scott, the leading revisionist of the crises, minimizes the importance of the Exclusion itself and argues for a larger crisis of 'popery and arbitrary government' in *Algernon Sidney and the Restoration Crisis 1677–1683* (Cambridge: Cambridge University Press, 1991).

19 Richard Ashcraft, *Revolutionary Politics and Locke's Two Treatises of Government* (Princeton: Princeton University Press, 1986); Melinda S. Zook, *Radical Whigs and Conspiratorial Politics in Late Stuart England* (University Park, Pennsylvania: Pennsylvania State University Press, 1999).

20 Ezerel Tonge, *The Northern Star the British Monarchy* (London, 1680), 'Dedication', and pp. 13, 52.

21 For techniques used to get oppositional messages across, see James Jacob, *Henry Stubbe*, and Steven N. Zwicker, *Lines of Authority: Politics and English Literary Culture, 1649–1689* (Ithaca: Cornell University Press, 1993).

22 For the Whig and Tory newspapers of this period, see James Sutherland, *The Restoration Newspaper and its Development* (Cambridge: Cambridge University Press, 1986).

23 Narcissus Luttrell, *A Brief Historical Relation of State Affairs from September 1678 to April 1714* (Oxford, 1857), vol. 1: 8; 'The Popish Courant', in *The Weekly Pacquet of Advice from Rome*, vol. 2, no. 20 (Friday, November 21 1679): 160. Others believed it was not Godfrey himself, but the Devil in his shape. BL Add. MS 61903 (Diary and Commonplace Book of Peter Le Neve), fo. 11r. For another appearance of Godfrey's ghost, see 'Extracts from the Papers of Thomas Woodcock (ob. 1695)', ed. G.C. Moor Smith, in *Camden Miscellany No. 11*, Camden Third Series no. 13 (London: Camden Society, 1907), p. 70.

24 Gadbury, *Ephemeris 1681* (London, 1681), 'To the Reader'.

25 See the broadside *A True and Perfect Relation of Elizabeth Freeman of Bishops Hatfield in the County of Hertford, Of a Strange and Wonderful Apparition which Appeared to Her Several Times, and Commanded Her to*

declare a Message to His Most Sacred Majesty (London, 1680); BL Add. MS 61903, fo. 84r; and Luttrell, *Historical Relation*, vol. 1: 66, 86. The Maid of Hatfield and other pro-Monmouth wonders were satirized in *A Choice Collection of Wonderful Miracles, Ghosts, and Visions* (London, 1681).

26 *True Protestant Mercury*, nos 11 (January 29–February 1, 1680/81) and 12 (February 1–5, 1680/81).

27 *The Loyal Protestant, and True Domestick Intelligence*, nos 13 (April 19, 1681) and 22 (May 21, 1681).

28 A similar account, although described as taking place on the 25th rather than the 17th, can be found in *The True Protestant Mercury*, no. 3 (January 1–3, 1680/81). For Oliver Heywood's reaction to this story see *Heywood Diary*, vol. 2: 298–9. Christopher Ness included this prodigy among others he thought were being treated with insufficient seriousness in *A Philosophical and Divine Discourse Blazoning upon this Blazing Star* (London, 1681), p. 23. Lilly's heir as almanac writer, Henry Coley, a timid Whig, also thought contemporary prodigies were not being taken seriously enough: see Coley, *Nuncius Coelestis, or the Starry Messenger for 1682* (London, 1682), 'Astrological Observations'.

29 *True Protestant Mercury*, no. 181 (September 27–30, 1682)r.

30 *Observator*, nos 204 (September 13, 1682) and 221 (October 11, 1682); *A New Song, on the Strange and Wonderful Groaning Board* (London, 1682), in *POAS*, vol. 3: 354–7; and *A New Ballad, or the True-Blue Protestant Dissenter*, in *POAS*, vol. 3: 367. *The Last Words and Sayings of the True Protestant Elm-Board* (London, 1682), *More Last Words and Sayings of the True Protestant Elm-Board* (np, 1682) and *A Sober Vindication of the Reverend Dr. and the Harmless Board Late Glew'd Together in a Profane Pasquil* (London, 1682) employed the board to satirize Gilbert Burnet, a frequent target of Tory ridicule. For Whig rejoinders, see *A Real Vindication of Dr. B—— from the Base and Scandalous Affronts put upon him, in the Scurrilous Pamphlets* (London, 1682) and *The Weekly Pacquet of Advice from Rome*, no. 6 (Friday, September 29, 1682), 'The courant'. *Notes Conferr'd: or a Dialogue Betwixt the Groaning Board, and a Jesuit* (London, 1682) was an anti-Catholic satire.

31 Wood, *Life and Times*, vol. 2: 29. Further references to 'groaning boards', by that time seen merely as entertainment, occur in Richard Steele's early eighteenth-century essay paper *The Tatler*. See Donald F. Bond, ed., *The Tatler* (Oxford: Clarendon Press, 1987), vols 1: 317 and 3: 303.

32 Nehemiah Grew, *The Anatomy of Plants* ([London] 1682), pp. 138–9.

33 *True Protestant Mercury*, no. 48 (June 18–22, 1681): verso and no. 127 (March 22–5, 1682): verso.

34 There was one of the old 'confederates' involved in both the *Mirabilis*

Annus affair and the Whig newspaper press of 1678–82, the Baptist bookseller Francis Smith. His newspaper *Smith's Protestant Intelligence*, however, published very little prodigy material.

35 *True Protestant Mercury*, no. 3 (January 1–3, 1680/81).

36 *Impartial Protestant Mercury*, no. 6 (May 12, 1681): verso.

37 *The New Anti-Roman Pacquet*, no. 3 (Friday, July 23, 1680): 22. This was one of the many temporary titles taken by the *Weekly Pacquet* to avoid the censorship.

38 For an argument that Rawlins functioned as an overall editor for a group of Tory writers, see Theodore F.M. Newton, 'The mask of Heraclitus: a problem in Restoration journalism', *Harvard Studies and Notes in Philology and Literature*, 16 (1934): 145–60.

39 *Observator*, no. 89 (January 14, 1681/82): verso.

40 *Observator*, vol. 2, no. 40 (April 5, 1684): recto. Sir Leoline Jenkins, a leading coordinator of the government's response to opposition forces during the crisis, was quoted as referring to Mather as 'that stargazer, that half deluded man'. See *Mather Papers*, p. 528.

41 *Observator*, vol. 2, no. 26 (March 6, 1683/84).

42 *Observator*, vol. 2, no. 73 (June 2, 1684): verso.

43 *Heraclitus Ridens*, no. 1 (February 1, 1681): verso. In addition to his newspaper, Harris printed at least one prodigy tract during the crisis, *Strange News from Lemster in Herefordshire* (London, 1679). It described the earth opening and things resembling hands, arms and saddles ascending to the sky, but had no discernible political meaning.

44 *Heraclitus Ridens*, no. 5 (March 1, 1681).

45 *Heraclitus Ridens*, no. 11 (April 12, 1681).

46 *The Charter*, in *POAS*, vol. 3: 425–6.

47 Thoresby, *Diary*, vol. 1: 142. For another attack on providential prodigy interpretation by a Church of England minister, in a less formal setting – a drinking session, or wake, following a funeral – see *Heywood Diary*, vol. 2: 278.

48 DWL Morrice MS P., p. 478.

49 *Dux Bonis Omnibus Appelans. The Swans Welcome to his Royal Highness the Duke. Or, Some Remarks upon that Note-worthy Passage, Mentioned in the True Domestick Intelligence, Dated Octob. 14. 1679. Concerning a Company of Swans, More than Ordinary Gathered Together, at his Royal Highness's Landing* (np, 1679); and *Prince-Protecting Providences: or A Collection of Some Historical Passages, Relating how Several Princes and Personages, (Born for Great Actions) have had Miraculous Preservations. Made Publick upon Occasion of the Late Memorable (and Miraculous) Deliverance of His Royal Highness, James, Duke of York* (London, 1682).

50 Included in *The Second and Third Parts of the Works of Mr. Abraham Cowley* (London, 1689).

51 *Heywood Diary*, vol. 2: 218.

52 The *DNB* article on Ness entirely omits his astrological activity. Genuth, *Comets*, pp. 78–81, discussed his work along with that of other prodigy interpreters of the crisis years, but he is not even mentioned in Curry's *Prophecy and Power*. Ness was also the author of an unsuccessful reply to John Dryden's *Absalom and Achitophel, A Key (with the Whip) to open the Mystery of Iniquity of the Poem Called, Absalom and Achitophel* (London, 1682).

53 A document purporting to give information on dissenting congregations in London and Westminster (*c.* 1676) refers to that of 'Mr. Nest, an Independent, frequented by some people of quality': see 'Particulars of Conventicles, &c., in London and Westminster', in HMC *Duke of Leeds MSS*, p. 12.

54 BL Add. MS 45675, fos 223–6.

55 *True Protestant Mercury*, no. 48 (June 18–22, 1681): verso and no. 127 (March 22–25): verso.

56 Ness, *A Distinct Discourse and Discovery of the Person and Period of Antichrist* (London, 1679), p. 54.

57 Ness, *The Signes of the Times* (London, 1681), pp. 9–13.

58 Christopher Ness, *A Protestant Antidote against the Poyson of Popery* (London, 1679), p. 14.

59 Ness, *Signes*, p. 37.

60 Ness, *Signes*, p. 79.

61 Ness, *Signes*, p. 75.

62 'Theophilus Rationalis', *Multum in Parvo, aut Vox Veritatis: Wherein The Principles, Practices, and Transactions of the English Nation: But More Especially and in Particular By Their Representatives Assembled in Parliament Anno Domini 1640, 1641: As also 1680, 1681. Are Most faithfully Examined, Collected and Compared together for the Present Seasonable Use, Benefit and Information of the Publick* (London, 1681), p. 49.

63 Ness, *Signes*, p. 56.

64 Ness, *Signes*, 'Dedication'.

65 Ness, *Signes*, p. 38.

66 Ness, *Signes*, p. 29.

67 Ness, *Signes*, pp. 59–60.

68 Ness, *Philosophical and Divine Discourse*, p. 20. The Baptist poet and hymnodist Benjamin Keach, who also interpreted the Popish Plot in prodigious and apocalyptic terms, challenged natural philosophers to explain 'Who sets the comet in the angry sky/ Those dismal Harbingers of Misery?' See Keach, *Sion in Distress*, p. 17.

69 Thus Ness explicitly linked *A True Account* to both *Signes* and an earlier comet treatise he had published in 1680, *A True Account of this Present Blasing-Star* (London, 1682): recto. Ness had published two

writings incorporating cometary material in 1680: *The Lord Stafford's Ghost, or A Warning to Traitors, With his Prophecie Concerning the Blazing Star* (London, 1680); and *A Full and True Account of the Late Blazing Star* (London, 1680). The reference is probably to the latter, which was republished as the first section of *A Philosophical and Divine Discourse Blazoning upon this Blazing Star* (London, 1681). The astrologer John Partridge made a similar attempt to link the providential interpretation of celestial prodigies, astrology and anti-Catholic politics in his *Vox Lunaris, Being a Philosophical and Astrological Discourse of Two Moons which were seen at London And the parts Adjacent, June the Eleventh, 1679* (London, 1679). Partridge claimed that a similar tract he had written on multiple suns had been suppressed for political reasons; see Partridge, *Almanac 1680*, 'Astrological Observations'. For more, see John Hill, *An Allarm to Europe by the late Prodigious Comet seen November and December, 1680* (London, 1680); and the anonymous *The Mystery of Ambras Merlins, Standardbearer Wolf, and last Boar of Cornwall* (London, 1683).

70 Ness, *An Astrological and Theological Discourse upon the Present Great Conjunction* (London, 1682), p. 41.

71 M. Marsin, *Some of the Chief Heads of the Most Miraculous Wonders* (London, 1694); and *The Near Aproach of Christ's Kingdom* (London, 1696). For Marsin, see William E. Burns, ' "By Him the women will be delivered from that bondage, which some have found intolerable": M. Marsin, an English seventeenth-century millenarian feminist', *Eighteenth-Century Women*, 1 (2000): 19–38.

72 Woodcock, 'Extracts from the Papers of Thomas Woodcock', pp. 73–4, and *The Flemings in Oxford*, vol. 2: 138. Future Jacobites also noted these omens: see George Hickes, in *Letters Written by Eminent Persons in the Seventeenth and Eighteenth Centuries* ed. John Walker, 2 vols (London, 1813), vol. 1: 213–14. The reign of James II was also marked by a great deal of excitement in Ireland, where James's vacillating but basically pro-Catholic policies produced hope on the part of the Catholic Irish, and a great deal of fear on the part of the Protestant English and Scottish settlers. One Irish prodigy of 1687, a woman who wept corn from her eyes, may have attracted political interest. James Bonnell, in his two letters to John Strype describing the incident, both times put the story of the girl immediately after visionary and prophetic incidents involving Irish politics. The girl was held and strictly examined in the household of the Protestant Bishop of Meath. See CUL Add. MS 1, nos 58 and 60, and Huntington Library Hastings MS 15978. For more Irish prodigies connected with political uncertainty, see *Letters of John Pinney*, pp. 19–20.

73 DWL Morrice MS P, pp. 486, 537.

74 *Publick Occurences Truly Stated*, no. 25 (August 7, 1688): verso.
75 *Publick Occurences Truly Stated*, no. 26 (August 14, 1688).
76 *Old Stories which were the Fore-runners of the Revolution in Eighty-Eight, Reviv'd* (London, 1719), a Jacobite anthology of false rumours accompanying the revolution, such as those impugning the legitimacy of the prince of Wales, included no forged prodigies, although it did include one ghost story (pp. 52–3).
77 *A Congratulatory Poem To His Royal Highness the Prince of Orange, On his Welcome to the City of London*, in *Pepys Ballads*, vol. 5: 34.
78 *A Collection of Papers Relating to the Present Juncture of Affairs in England* ([London], 1688), p. 22. A post-revolutionary periodical, *The Gentleman's Journal: or the Monthly Miscellany* (1693), pp. 54–5, traced this story to the original French version of a history of the persecution of the Protestants in the Principality of Orange written by Pineton de Chambrun and translated into English under the title *The History of the Persecutions of the Protestants by the French King in the Principality of Orange* (London, 1689). The writer claimed that the story, along with other material favourable to William, had either been suppressed by James's government or omitted by the translator for fear of offending it, presumably while the work was being prepared for the printer before the revolution.
79 Although not prodigies, there were some omens with a Suetonian flavour connected to the death of Queen Mary. See Russel J. Kerr and Ida Coffin Duncan, eds, *The Portledge Papers* (London, 1928), p. 193.
80 For examples of Whig prodigies showing God's support for William and Mary, see *Strange and Wonderful News from Holbitch in Lincoln-Shire* (London, 1693), which used the recent washing up on the shore of two monstrous fish, a male and a female, as a sign that God had destined the sovereignty of the seas to the British monarchs William and Mary. For another Whig prodigy of the 1690s, see *The Westminster Wonder*, in *Pepys Ballads*, vol. 5: 144.
81 Blair Worden's Introduction to *A Voyce from the Watch Tower*, pp. 22–34, makes a strong but circumstantial case for Toland being the editor of the *Memoirs*.

4

'A warning to all to repent': prodigies and moral reform in the 1690s

The revolution of 1688 was followed by a vigorous campaign for moral reform, much of it ultimately emanating from the court of the new sovereigns, and leading to the formation of societies for the reformation of morals throughout much of England.[1] Closely related to the struggle to purify England's morals was the struggle against deism and Socinianism. Many thought that the denial of the trinity or the Christian gospel by deists fostered scepticism towards religion generally, contributing to vice and immorality and ultimately to well-merited providential punishment of the offending nation.

Providential prodigy interpretation and moral reform were old allies, going back to a time before the Reformation, and linked in sermons, pamphlets and ballads.[2] Moral reform and the struggle against atheism had been part of Poole's agenda, and, while sectarian and political debate dominated the prodigy literature of the Civil War and the Restoration, the tradition of moralistic prodigy interpretation had certainly never disappeared. Prodigies continued to play a prominent role in the 'culture war' of the reigns of William and Mary. Most published providential prodigy interpretation in the 1690s was not ostensibly aimed at advancing one group of Christians over another, and still less at heralding the coming of the millenium. Instead, just as Poole had sought in the 1650s to combat atheism by collecting and publishing accounts of prodigies and remarkable providences, prodigy interpreters of the 1690s sought to vindicate Christianity in general from the assaults of deists and atheists, and to oppose sinful debauchery, carrying out at the level of popular culture some of the same work that the Boyle lecturers were carrying out at a high culture level. Prodigies became part of the apologetics of the late seventeenth century which sought to support belief in the existence of God through empirical demonstration of the existence of non-material forces such as witchcraft, ghosts and angels. This type of providential interpretation no longer treated the prodigy as a phenomenon with a decodable meaning for the future, but rather as one enabling the beholder or reader to draw general conclusions concerning the existence of God and the inevitable punishment of sin. As such, the prodigious began to lose its status as an independent category and to be subsumed simply under the heading of a remarkable or special providence.

The leaders of the effort to adopt prodigies and remarkable providences as vehicles of moral reform at the end of the seventeenth century comprised a group of moderate Church of England men and dissenters, of whom the most influential were the London book-trade figures Nathaniel Crouch (?1632–?1725) and John Dunton (1659–1733). Both had been peripheral figures on the Whig side of the Popish Plot and the Exclusion agitation, and there learned to avoid mixing prodigies and oppositional politics. Crouch and Dunton produced and sold books and periodicals setting forth a new providential picture devoid of apocalypticism and prodigies with an easily decodable partisan meaning.

Crouch and Dunton were both pioneers in the development of a publishing industry directed at the less educated classes. In their targeting of moralistic prodigy interpretation at the lower classes, the claim made by some opponents of providential interpretation that providential prodigy belief was a characteristic specific to the 'superstitious vulgar' became closer to an accurate description of reality. But their projects had been anticipated by more learned men – by Poole, the American Increase Mather and an Anglican clergyman named Simon Ford.

Simon Ford and magisterial prodigy gathering

This new moralistic prodigy interpretation had been anticipated in 1678 in the attempt by an Anglican divine to save prodigies as divine signs by emphasizing the division between valid private judgements and the invalid application of prodigies to public issues. The Reverend Simon Ford's *A Discourse Concerning God's Judgements* was based on the case of the Duncalf man whose hands had rotted away after he had stolen a Bible, a case particularly useful for moralizing purposes because of its very obviousness.[3] Ford used this incident to set forth a narrow set of criteria for determining whether or not a given phenomenon is a judgement from God and to propose yet another scheme for gathering accounts of prodigies and providences.

Ford presented himself as treading the narrow path between those who would cry up every unusual happening as a divine sign and those who would entirely deny the connection between God's will and natural phenomena, between fanatics and Catholics on the one hand and atheists on the other. Most of his energy, however, went into refuting the first position. Principally, he attacked the perversion, as he saw it, of God's judgements to the benefit of a party or faction. Rather, divine judgements must have a meaning apparent to a consensus of Christians, or, better yet, all mankind. For this to be accomplished, judgements must be distinguished from the ordinary disasters that are part of life. To truly be direct strokes of God, judgements should have something 'in them, that appears to be either above, or contrary to, or but besides the wonted course of Nature, and so is either miraculous or prodigious'.[4] The Duncalf case was of particular use, as the thief had been punished in the hands, the part that had been used in the commission of the sin. 'A far greater evidence is given in this case many times, to make Divine Judgements manifest, by the fair and legible Impression and Image of the very offence it self, upon the punishment inflicted'.[5] This case functioned as a rare unambiguous example of a prodigy of judgement on an action universally condemned. The appeal to consensus itself nullified the possibility of using prodigies in a partisan way to promote one side or another in differences between Christians. The requirement that a prodigy or judgement be clearly and unambiguously related to an offence would also shrink their number.

Invoking Bacon, Ford called for a history of providences.[6] This call differed from those made by the dissenting clerics Poole and Mather, however, in that the primary gatherers of accounts of prodigies were to be not ministers, nor even Anglican clergymen, but magistrates. Although magistrates had a long history of involvement in prodigy accounts as administerers of oaths to alleged witnesses, and sometimes as investigators, the principal role royalists had assigned to them in the 1660s had been the negative one of disproving, denying and suppressing prodigies, as in the claim of the *Kingdom's Intelligencer* that magistrates had denied all the alleged prodigies.[7] Ford went beyond this to envision a positive and active role for the magistracy in prodigy collection. Exhibiting the scepticism regarding testimony that was one result of the *Mirabilis Annus* affair, he argued that magistrates were in the best position to carry out such a project as they had the ability to force people to take oaths and to punish liars.[8] The magistracy was also the only conceivable rival to the clergy in the ability to cover the entire nation. Ford did not add that collection by magistrates would ensure that accounts of prodigies and judgements would not be used to subvert the State, but, given his concern to deny prodigies' public meanings, the implication was clear. Ford's project seems more designed to screen false prodigies than to gather true ones.

One prodigy pamphlet issued shortly after Ford's work that made explicit its connection with the authority of a JP in its title was *A Very Strange, but True Relation of the Raining a Showre of Blood at Shewall in the Parish of Stoake Idith in the County of Hereford, on the 16th Day of this Instant July, 1679. The Examination whereof was taken upon Oath the 18th of this Instant July before Richard Hopton Esq. One of His Majesties Justices of the Peace for the said County* (1679). The text of the pamphlet was a statement by one Mary Godsall sworn before a JP, and began: 'The Examinant saith'.[9] The story of some drops of blood falling on Godsall as she was milking a cow, and her calling some of the neighbour women to witness this event, was followed by the words: 'This is an exact Copy of the Examination taken before the said Worshipful Justice of the Peace, concerning this Miraculous Relation, and is published to prevent False Reports.'[10] In addition to enclosing the narrative within the legal category of an examination, the closing statement also identified the purpose of publication as the prevention of the dissemination of false rumours, through the phrase 'prevent False Reports', often identified with government-sponsored means of circulating information such as official newspapers. Naturally, the pamphlet included no speculation as to the political or theological import of the shower of blood, which was presented in colourless and undramatic terms, possibly indicating that one reason why magisterial prodigy accounts never caught on was simply that they were dull.

The lead that Ford had given the magistracy did not result in a nationwide network of magisterial prodigy-collectors. English magistrates, being both servants of the State and leaders in their local communities, were not easy to organize centrally, nor did the majority seem to have had much interest in serving as prodigy-collectors. The central government was also indifferent or hostile to prodigy collection. However, other people would answer Ford's call for a collection of prodigies based on moralistic rather than political or controversial principles.

'Wonderful Prodigies, Surprizing Miracles, and Admirable Curiosities': Nathaniel Crouch the prodigy-monger

Nathaniel Crouch, a London bookseller, published many books of history and other kinds of factual information for a popular audience, usually in duodecimo and selling for one shilling.[11] Crouch published under the pseudonym Robert Burton or 'R.B.', and included prodigy material in many of his compilations, such as *Wonderful Prodigies of Judgement and Mercy, Admirable Curiosities, Rarities, and Wonders in England, Scotland, and Ireland* (1682) and *The Surprizing Miracles of Nature and Art* (1683). The titles were frankly commercial in their purpose, and called for an emotional reaction of surprise and wonder on the part of the reader. All of them went through many editions in the late seventeenth and eighteenth centuries. Clearly, there was a market for stories of wonders and prodigies among the 'ordinary Londoners', the unschooled and those with no Latin, whom Robert Mayer identifies as Crouch's target audience.[12]

At the beginning of his career, Crouch had been apprenticed to Livewell Chapman, and during the Popish Plot he had had close ties to the Whig newspaper press. In particular Crouch was linked to Benjamin Harris's *Domestick Intelligence* – to which he contributed and in which he advertised his *Wonderful Prodigies* – and to Henry Care and Thomas Vile's *Impartial Protestant Mercury*, which advertised both *Wonderful Prodigies* and *Admirable Curiosities*.[13] That his works were not unconnected with the politics of the time is evident from the Preface to *Surprizing Miracles*, Crouch's most wonder-oriented compilation, in which he situated the work in the context of recent British history, beginning roughly with the outbreak of the English Civil War:

> There is no Person of any Age or Understanding, but must needs acknowledge that the last Forty Years has been as it were an Age of Prodigies and Wonders in these three Kingdomes, so that it may be no former time can parallel so many strange Transactions as have happened in so little space, and therefore as an Ingenious Person says, A Book of Prodigies is fit/ In time Prodigious to be writ.[14]

Surprizing Miracles appeared in 1683, in the wake of Whig defeat. It was divided into two parts, the larger dealing with prodigies and the smaller with 'Miracles of Art', mostly buildings. Crouch's practice was to create his books as abridgements and simplifications of standard English-language or translated sources. He himself, like his readers, lacked an advanced education. The principal sources for the first part of *Surprizing Miracles* were the prodigy works of Gadbury, *Natura Prodigiorum* and *De Cometis*. Crouch's use of the writings of the royalist and Catholic Gadbury indicates his willingness to reach outside the permitted Whig canon, although he also divested Gadbury's work of its proto-Toryism.

Strong providentialism and anti-Catholicism were apparent in *Surprizing Miracles*. Despite Crouch's titular reference to nature, his treatment of prodigies was entirely providential, although not apocalyptic. His providentialism was explicitly stated in the Preface:

> And if we consult History, we shall find, that there hath never been any notable Apparition or Prodigy, seen in the Heavens, but it hath been attended with more than Ordinary Changes or Troubles here on Earth; Neither is there any one except he hath no Religion, who is not affrighted at Lightning, the clashing noise of Thunder, or an horrible Comet; For God speaks to men not only with the Tongues of men by Prophets, apostles, and Teachers, but sometimes also by the Elements, and other Extraordinary signs in the Heavens, Earth, or Sea.[15]

The arrangement of the prodigies, following Gadbury, was chronological, with many passages, like the following, blurring together prodigies and other historical events without making explicit their connections:

> In 507 there fell a great and fiery dart from Heaven in Africa, and dark spots were observed in the body of the Sun. The Emperor gives the Goths money to depart his Dominions, Clovis warreth against Alaricus for Religion, and Italy is wasted by Clorus with an hundred ships, and eight thousand men. In 529 happened wonderful Lightning at Antioch, and an Earthquake at Constantinople; Legible Letters are seen in the Air at Rome, it rained blood in the Valleys of Lucern and Piedmont four days together. The Persians war against the King of Colchos, and the Emperor; the Vandals put their General to death, the Jews are suppressed, the Emperors General Mundus defeateth the Goths who wasted Thrace.[16]

Substantial digressions in Crouch's chronological narrative covered particular historical episodes. One covered the obligatory topic of Josephus and the Jewish Wars. Another covered the prodigies and events of the Thirty Years War from a strongly anti-Catholic viewpoint.[17] This contrasts with the relatively perfunctory treatment of Britain's Civil War, on which Crouch had written a separate work. The treatment of the Thirty Years War, and also that of the Irish massacres of Protestants in 1642, indicate Crouch's desire to disseminate anti-Catholic propaganda. A more direct statement of Crouch's Whig and dissenting viewpoint came in his discussion of the reign of the Emperor Constantine. He spoke of 'the extraordinary Indulgence of Constantine the Emperor, toward the Christian Bishops, and his heaping Estates, Riches, and Honours upon them, whereby they soon after lost their former Piety and Humility'.[18] Such direct indications of Crouch's bias were rare, however, and most of his work adhered to a 'safe' anti-Catholicism that did not accuse any party within the established Church or the State of sympathy with Rome.

Wonderful Prodigies employed a more explicitly providential but non-controversial approach, also claiming to combat atheism. Crouch's compilation of the horrible fates of sinners, blasphemers and atheists drew heavily on the tradition of judgement compilations, relying particularly on Beard's *Theatre of God's Judgements* and the works of the Puritan divine Samuel Clark, whose less controversial *A Mirror or Looking Glass for Saints and Sinners*. *Admirable*

Curiosities included both prodigy stories and judgements along with other information on the English counties and British kingdoms. Many of the prodigies included in Crouch's works were defanged in respect of their original meaning in religious politics. A good example of this process is the destruction of a church in Withicombe in 1638, which the Puritan propagandists John Vicars and Lewis Hughes had, shortly after, claimed to be a demonstration of God's anger at Laudian innovations.[19] Crouch's narrative, by contrast, emphasized the courage shown by the minister and God's mercy in sparing most of the congregation.[20] The issue of the arrangement of the church, such as the placement of the altar, or of the Laudian innovation did not arise. For Crouch the Withicombe church incident simply endorsed an uncontroversial Christian faith.

Crouch's willingness to draw from a variety of sources, ranging from the works of the royalist astrologer Gadbury to those of the Presbyterian minister Clark, indicates that he tried to avoid partisan involvement in the political issues of late seventeenth-century England. In attacking sin, atheism and, in a generalized way, Catholicism, Crouch reflected a consensus of the majority of England's respectable society. Unlike those of most of his predecessors, Crouch's prodigies were presented not to exacerbate existing tensions or to promote a particular programme, but to sell many copies and put money in Crouch's pocket. Crouch's non-political approach, and his deliberate appeal to a less educated populace, gave his frequently reprinted works more staying power than other providential prodigy writings of the late seventeenth century, indicating that tales of wonder, providential or not, maintained a large popular audience.

John Dunton, William Turner and prodigy collecting in the 1690s

The last of the large collections of prodigies and other remarkable events to have been influenced by a providential view was William Turner's *A Compleat History of the most Remarkable Providences, Both of Judgement and Mercy, which have hapned in this Present Age* (1697). Directed at a more sophisticated and wealthier audience than Crouch's compilations, Turner's project was far more learned, bulky and expensive. The creation of *A Compleat History* was intimately connected with a periodical, John Dunton's *Athenian Mercury*. The *Athenian Mercury* involved such well-known figures as Sir William Temple and Jonathan Swift, lasted for five years, an unusually long time for a seventeenth-century periodical, and spawned a host of imitators.[21] An examination of the treatment of prodigies in both the *Athenian Mercury* and *A Compleat History* reveals the adaptation of the providential prodigy to the climate of post-revolutionary England.

Dunton's *Mercury* was a twice-weekly paper, printed on both sides of an unnumbered folio half-sheet, and was principally devoted to answering queries sent in by its readers – an innovation in which Dunton took particular pride. Dunton explicitly positioned the *Mercury* to make money and to advertise his other publications, but also as an instrument to combat certain cultural and political trends he found deplorable. The *Mercury* firmly supported the revolution settlement, adulated King William and Queen Mary, proclaimed its devotion to the Church of England, and fiercely opposed libertinism. Intellectually, it sought to combat four distinct tendencies: Protestant Nonconformity; high church Jacobitism; Roman Catholicism; and the menace of free-thinking deists and atheists.

Despite the Church of England position of the *Mercury*, which aligned it with the largest group of potential customers, Dunton, like many who showed an interest in prodigies in the later seventeenth century, had strong dissenting connections. He refused to identify himself in his autobiography either as a Church of England man or as a dissenter, expressing esteem for moderates of both groups. He had married the daughter of an eminent dissenting minister, Samuel Annesley, who decades earlier had been proposed by Richard Baxter to Matthew Poole as a participant in his scheme of providence collecting.[22] Dunton published many works of devotion by Dissenters, including those of his father-in-law and Baxter, and even, early in his career, Ness's *The Devils Patriarck*.[23] Like Crouch, for whom he claimed to have 'a hearty Friendship', Dunton had been a firm Whig during the Popish Plot and Exclusion Crises.[24]

Like other late seventeenth-century opponents of atheism, the *Mercury* published many accounts of varied supernatural occurrences such as ghosts and visions to demonstrate the existence of an immaterial substance, or soul. It also received many inquiries concerning such prodigies as celestial apparitions and monstrous births. The *Athenian Mercury* gave its position on prodigies and wonders in a series of questions and answers in 1692. It defined prodigy as 'Any unaccountable or very unusual Phaenomenon in Nature, presented to the World by the Interposition of some supernatural Agent'. Prodigies, like other supernatural occurrences, could therefore be employed in demonstrating God's existence, but they needed to be used with great care, to avoid association with the views of dissenting radicals. The *Mercury* proclaimed its belief in the existence of prodigies, but the evidence it gave for them was safely in the past, from the Old Testament to the fall of Jerusalem. The key statement of the *Mercury*'s position on contemporary prodigies was in response to the question 'When Prodigies happen in a Countrey where there are two different sides and Professions in Religion, how it may be known whether of them they concern?' The answer skilfully dodged the issue: 'Undoubtedly they concern both, they are sent to the Community, and are a Warning to all to Repent.' Prodigies, therefore, should not be employed in religious controversy, but only to induce a non-specific repentance.[25] Dunton's association with prodigies extended to other projects, as he was the publisher of the anonymous tract *A Practical Discourse on the Late Earthquakes, with An Historical Account of Prodigies and their Various Effects.*[26]

Dunton, or his staff of writers, were always sceptical, or claimed to be, of prodigies with an alleged political import. The *Athenian Mercury* mocked prodigies such as the Groaning Board, and ascribed belief in portents to 'wise Mr. Mob'.[27] Even prodigies testifying to the virtue of causes that Dunton strongly supported were treated sceptically. For example, the *Mercury*, a passionate advocate on behalf of the persecuted Protestants of France, suggested that the mysterious hymn-singing heard in the air in the Cevennes was an echo, adding that 'it becomes such as wou'd search after Truth, not to be too credulous in the belief of such things as seem visibly to surpass the ordinary Powers of Nature'.[28] Despite the *Mercury*'s generally royalist treatment of the Civil War, it also emphasized a need for scepticism when discussing a celestial battle between two armies, one led by a headless general who suddenly regained his head, that was alleged to have taken place shortly before the death of Charles I.[29]

The *Athenian Mercury* also provided a handy venue for Dunton to advertise and promote his other book-selling projects. Two of these involved prodigies. One was *A Practical Discourse* and the other was Turner's *Compleat History*. Turner's work was actually a joint-project of Turner and Dunton, the latter describing himself as the 'Undertaker' of the work.[30]

Although holding a living in the Church of England by the time of the compilation of the *Compleat History*, William Turner (1653–1701) had come from a background of conservative dissent. He had been a pupil of the Presbyterian minister Philip Henry, an avid reader of the *Mirabilis Annus* tracts.[31] Turner was supplementing his clerical income by working as a compiler, having previously written a work, published by Dunton, on the world's religions.[32] The massive *Compleat History* took several years' work from its first announcement to the actual printing, and even so showed marks of haste, including no less than seven paginations.

Turner initially set forth the plan for his project in a work published by Dunton, *An Essay on the Works of Creation* (1695). This essay was primarily concerned to glorify God with an emphasis on the regularity and continuity of celestial phenomena. Like the expounders of natural theology, Turner emphasized God's power and providence, but in doing so he set himself in opposition to 'the Philosophers', attacking the idea of secular explanations of natural phenomena, expatiating on human ignorance and presumption, and even proclaiming his adherence to the geocentric cosmos.[33]

When the time came to actually collect and compile the accounts of prodigies, providences and remarkable events called for by Turner's *Essay*, the *Athenian Mercury* not only advertised subscriptions but solicited prodigy stories and other accounts. Dunton printed a plan for the work and a call for contributions in the *Mercury* at an early stage. The existing system of gathering inquiries to be answered in the *Mercury* was admirably adapted for the gathering of prodigy accounts, and the advertising columns were a way of communicating with contributors.[34] The fact that this project could be carried out openly indicates the greater extent of press freedom since the time of the *Mirabilis Annus* affair and that providential prodigies were no longer considered as politically dangerous as they had been during the Restoration, when prodigy-story gathering itself had been considered subversive.

Turner's work, like Increase Mather's, was presented – and

advertised – as the completion of the Poole project, by then over thirty years old.[35] However, it differed from Poole's and Mather's projects, and from Ford's plan, in several ways. Turner and Dunton did not set up a centralized organization to evaluate prodigy accounts, but simply printed those that had been sent in, as well as those gathered from other printed texts and Turner's own experiences. The *Compleat History*, despite its titular reference to 'the present age', was also not as focused on the present as was the Poole project. It included a variety of providences from all historical eras, drawn from an exhaustive reading of histories, travel literature, medical works and compilations, including the works of Nathaniel Crouch.[36] The most important difference from Poole and Mather, however, was that Turner and Dunton abandoned the idea of a profession with specific expertise or credibility to evaluate prodigies, or even the idea of evaluating prodigy accounts at all. Poole and Mather had assumed that educated and Godly ministers would collect and evaluate accounts of remarkable providences, with, in Poole's case, occasional help from magistrates. Turner and Dunton relied on the *Mercury*-reading public, with its varying religious positions and levels of education. The *Compleat History* also differed from the Poole project in that its primary ideological mission was defensive, combating the threat of atheism, as opposed to discerning God's specific purposes.

The work was divided into three main parts. The first, and by far the largest, was the compilation of remarkable providences, instances of God's direct actions, including judgements and instances of outstanding piety and virtue as well as prodigies. The second part was devoted to the wonders of nature, but these wonders were also meant to demonstrate God's existence by offering evidence of design.[37] The brief third section, the wonders of art, testified to God's achievements through the greatness of his creation, man. In this section, Turner took a much more positive attitude towards contemporary natural philosophy than he did in the *Essay*, including a variety of recent achievments as evidence of the progress of medicine and natural philosophy.[38]

Turner's treatment of the standard canon of providential prodigies is revealing. Although Turner was one of the few English prodigy writers of the seventeenth century to use Stephen Batman's Elizabethan compilation *The Doome, Warning All Men to the Judgement*, as a source, he took a somewhat defensive attitude towards divine prodigies.[39] In discussing battles in the air, Turner was careful to disassociate himself from the excessively credulous: 'I confess, they are often mixed with false incredible Relations, yet not therefore all to be rejected.'[40] Significantly, chapters treating such classic providential prodigies as monstrous births and comets were included in the section on the wonders of nature rather than in that on God's providences.

However, the extent of Turner's departure from the the tradition of providential prodigy interpretation should not be exaggerated. He was capable of making political interpretations of quite recent prodigies, linking a strange noise heard in the air i n 1680 to the Popish Plot and an earthquake both to the revolution of 1688 and the wars of Louis XIV.[41] Unlike Dunton, Turner, strongly anti-Catholic, expressed no doubt concerning the wonders associated with the persecution of the French Protestants.[42] Turner took no explicit position on the Civil War, but included accounts of both royalist prodigies on the death of the king and pro-parliamentarian divine interventions from Samuel Clark and other writers of the period.[43]

Turner and Dunton's work shows the survival of a providential conception of prodigies into the later seventeenth century, particularly among those personally connected to or politically allied with dissent.[44] Their efforts also show a growing reluctance to employ prodigious evidence in defence of or attack on contested religious and political positions.

Another person active in the Whig newspaper press during the Popish Plot ventured into periodical publishing, although much less successfully. Anne Baldwin had been the business partner and wife of Richard Baldwin, publisher of the Exclusion-era Whig propaganda sheet *Protestant Courant*.[45] Her periodical, launched in the first year of the eighteenth century, was the curious and shortlived (two issues) *Memoirs for the Curious: Or, an Account of What Occurrs that's Rare, Secret, Extraordinary, Prodigious, or Miraculous, through the World; Whether in Nature, Art, Learning, Policy or Religion*. The publication endorsed moralistic and even apocalyptic prodigy interpretation, combining popularized science with a cautious leaning towards millenarianism. In its short life, *Memoirs for the Curious* published providential accounts and interpretations of such classic prodigies as the boy with *DEUS MEUS* around his irises and the worm found in the heart of John Pennant which some had viewed as presaging the Civil War.[46] *Memoirs for the Curious* was far more explicitly providential than Dunton's or Crouch's work, which never showed any interest in relating prodigies to the millenium. Unsurprisingly, given the decline of millenarianism and apocalypticism in the late seventeenth century, *Memoirs for the Curious* failed to find an audience.[47]

Earthquakes and topknots, and the reformation of manners

There were several widely noted earthquakes in the British Isles, Europe and Britain's possessions overseas during the 1690s.[48] Indeed, the earthquake took over the position of paradigmatic prodigy from the comet during this period.[49] Like blazing stars, earthquakes played a prominent role in Revelations, and, like the blazing stars of the Restoration, they were interpreted as providential signs.[50] Dunton's publication *A Practical Discourse on the late Earthquakes, with An Historical Account of Prodigies and their Various Effects* (1692), by a 'Reverend Divine', was one of the many works inspired by the London earthquake of 1692, which evoked a variety of providential responses.[51] This particular earthquake, like other English earthquakes, not terribly destructive in itself, had an unusually strong cultural impact due to its following the destructive Jamaica earthquake the same year, and being followed by terrifying and destructive earthquakes in Sicily and Malta.[52] *A Practical Discourse* took a strongly providential line, placing itself in the tradition of early seventeenth-century Anglican divines and particularly Thomas Jackson.[53] The writer asserted that prodigies were 'above the usual Laws and Power of Nature' and were caused solely by God's will.[54] Without naming Spencer, *A Practical Discourse* positioned his way of thinking about prodigies against Jackson's and claimed that it led to atheism.[55] In addition to the earthquake itself, the tract enumerated a variety of standard prodigies including comets and even battles in the sky (although it omitted monstrous births[56]). *A Practical Discourse* was affected by the late seventeenth-century tendency away from political and apocalyptic prodigies, claiming to eschew predictions on the fate of individual nations or giving comfort to 'Male-contents'.[57] Rather than theological or high-political conflict, *A Practical Discourse* was driven by the crusade against immorality characteristic of England in the 1690s.

Another work treating the earthquake as a prodigy was a sermon of the dissenting minister Samuel Doolittle, *A Sermon Occasioned by the Late Earthquake Which happen'd in London, And Other Places on the Eighth of September 1692. Preached to a Congregation in Reading* (1692). Doolittle treated the earthquake less as a prodigy and more as a judgement, that is as a punishment for London's sins rather than as a sign of possible future punishments. In the one passage where he did treat the earthquake as a sign, he disavowed any pretence of interpreting it: 'The Book of Providence be very mysterious, and dark, and cannot be unriddled.'[58]

Most interpretaters of the earthquakes avoided apocalyptic predictions. One exception was Thomas Beverley, a veteran millenarian dissenter, whose many apocalyptic works fixed the date for the second coming of Christ at 1697. His 1693 *Evangelical Repentance Unto Salvation not to be Repented Of* identified the earthquakes both as apocalyptic signs and as warnings to repent. Beverley asserted that prodigies were indeed providential signs, attacking the natural philosophers who would treat divine explanations as inconsistent with natural ones.[59]

Providential interpretation of earthquakes was not a dissenting monopoly. Anglicans such as John Evelyn and Thomas Watson, the bishop of St David's, interpreted earthquakes as warnings from God.[60] The earthquakes were also invoked in the literature of the Societies for the Reformation of Manners. These groups, which brought together Anglicans and dissenters, presented their case for moral reformation in a heavily providential context, claiming that unless the nation's morals were reformed God would punish it. The mild London earthquake was but a foretaste, and if it was not followed by speedy national repentance, it might be followed by the kind of destruction an angry God had wrought on Jamaica and Sicily.[61] So great was the fear that God would repeat in London what he had done in Jamaica that the lord mayor shut down a show on the Jamaica earthquake at Southwark Fair.[62] The Jamaican earthquake had been so destructive that some of the letters from residents sent by Hans Sloane to *Philosophical Transactions* mused on its providential import, although none called for moral reform.[63]

Earthquakes were one of the few prodigies which retained a providential meaning into the eighteenth century. Their advantage over other prodigies was their sheer destructiveness – unlike rains of blood, their reality was hard to deny, and unlike comets they could be expressions as well as signs of the wrath of God. The famous London earthquake of 1750 showed the continued power of earthquakes to call forth providential responses, the most famous being the refusal of a publisher to go into a second edition of David Hume's *Enquiry Concerning Human Understanding*.[64]

At the opposite end of the scale of destructiveness from earthquakes was an almost parodic example of the moralistic interpretation of prodigies in the 1690s, the craze for monstrous births with topknot-like lumps of flesh attached to their heads.[65] This interest, with which Dunton and Turner had a peripheral involvement, was part of the larger controversy over the propriety of female topknots. Ballads such as *A Fair Warning for Pride: By a Foal which is Lately said to come into the World with a Top-Knot on its Head of Several Colours, at Chelcknom in Glocester-Shire* (?1691) and *The Somersetshire Wonder: Being a True Relation of a Cow withing 8 mile of Bathe, who Brought forth a Calf, with the Likeness of a Womans Head-Dress, being a Commode, near Half a Yard high, which Calf will be Shortly Brought to the Tower of London, there to be Exposed to all Curious Spectators* (?1691) combined with pamphlets and broadsheets such as those by 'G.V.', *An Account of a Child Born at Iurbick in Darbyshire, the 19th of January 1694. with a Top-knot and Rowle upon its Head, of Several Colours* (1694) and *The Vanity of Female Pride* (1691) (on a Wiltshire sow with seven monstrous topknotted piglets) to convey a moral and misogynist message, rebuking the vanity of women with topknots.[66] Another ballad, *The Farmers Wifes Complaint against the Ladys Commodes and Topknots*, blamed the monstrosity of the calf on the cow catching sight of a lady's topknot at the moment of conception.

So moralistic were these works that the prodigies themselves sometimes seemed secondary to the moral denunciation; one pamphlet on a monstrous child devoted only one paragraph in four pages to the actual monster. *The London Ladies Vindication of Top-Knots*, an answer ballad produced by the same publishers as *The Somersetshire Wonder*, dismissed the monster in a single line: 'They talk of a calf which was seen in our dress'. The *Athenian*

Mercury's discussion of the Somersetshire calf reflected Dunton's philogyny and intermittent scepticism regarding divine prodigies, suggesting that the true explanation was the power of the imagination rather than God's rebuke of female vanity.[67]

The moralistic and commercial prodigy writers of the 1690s demonstrated the continued viability of providential prodigy interpretation in a field ostensibly removed from party politics. However, they were also limited by the short-term nature of the fashion for moral reform. The atmosphere of moral crisis on which reformers thrived did not last very long. The reform campaign was also a victim of the revival of Church versus dissent politics in the first decade of the eighteenth century. The kind of cooperation between churchmen and dissenters embodied in the Societies for the Reformation of Manners and the campaign against 'atheism' could not last. Moralistic prodigy intepretation had diminished along with moral reform itself by the end of King William's reign. However, it proved more durable at the popular level than at the learned. Crouch's tracts in particular went into a myriad cheap editions appealing to the lower classes of the literate population, increasingly aimed at evoking wonder rather than generating moral reform. Although Turner attempted it, there was no high culture equivalent of Crouch, and the moral interpretation of prodigies faded in importance among the educated men and women of the Augustan era. Instead, during the 'rage of party', prodigies were once more – and for the last time – interpreted in terms of party politics.

Notes

1 For discussion of the drive to moral reform in the 1680s, see Dudley W.R. Bahlmann, *The Moral Revolution of 1688* (New Haven: Yale University Press, 1957), Tony Claydon, *William III and the Godly Revolution* (Cambridge: Cambridge University Press, 1996) and John Spurr, 'The Church, the societies and the moral revolution of 1688', in John Walsh, Colin Haydon and Stephen Taylor, eds, *The Church of England c.1689–c.1833: From Toleration to Tractarianism* (Cambridge: Cambridge University Press, 1993), pp. 127–42.

2 Walsham, *Providence*, pp. 135–42.

3 In addition to the previously discussed use of this story by Robert Plot, it was also recounted in James Illingworth, *A Just Narrative or*

Account of the Man whose Hands and Legs Rotted Off: in the Parish of Kings-Swinford, in Staffordshire (London, 1678).

4 Simon Ford, *A Discourse Concerning God's Judgements* (London, 1678), p. 4.

5 Ford, *Discourse*, p. 25.

6 Ford, *Discourse*, p. 52.

7 For an example of a magistrate fufilling the traditional role of swearing witnesses to an apparition in the early 1660s, see Marjorie Hope Nicolson, ed., *The Conway Letters: The Correspondence of Anne, Viscountess Conway, Henry More, and their Friends*, revised edition with an Introduction and new material edited by Sarah Hutton (Oxford: Clarendon Press, 1992), pp. 199–200. Another prodigy account circulating with the authority of a magistrate is in Josten, *Ashmole*, vol. 3: 1084. For a case in which local authorities got involved in an alleged sighting of triple moons, '2 of a more bloodyish colour', see two letters of Nathaniel Fairfax to Henry Oldenburg in *Correspondence of Henry Oldenburg*, vol. 3: 320–1, 386–7. Fairfax found the reaction of the bailiffs to be unsatisfactory in that they failed even to get the alleged witness's name.

8 Ford, *Discourse*, p. 52.

9 *A Very Strange, but True Relation of the Raining a Showre of Blood* (London, 1679), p. 1.

10 *A Very Strange, but True Relation*, p. 2.

11 For Crouch and the appeal of his works to the literate lower classes, see *DNB*; J. Paul Hunter, *Before Novels: The Cultural Contexts of Eighteenth-Century English Fiction* (New York and London: W.W. Norton & Company, 1990), pp. 210–14; and Robert Mayer, 'Nathaniel Crouch, bookseller and historian: popular historiography and cultural power in late seventeenth-century England', *Eighteenth-Century Studies*, 27 (1994): 391–419.

12 Mayer, 'Nathaniel Crouch'.

13 Crouch was briefly in legal trouble over his participation in Harris's paper; Sutherland, *Restoration Newspaper*, 209. For newspaper advertisements of Crouch's works in the Whig press see *Domestick Intelligence*, nos 130 (August 17–21, 1682): verso; 140 (September 21–5, 1682): verso; 149 (October 23–6, 1682): verso; and 150 (October 26–30, 1682): verso; and *Impartial Protestant Mercury*, nos 77 (January 13–18, 1681/82): verso; 91 (March 3–7, 1682): verso; 102 (April 11–14, 1682): verso; 106 (April 25–8, 1682): verso; 108 (May 2–5, 1682); 109 (May 5–9, 1682): verso; and 113 (May 19–23, 1682): verso. Crouch also published Keach's *Distressed Sion Relieved*.

14 'R.B.' (Nathaniel Crouch), *The Surprizing Miracles of Nature and Art* (London, 1683), 'To the Reader'.

15 (Crouch), *Surprizing Miracles*, 'To the Reader'.
16 (Crouch), *Surprizing Miracles*, pp. 64–5.
17 (Crouch), *Surprizing Miracles*, pp. 97–145.
18 (Crouch), *Surprizing Miracles*, p. 61.
19 John Vicars, *Prodigies and Apparitions* (London, 1642), and Lewis Hughes, *Certain Grievances, or, the Popish Errors and Ungodlinesse of so much of the Service-Book as is Antichristian* (np, 1642), pp. 41–4.
20 'R.B.' (Nathaniel Crouch), *Admirable Curiosities, Rarities, and Wonders In England, Scotland, and Ireland* (London, 1682), pp. 55–6.
21 Dunton left an autobiography, *The Life and Errors of John Dunton* (London, 1705). His life and the popularity and influence of his *Athenian Mercury* are discussed in Walter Graham, *English Literary Periodicals* (New York: Thomas Nelson & Sons, 1930), pp. 32–7; Gilbert McEwen, *The Oracle of the Coffee House: John Dunton's Athenian Mercury* (San Marino: Huntington Library, 1972); and Hunter, *Before Novels*, pp. 12–17. Bertha-Monica Stearns, 'The first English periodical for women', *Modern Philology*, 28 (1930): 45–59, argues that the *Athenian Mercury* was the first periodical consciously aimed at a female audience.
22 Baxter to Matthew Poole, August 31, 1657, in DWL Baxter Correspondence. For Annesley's interest in moralistic monstrous birth stories see Thomas Woodcock, 'Extracts from the Papers of Thomas Woodcock', pp. 68–9.
23 Dunton listed the dissenting authors he published in *Life and Errors* (pp. 230–7, mispaginated 732), referring to Ness as 'a man of considerable Learning' who 'Labours under some Unhappyness in his Stile', (p. 236).
24 Dunton, *Life and Errors*, p. 282. Dunton (p. 439) spoke highly of Francis Smith, although in terms that do not suggest much personal acquaintance. Dunton also had at least indirect exposure to the prodigy literature immediately preceding the *Mirabilis Annus* tracts. A subsequent Dunton periodical (*Athenian News, or Dunton's Oracle*, 1, no. 20 (May 9–13, 1710): 4) included among other sudden deaths the story of the Clerk of Brokington's Daughter, which had appeared in *Strange and True News from Gloucester* and *The Lord's Loud Call to England*.
25 *Athenian Mercury*, 8, no. 3 (July 19, 1692): verso. This is very close to a passage in L. Brinckmair, *The Warnings of Germany* (London, 1637), sig. **3v.
26 Dunton (*Life and Errors*, p. 454) also held in high regard another earthquake pamphleteer, the dissenting minister Samuel Doolittle high regard. Doolittle was the author of *A Sermon Occasioned by the Late Earthquake Which Happen'd in London, And Other Places on the Eighth*

of September 1692. Preached to a Congregation in Reading (London, 1692).

27 *Athenian Mercury*, 6, no. 1 (February 2, 1692): recto; 10, no. 2 (April 1, 1693): recto.

28 *Athenian Mercury*, 2, no. 30 (nd): verso. For these prodigies, see Hillel Schwarz, *The French Prophets: The History of a Millenarian Group in Eighteenth-Century England* (Berkeley: University of California Press, 1980), p. 16. Other prodigy and miracle stories concerning Louis XIV's persecution of the Huguenots were circulated widely in England: see DWL, Morrice MS P, p. 498; *Strange News from France* (London, 1678); and *A Relation of Several Hundred of Children and Others that Prophesie and Preach in their Sleep, &c. First Examined and Admired by several Ingenious Men, Ministers and Professors of Philosophy at Geneva, and sent from thence in two Letters to Rotterdam* (London, 1689).

29 *Athenian Mercury*, 3 no. 6 (August 15, 1691): verso. I have found no source for this prodigy story.

30 *Athenian Mercury*, 17, no. 18 (June 1, 1695): verso. For Turner and Dunton's business relationship, see *Life and Errors*, p. 225.

31 Dunton, *Life and Errors*, p. 225; and see *Diary of Philip Henry*, p. 231, for the connection between Henry and Turner. Turner claimed that a story of an apparition had been recounted to him by Henry, to whom he referred as 'a very Learned and Pious Divine'. Turner, *Compleat History*, second pagination, p. 75.

32 William Turner, *The History of All Religions in the World* (London, 1695).

33 William Turner, *An Essay on the Works of Creation* (London, 1695), pp. 22–3, 61–2.

34 For correspondence concerning prodigy accounts sent in from various sources for inclusion in the project see *Athenian Mercury*, 17, nos 16 (May 25, 1695): verso and 19 (June 4, 1695): verso; 18, nos 2 (July 20, 1695): verso and 6 (August 4, 1695): verso.

35 *Compleat History*, Title Page and 'To the Courteous Reader'; *Athenian Mercury*, 20, no. 1 (May 14, 1697): verso and *The Post-Man*, no. 408 (December 11–14, 1697): verso. Turner was also aware of Mather's project: *Compleat History*, 'To the Courteous Reader'. Dunton had met Mather in a visit to New England: Dunton, *Life and Errors*, p. 125.

36 For Turner's use of Crouch, see *Compleat History*, second pagination, pp. 43, 69–70; and fourth pagination, p. 15.

37 Turner, *Compleat History*, 'Preface to the Wonders of Nature'.

38 Turner, *Compleat History*, seventh pagination, p. 6.

39 Turner, *Compleat History*, sixth pagination, p. 26.

40 Turner, *Compleat History*, first pagination, p. 9.

41 Turner, *Compleat History*, second pagination, p. 70; sixth pagination, p. 80.

42 Turner, *Compleat History*, fourth pagination, pp. 162–3.
43 Turner, *Compleat History*, second pagination, pp. 77–8, 80–1; fourth
   pagination, pp. 15–16; sixth pagination, p. 73.
44 Dunton and Crouch were also involved in publicizing a series of
   miraculous cures of London's dissenting women in the early 1690s.
   These were described as miracles rather than prodigies, however.
   Dunton was one of the publishers of *A Narrative of the Late Extraordinary Cure Wrought in an Instant upon Mrs. Eliz. Savage, (Lame from her
   Birth) Without the Using of any Natural Means* (London, 1694), and
   Crouch recounted miraculous cures of Savage, a Huguenot girl
   named Mary Maillard and a shepherd named David Wright in 'R.B.'
   (Nathaniel Crouch), *The General History of Earthquakes* (London, 1694),
   pp. 172–5. Dunton's interest in circulating accounts of remarkable
   providences continued after the *Mercury*. The *Post-Angel*, an unsuccessful periodical project, included 'The Remarkable Providences of
   Judgment and Mercy that Happened Monthly': Dunton, *Life and
   Errors*, p. 267.
45 On the Baldwins, see Rostenberg, *Literary, Political, Scientific, Religious,
   and Legal Publishing*, pp. 369–415.
46 *Memoirs for the Curious: Or, an Account of What Occurrs that's Rare,
   Secret, Extraordinary, Prodigious, or Miraculous, through the World;
   Whether in Nature, Art, Learning, Policy or Religion*, nos 1 (January
   1701): 1–8 and 2 (February 1701): 45–6.
47 Another, even shorter-lived (one-issue), periodical which included
   providential prodigies was *Memoirs for the Ingenious, or the Universal
   Mercury* (January, 1694).
48 In a letter of October 18, 1690, Richard Lapthorne referred to 'a
   discourse of Earthquakes in many places within his Majestie's
   dominions', including Ireland as well as England: *Portledge Papers*,
   pp. 87–8. For an earthquake in Scotland late that year see *The
   Portledge Papers*, pp. 94–5, and San Marino, Huntington Newsletters,
   no. 16. See also CUL MS Oo.VI.115, fos 149–50. Earthquakes occurred
   in England in earlier decades, but the last one to be extensively publicized or commented on had been in 1580. For that earthquake, see
   Walsham, *Providence*, pp. 130–5. An earthquake in 1683 attracted some
   attention. See *Strange News from Oxfordshire: Being a True and Faithful
   Account of a Wonderful and Dreadful Earthquake that Happened in those
   Parts on Monday the 17th of this Present September, 1683* (London, 1683);
   Heywood Diary, vol. 1: 264; vol. 2: 191–2; and DWL Morrice MS P,
   p. 383.
49 Although there were no significant comets in the 1690s, there was a
   noted eclipse in 1699. It was something of a fiasco, possibly due to
   cloudy conditions that impared visibility, and it produced little pro-

vidential interpretation. See *Letters Written by Eminent Persons*, ed. John Walker, vol. 1: 97 and Edward Ward, *The London Spy* 11 (September, 1699).

50 Revelations 11:13 and 16:8.

51 For the relation drawn between the earthquake, God's anger and moral reform, see Bahlmann, *The Moral Revolution of 1688*, p. 9. Reactions to the earthquake are discussed in *The Tatler*, 240 (October 21, 1710), in Bond, ed., *The Tatler*, vol. 3: 235. Burnet (*History*, vol. 4: 181) claimed the earthquake along with others occurring around the same time prompted apocalyptic speculation. For another reaction to the earthquake as a judgement, see the letter of Sir Edmund King to Christopher Hatton, in *Correspondence of the Family of Hatton*, ed. Edward Maunde Thompson, Camden Society New Series nos 22–3 (London: Camden Society, 1878), vol. 2: 184. See also *Correspondence of John Locke*, vol. 4: 517–18, and *Portledge Papers*, pp. 146–7.

52 For the fear caused by the connection between the Jamaica and London earthquakes, see *The Autobiography of Sir John Bramston, K.B.*, Camden Society First Series no. 32 (London: Camden Society, 1845), p. 371. Bramston, a pro-revolution Tory, claimed regarding earthquakes: 'I looke not on them as judgments from God, but as proceeding from natural causes' (p. 372). It was claimed, in relation to the Jamaican earthquake, that 'if it continue its feared the Island will quite be depopulated': Clark Memorial Library Newsletters Box 2, no. 20. See also *Portledge Papers*, p. 144, and John Tutchin, *The Earth-Quake of Jamaica, Describ'd in a Pindarick Poem* (London, 1692).

53 *A Practical Discourse on the late Earthquakes, with An Historical Account of Prodigies and their Various Effects* (London, 1692), p. 5.

54 *Practical Discourse*, pp. 14–15.

55 *Practical Discourse*, p. 25.

56 *Practical Discourse*, p. 15.

57 *Practical Discourse*, 'Preface'.

58 Doolittle, *Sermon*, p. 20. For Doolittle and his influence on New England earthquake sermons, see Maxine Van de Wetering, 'Moralizing in Puritan natural thought: mysteriousness in earthquake sermons', *Journal of the History of Ideas*, 43 (1982): 417–38. Another work inspired by the 1692 earthquake was J.D.R.'s 'French Minister', *The Earth Twice Shaken Wonderfully* (London, 1693/94), which, in addition to giving an Aristotelian explanation of the physics of earthquakes, treated the quake as a providential sign, while refusing to say of what. It was reprinted later in 1694, with a new title page linking it to a recent earthquake in Naples, as *Observations upon Three Earthquakes*, although the text was not changed to reflect this. (For a contemporary notice, see *The Gentleman's Journal: or the Monthly*

Miscellany, March (1694): 63.) The other earthquakes of the early 1690s in Sicily and Jamaica also evoked providential responses. See Evelyn, vol. *Diary*, 5: 133; and, arguing against theories of both divine and astrological causation, *The Gentleman's Journal, or the Monthly Miscellany*, August (1692): 18–21.

59 Thomas Beverley, *Evangelical Repentance unto Salvation not to be Repented of, upon 2. Cor 7.10. And as most Seasonable; Short Considerations on that great Context Hebr. 12.26. Yet Once more I shake not only Earth, &c. Upon the Solemn Occasion of the Late Dreadful Earthquake in Jamaica; and the Later Monitory Motion of the Earth in London, and other parts of the Nation, and Beyond the Sea. Whereunto is Adjoined a Discourse on Death-Bed Repentance, on Luc. 22.39* (London, 1693), p. 142.

60 Thomas Watson to the earl of Huntingdon October 8, 1690 (Hastings Manuscript 13083, Huntington Library), and John Evelyn to Archbishop Thomas Tenison, October 15, 1692, in *Diary and Correspondence of John Evelyn*, vol. 4: 467–72. This letter is primarily devoted to natural-philosophical hypotheses explaining earthquakes, but Evelyn also acknowledges that they are warnings or chastisements from God.

61 *Proposals for a National Reformation of Manners* (London, 1694), 'Preface' and pp. 1, 9 and 29; Josiah Woodward, *An Account of the Rise and Progress of the Religious Societies in the City of London, etc. And of the Endeavours for Reformation of Manners that have been Made therein. The Second edition, enlarged* (London, 1698), p. xiii. Dunton printed both works.

62 San Marino, Huntington Newsletters no. 25 (September 15, 1692), and Clark Memorial Library Newsletters Box 2, no. 39 (September 15, 1692). There was also a controversial show at Bartholomew Fair: see *Proposals for a National Reformation*, p. 17,

63 *Philosophical Transactions*, 18, no. 209 (March–April 1694): 78–100.

64 Among many other examples of providential reactions, see *Memoirs of William Stukeley*, vol. 1: 479–82. For a discussion of the tension between providential and natural-philosophical uses of the earthquake, see Simon Schaffer, 'Natural philosophy and public spectacle in the eighteenth century', *History of Science*, 21 (1983): 15–21.

65 The comparison of monstrous growths on heads to topknots was not new, see (Matthew Prior and Charles Montague) *The Hind and the Panther Transvers'd* (London, 1687), p. 11. Benjamin Keach anticipated the strategy of rebuking women's headresses by likening them to monsters in *Distressed Sion Relieved* (London, 1689) p. 50: 'Should any women have such children born/with such attire as in their Heads are worn/would it not them affright and terrifie/God may do so if you don't speedily/Reform your lives, and cast your Fashions off'.

66 Luttrell, *Historical Relation*, 2: vol. 233 (May 30, 1691): 'Letters from Somersetshire bring a strange account of a monstrous calf, that was calved last March near Bath in that County, with the form of a womans commode or headdresse near half a yard high growing on it's head.' This is found nearly word-for-word in Turner, *Compleat History*, sixth pagination, p. 26, indicating a common source, probably a newsletter. The topknot craze extended to Ireland, where it was reported: 'a hen has layd an Egg, which at one end represents a Ladyes Comode, and both rich and poor flock there to see', Clark Memorial Library Newsletters Box 2, no. 53: verso.

67 *Athenian Mercury*, 2, no. 2 (May 30, 1691): recto.

5

'The poor comfort of prodigies and old women's fables': political prodigies in the early eighteenth century

The reign of Queen Anne (1702–14) was highly polarized politically and religiously, and saw a voluminous outpouring of political and satirical writing, much of it dealing with prodigies. Many 'Augustan' writers situated the party struggles of Anne's reign – the 'rage of party' – in a historical framework, tracing the differences of contemporary Whigs and Tories to the Civil War and the Exclusion Crisis of the previous century. Given the importance of prodigies in these conflicts, questions of the significance of prodigies were revived and debated during this period. Even the *Mirabilis Annus* controversy of forty years earlier was not forgotten. Anonymous Tory pamphlets and satires revived the *Mirabilis Annus* tracts in order to link their contemporary Whig and dissenting opponents with the radical Fifth Monarchists of the Restoration. One collection, usually ascribed to the lawyer and high-church propagandist John Brydall, went through two editions with different titles in 1707 and 1708. *The Oracles of the Dissenters: Containing Forty-Five Relations of Pretended Judgements, Prodigies, and Apparitions, In Behalf of the Non-Conformists* was a reprinting of judgements and prodigies selected from *Mirabilis Annus Secundus* together with hostile commentary.[1] The fact that the writer of *The Oracles of the Dissenters* had to go back over fifty years to find a dissenting prodigy tract to attack is testimony both to the persistent cultural presence of the *Mirabilis Annus* tracts and to the paucity of Whig and dissenting prodigy material from the writer's own time. (One reason for using the *Mirabilis Annus* material in 1708 was that the tracts denounced those who compromised with the rituals and ceremonies of the re-established Church of England, showing many of them to have suffered providential punishment. Brydall used the evidence of the tracts to show that early eighteenth-century dissenters were hypocrites in their use of Occasional Conformity, the practice of taking the Anglican Sacrament so as to qualify for public office under the provisions of the Test Act.[2]) Brydall did not display any particular knowledge of the *Mirabilis Annus* outside of the tracts themselves, making no reference to any of the individuals involved in their compilation, printing or distribution, but Civil War and Restoration issues did persist in his work – he referred to William Lilly, dead nearly thirty years, as 'The Dissenter's Oracle'.[3]

The Oracles of the Dissenters used several strategies to discredit the stories it included, but did not mark an advance in the anti-providential argument from that of the original controversy surrounding the tracts. Like the royalists of the 1660s, Brydall attacked the *Mirabilis Annus* compilers for lack of charity, and for providing no or inadequate testimony in corroboration of their prodigies and judgements.[4] He also put forward alternative, non-providential, explanations for the phenomena recounted in the original tract, and denounced the idea that anyone should be at liberty to interpret judgements and prodigies 'according as it suits best with his Opinion and Interest'.[5] *The Oracles of the Dissenters* also attacked the accounts' truth-claims, particularly their lack of circumstantial detail.[6]

A Protestant Monument, Erected to the Immortal Glory of the Whiggs and the Dutch (1713) had a more specific agenda. It was produced at the close of the war of the Spanish Succession, a time of frenzied debate over the claims of Britain's allies, particularly the Dutch, to be considered in the peace. The Tories supported the British government's position in favour of the Treaty of Utrecht, while the Whigs argued for 'no peace without Spain', a slogan which indicated a willingness to continue the war with France until Philip V of Spain, the grandson of Louis XIV, was driven from the Spanish throne. The Tories replied that this policy subordinated British interests to those of the holy Roman emperor and the Dutch, appealing to xenophobia to support the policies of the government which was negotiating the Treaty of Utrecht. *A Protestant Monument* attempted to revive the hostility towards the Dutch which had been characteristic of the commonwealth and the reign of Charles II, the period of the Anglo-Dutch war.

To this end, the author argued that the Fire of London had been a plot of the Whigs and the Dutch, a plot laid out in the *Mirabilis Annus* tracts. The description of this plot in *A Protestant Monument* was much more circumstantial than that in *The Oracles of the Dissenters*, although the author of *A Protestant Monument* also named no names. He or she alleged that in the year 1660 a secret club of 'whiggish protestants' set up a network of correspondents covering the British Isles which was dedicated to the fabrication of prodigies and judgements 'on purpose to debauch the people from their allegiance'. The tracts's prodigy narratives allegedly encoded a plot against England on the part of the Dutch and the Whigs.[7] When decoded, these descriptions were actually of the disasters of the Fire of London *and* the Dutch war.[8]

In the conflict between Whigs and Tories in Queen Anne's reign, satire was particularly important to the Tory cause. An examination of Tory satire of the period reveals that Tories like Jonathan Swift and the members of the Scriblerian Club, including such distinguished figures as Alexander Pope and John Gay, often attacked their Whig rivals, for example the astrologer John Partridge, by depicting them as believers in the providential interpretation of prodigies.[9] This was a particularly useful strategy in that it reinforced the connection of Whigs, dissenters and seventeenth-century revolutionaries that was central to Tory propaganda.[10]

Although both Tory satirists and natural philosophers continued to attack the providential interpretation of prodigies, they were seldom intentional allies. Natural philosophers, or 'virtuosi', remained frequent objects of satire themselves, whether from the Whig dramatist Susanna Centlivre in her play *The Basset-Table* or, more commonly, from Tories such as John Arbuthnot and his fellow Scriblerians in *Martinus Scriblerus*.[11] Prodigies and monsters often figured in these satires as objects of ridiculous curiosity on the part of natural philosophers, just as the absurd 'virtuoso' Scriblerus married conjoined female twins.[12] However, whether or not they realized it, satirists and natural philosophers were united in ridiculing providential prodigy interpretation.

Although some prodigy-writing in the providential tradition did appear in the Whig press, prominent elite Whigs like Joseph Addison did not try to defend providential interpretation.[13] In his best-known and most successful essay paper, *The Spectator*, which he and Richard Steele wrote during Anne's reign, Addison declared that the providential interpretation of prodigies was out-moded. He linked providential prodigy belief with fairy lore and belief in witchcraft and enchantment as relics of the time 'before the world was enlightened by Learning and Philosophy'.[14] For Addison, the making of connections between prodigies and notable subsequent events was legitimate only in such poetry as Milton's *Paradise Lost*.[15] But the anti-prodigious position of Addison and other Whigs went beyond that, into using accusations of credulity against their Tory opponents, despite the little use Jacobites and Tories made of prodigies. The Catholicism of the exiled Stuarts and some of their foreign and domestic supporters certainly made their identification with superstition and barbarism more credible to Whig minds, and as Tories identified credulity with Protestant dissent, so Whigs identified it with Catholicism. As both Whigs and Tories were now attacking each other as believers in or manipulators of the providential interpretation of prodigies, there was little space for its straightforward employment in politics.

'Surprizing phaenomena of light': the wonder years 1715 and 1716

Despite, or because of, the decline of the political prodigy, prodigies were important in the Whig, Tory and natural philosophy literature created by the conjunction of some unusual celestial phenomena with the tumultuous period from the death of Anne in 1714 to the execution of the Jacobite rebels against the new monarch George of Hanover in 1716.[16] The polemical use of these prodigies marked a fundamental shift in Whig rhetoric. Rather than use the prodigies to show divine favour for the Whig cause, most Whig writers now seized the opportunity presented by the eclipse and the aurora to associate Tories and Jacobites with providential prodigy belief. Rather than assimilating their attacks on providential prodigy belief to the Tory and Anglican critique of Whig and dissenting 'enthusiasm', Whigs incorporated their attacks into their own critique of Tory, high church and, ultimately, Catholic 'superstition'.

The total eclipse of the sun in 1715 occurred shortly after the death of Queen Anne and the coming in of King George, and the

aurora borealis followed by a few days the execution of the
Jacobite rebels Lords Kenmure and Derwentwater.[17] (Subsequent
auroras were sometimes referred to as 'Lord Derwentwater's
Lights'.) These remarkable phenomena were interpreted in Whig,
Tory and non-political ways, as well as studied and expounded
by natural philosophers.[18] Discussion of the aurora was particularly important, marking the transition from the politically significant 'battle in the sky' to the apolitical 'Northern Lights'. The
1716 aurora was a dramatic event, as can be gathered from this
description by a contemporary observer, Mary, Countess Cowper.

> First appeared a black Cloud, from whence Smoke and Light
> issued forth at once on every Side, and then the Cloud opened, and
> there was a great Body of pale Fire, that rolled up and down, and
> sent forth all Sorts of Colours like the Rainbow on every Side; but
> this did not last above two or three Minutes. After that it was like
> pale elementary Fire issuing out of all sides of the Horizon, but
> more especially at the North and Northwest, where it fixed at last.
> The Motion of it was extremely swift and rapid, like Clouds in their
> swiftest Rack. Sometimes it discontinued for a While, at other
> Times it was but as Streaks of Light in the Sky, but moving always
> with great Swiftness. About one o'Clock this Phaenomenon was so
> strong, that the whole Face of the Heavens was entirely covered
> with it, moving as swiftly as before, but extremely low.[19]

Addison's response to the aurora exemplifies one early
eighteenth-century Whig interpretation of the relation of prodigies, journalism and civil discord. At this time, Addison was an
active Whig propagandist and politician, and instead of the rather
apolitical critique of providential prodigy belief characteristic of
the ostensibly non-partisan *Spectator* he now aggressively associated superstitious belief in providential prodigies with Tories and
Jacobites.

Addison's new government-subsidized periodical *The Freeholder* was much more explicitly political and Whig than *The
Spectator*. It was issued during the foreign and domestic peace following the Treaty of Utrecht, the accession of King George,
and the defeat of the Jacobites. In *The Freeholder* Addison linked
'superstitious' prodigy belief with 'superstitious' Jacobite divine-
right politics. In doing so, Addison shows how Whigs in power
during the Georgian period adapted Tory arguments about prodigies from the later Stuart period.[20] Jacobite use of the aurora as a

prodigy he claimed to be a ploy particularly characteristic of these opponents of 'our present happy establishment', just as similar accusations against dissenting malcontents had been made by royalist and Anglican defenders of the 'happy establishment' of the 1660s. But, unlike the royalist opponents of the *Mirabilis Annus* tracts, who had portrayed the use of prodigies by political malcontents as a dangerous tactic, Addison treated the alleged Jacobite attempt to exploit the aurora as the final ridiculous shift of a defeated and discredited faction: 'The Party, indeed, that is opposite to our present happy Settlement, seem to be driven out of the Hopes of all human Methods for carrying on their Cause, and are therefore reduced to the poor Comfort of Prodigies and Old Women's Fables. They begin to see Armies in the Clouds, when all upon the Earth have forsaken them.'[21] (This passage was used to define 'prodigy' in Dr Samuel Johnson's *Dictionary*.)

Political prodigy interpretation was no longer a dangerous foe to be combated. Instead, imputing political prodigy belief to Addison's political targets was way of denigrating them:

> It is an old observation, that a time of Peace is always a Time of Prodigies; for as our News-Writers must adorn their Papers with that which the Criticks call the Marvellous, they are forced in a dead Calm of Affairs to ransack every Element for proper Materials, and either to astonish their readers from time to time with a strange and wonderful Sight, or be content to lose their Custom. The Sea is generally filled with Monsters, when there are no Fleets upon it. Mount Aetna immediately began to rage upon the Extinction of the Rebellion: and woe to the People of Catanea, if the Peace continues; for they are sure to be shaken every Week with Earthquakes, till they are relieved by the Siege of some other great Town in Europe. The Air has likewise contributed its quota of Prodigies. We had a blazing star by the late Mail from Genoa; and in the present Dearth of Battles have been very opportunely entertained, by Person of undoubted Credit, with a civil war in the Clouds, where our sharp-sighted Malecontents discovered many Objects, invisible to an Eye that is dimmed by Whig-Principles.[22]

Clearly, this is not the Whiggism of Christopher Ness. Despite Addison's claim that his is an 'old observation', what is immediately striking is its inversion of the earlier approach to the relation of prodigies to politics. Rather than being heralds and accompaniments of war, prodigies were now the products of peace, and the production and circulation of prodigy accounts was evidence of peace. In times of war, presumably, more important issues dominated discussion. 'Malecontents' are not portrayed in this passage as distributing prodigy accounts as part of their consistent strategy of destabilizing the regime; here they have become consumers of marvels as a consolation in the wake of political failure. The distributors of the prodigy accounts were not rebels attacking the State, which had just survived a rebellion, but vendors of news looking for material to fill their pages and attract the attention of their naive and ignorant readers. Continuing the trend set by the Tory satires of the Exclusion period, an anti-commercial critique of prodigy literature was beginning to dominate the political one, with newswriters rather than balladeers the prototypical prodigy-mongers. Countess Cowper, like Addison a Whig, took a similar position, describing the aurora in abstract and non-metaphorical terms, and ascribing its representation as a celestial battle to 'Papers printed and sold . . .'.[23]

Despite the scepticism of Countess Cowper, and doubtless of many other women, Addison presented women as particularly vulnerable to unscrupulous Jacobite prodigy mongers. His use of gender as a category was a heightening of a previous trend in attacks on providential prodigy interpretation. Classic attacks on providentialism, such as Spencer's *Discourse*, had used gender as a category, but they had preferred to associate providential prodigy belief with the uneducated and fanatical rather than with women *per se*. The credulity of women was more central to Addison's analysis. 'There has been another Method lately made use of, which has been practised with extraordinary Success; I mean the spreading abroad Reports of Prodigies, which has wonderfully gratified the Curiosity, as well as the Hopes of our fair Malignants.'[24] The ridiculing of politically active Jacobite women was an obsession of Addison in *The Freeholder*, and the association of providential prodigy belief with disloyal women served the purpose of discrediting prodigies, Jacobites and politically active women.

Some Whigs offered alternative, pro-Whig, providential interpretations of the aurora, such as that made in *A Dialogue Between a Whig and a Jacobite, Upon the Subject of the Late Rebellion; and the Execution of the Rebel-Lords, &c. occasion'd by the Phaenomenon in the Skie, March 6, 1715–16*. This pamphlet used Jacobite credulity regarding prodigies mostly as a hook to begin a dialogue about non-prodigy-related political concerns, but concluded with the Whig's claim that the heavens were draped with light in honour of King George. Another Whig, Anthony Corbière, described in a letter to Horatio Walpole an exchange he had had with a member of the 'rabble', who had claimed that the aurora 'was looked upon as a judgment upon the King for intending to execute the Lords the next day'. Corbière claimed he had replied that, on the contrary, 'it was a judgment because they were not to dye although they had so much deserved it'.[25] Lady Cowper, closely connected to the Hanoverian Court as lady of the bedchamber to the princess of Wales, gave a somewhat different Whig interpretation of the aurora: 'Both Parties turned it on their Enemies. The Whigs said it was God's Judgment on the horrid Rebellion, and the Tories said that it came for the Whigs taking off the two Lords that were executed.'[26]

There were Whig interpretations of the eclipse as well as the aurora. A leading Whig newspaper, *The Flying Post*, alleged that Jacobites, in a tactic reminiscent of the use of historical parallels in the *Mirabilis Annus* tracts, had claimed that a total solar eclipse had not been seen in England since the reign of King Stephen, as much a usurper as was King George. The newspaper replied that Stephen as a false claimant was a parallel to the Pretender, and that if the eclipse portended disaster to anyone, it was probably the Jacobites' ally the Sun King Louis XIV, or possibly their other ally the king of Sweden.[27] The same newspaper printed a letter following the aurora, linking the comet of 1680, the eclipse and the aurora in a Whig providential narrative displaying the 'Light, Beauty, and Security' emanating from King George.[28]

Despite the fact that both events could be interpreted as a positive omen for the Whig cause, Whigs rarely explicitly endorsed such providential interpretations. They attributed these interpretations to unnamed speakers or else qualified them with phrases like 'But whether there be anything Preternatural in Eclipses or not'.[29] By disassociating themselves from these interpretations, Whigs who engaged in public writing in newspapers and pamphlets operated on two levels. Whig writers provided the providentially-minded or the uncertain Whig reader with a reassuring explanation of the meaning of a prodigy.[30] On another level, they demonstrated that Whig interpretations were as easy to make as Jacobite ones, reinforcing the idea that all providential prodigy interpretation was arbitrary and erroneous and, in the mind of the non-providential Whig, associated the Jacobites with folly and superstition.[31]

Whig use of providential prodigy belief to associate Tories and Jacobites with superstition paralleled another development of the Augustan period: Whig use of witchcraft to the same ends. The most prominent instance of this phenomenon was the case of Jane Wenham, discussed in Bostridge's *Witchcraft and its Transformations*. Bostridge identifies the 1712 trial, condemnation and eventual pardon of the Hertfordshire witch Jane Wenham as the moment when witchcraft belief became inextricably enmeshed in partisan politics.[32] Whigs, such as Francis Hutchinson, author of *An Historical Essay Concerning Witchcraft* (1718), identified belief in witches (and prodigy interpretation) as Tory superstition, and repudiated the moderately sceptical position taken earlier by Addison in *The Spectator* in denying the existence of witchcraft altogether. This was expressed by Addison himself in his play mocking belief in witches, *The Drummer* (1716). The development of Addison's attitudes to prodigies, from the apolitical scepticism of *The Spectator* to the fierce attacks of *The Freeholder*, parallels the development of his attitude to belief in witches.

Despite the dominance of ridicule in Whig responses to political prodigy interpretation, older discourses which treated prodigies as serious threats to the political order persisted in some Whig writings. One published Whig sermon of the early eighteenth century which took the older view was Elisha Smith's *The Superstition of Omens and Prodigies; with the Proper Reception, and Profitable Improvement. A Divinity Lecture upon the Surprizing Phaenomenon of Light, March. 6. 1715. on the Sunday after* (1716). This work went through subsequent editions in 1717 and 1719. Smith's view of the relation of prodigies to political dissent was similar to that obtaining among Restoration conservatives. Like Addison, Smith, a prolific 'Court Whig' cleric and author, portrayed the Jacobite opponents of the government as superstitious believers in the providential interpretation of prodigies. Unlike Addison, Smith viewed providential prodigy belief as at least a potentially serious political danger:[33] 'Some, perhaps, will be so Maliciously and Prophetically given, as to presage from hence, the Subversion and Funeral of the present Settlement, and if any

can be encouraged and perswayded that the Heavens declare
against the Government, the next Inference is, that vain is the
Help of Man to defend it.'[34]

Smith's anti-providential arguments added little to those of
Spencer, whose work he did not specifically credit. He presented
himself in the role of an enlightener removing superstitious fear,
a superstitious fear that continued to dominate the minds of the
majority:

> I have seen, I have heard it had left upon the Minds of most
> People such surprise, Doubt, superstitious Fear, and Apprehension
> of some great Prognosticated Event, that I could not deny my
> Endeavours of offering some Ease and satisfaction; nor defer the
> Opportunity, first of removing false Superstitious Impressions;
> then of imprinting some due Improvement and solid Benefit, as the
> proper Influence of it upon our Hearts and Lives.[35]

Another sermon, this one Nonconformist, which was ambivalent
toward the providential use of prodigies was Joseph Burroughs's
*A Sermon Occasion'd by the Total Eclipse of the Sun, Upon April the
22d, 1715* (1715). Preaching on the old anti-divinatory text of
Jeremiah 10:2, and arguing that the predictability of eclipses precluded providential meaning, Burroughs divided the receivers of
the eclipse into three categories. Those making the right use were
reminded of the 'Power and Wisdom of God'. Others were dupes,
superstitiously fearing dire events portended by the eclipse; while
a third group felt 'a malicious Joy' caused by 'so favourable an
occasion for spreading fears of this nature throughout the Land'.[36]
The hopes of this third group were specifically related to their
opposition to the accession of the House of Hanover, providence's
true favourites.[37]

The fact that Whigs portrayed Jacobites as superstitious believers in prodigies, or else as unscrupulous manipulators of
popular superstition, does not mean that Jacobites did indeed
attribute providential meanings to the aurora or eclipse. Unmedi-
ated Jacobite responses are hard to recover, and may have varied
with the social class and level of education of individual Jacobites.
Dudley Ryder, a young Whig man-about-town, described with
some amusement two lower-class sisters' Jacobite interpretations
of the aurora as 'a prodigy portending great things' and a reason
for the king's possible pardon of the rest of the prisoners, com-

menting 'So very ignorant are the people and so easy to be imposed [upon] by supersition'.[38] A physician told Ryder the story of a precious stone inscribed with an indelible representation of the Pretender. Since this interlocutor was presumably 'learned', Ryder ascribed his story to Jacobite unscrupulousness rather than to superstition. The Jacobite Oxford scholar Thomas Hearne spoke of 'frightfull Appearances' while ascribing no political meaning to the aurora, and the Jacobite Catholic squire Nicholas Blundell treated both the eclipse and the aurora as spectacles rather than politically meaningful events.[39] However, Henry Prescott, the bibulous deputy registrar of the diocese of Chester, in the process of moving to Jacobitism from high-church Anglicanism and a grudging acceptance of the revolution, was sufficiently intrigued by the aurora and its possible providential cause to research the strange lights that had accompanied the disasters which frustrated the Emperor Julian's attempt to rebuild the Temple in Jerusalem in the fourth century.[40] The periodical *News from the Dead*, mildly sympathetic to the Stuart cause, argued that the 'gloomy and dark scene' of the eclipse could easily have been caused by God's wrath at national sin, despite God's working through natural causes.[41]

The poet Richard Savage produced a more explicitly Jacobite response, claiming the apparition in the sky along with other natural disasters was a specific attack on King George and linking the apparition with the execution of the Jacobite lords.[42] It is difficult to know the sincerity of this effort, particularly since Savage later abandoned both Jacobitism and providential prodigy interpretation.[43]

Another eclipse-related work which sought to discern benefits in what the eclipse portended was a pamphlet attributed to Daniel Defoe, *The Second-Sighted Highlander. Being Four Visions of the Eclypse, And Something of what may Follow*, part of a series on the alleged supernatural gifts of Scotland's Highlanders.[44] This work had a unique slant on prodigy interpretation in the English context, associating correct prodigy interpretation with the possession of supernatural gifts. It argued that the Highlander's God-given gift of second sight made him uniquely qualified to interpret the 'portentuous Significations' of the eclipse, and poured considerable scorn on astrologers.[45] Defoe gave somewhat more respect to natural philosophers, but the author argued:

'Signs in the Heavens, and in the Earth, are not wholly to be neglected, although the natural Causes thereof may be accounted for, and that Providence frequently warns the World of approaching Judgments, by such Events . . .'.[46] The second-sighted Highlander's actual prophecies were safely Whig and Protestant, predicting the imminent death of Louis XIV, the conversion of France to Protestantism and the downfall of Catholicism.[47]

'There is nothing in it more than Natural': natural philosophers in the wonder years

The author of *The Second-Sighted Highlander* was correct in claiming that 'Philosophers being able to give a clear Account of the Nature, as well as courses of Eclypses, make sport with, and ridicule all the Notions of their being portentuous and predicting'.[48] Natural philosophers and natural philosophy did indeed struggle against providential and portentuous explanations of the phenomena of the wonder years. Not only did natural philosophers themselves give non-providential explanations of the phenomena, but others wishing to do so employed arguments characteristic of philosophy of nature. The periodical *Chit-Chat*, probably authored by Addison's old associate and fellow Whig Sir Richard Steele, began its description of the aurora by asserting that its readers were too intelligent to be troubled with 'the ridiculous Construction that the Disaffected put on the late Lightning', before giving an elaborate naturalistic explanation based on the earth's release of pent-up vapours.[49]

The most conspicuous examples of natural philosophers working to deprive the eclipse and the aurora of providential and political meanings potentially harmful to the Hanoverian dynasty were two leaders of the Newtonians, the moderate Tory Edmond Halley (1656–1742) and the Unitarian Whig and friend of Addison and Steele William Whiston (1667–1752).[50] Halley, who probably owned a copy of the 1665 edition of Spencer's *Discourse Concerning Prodigies*, effectively employed popularized natural philosophy against politically destabilizing providential prodigy belief in connection with the eclipse of 1715.[51] In one broadside, a medium particularly useful for addressing a large public, Halley gave a picture of the shadow cast by the moon on a map of Great Britain and a simple explanation of the phenomenon. The purpose of the broadside was made explicit:

> The like Eclipse having not for many Ages been seen in the Southern Parts of Great Britain, I thought it not improper to give the Publick an Account thereof, that the suddain darkness wherein the Starrs will be visible about the Sun, may give no surprize to the People, who would, if unadvertized, be apt to look upon it as Ominous, and to Interpret it as portending evill to our Sovereign Lord, King George and his Government, which God preserve. Hereby they will see that there is nothing in it more than Natural, and no more than the necessary result of the Motions of the Sun and Moon.[52]

The Whigs who remembered Halley's support of the previous Tory government were not necessarily eager to accept his support of King George, which one Whig described as 'a Piece of designing Officiousness'.[53]

Halley's description of the 1716 aurora, in *Philosophical Transactions*, was addressed to a more philosophically sophisticated and socially elite audience, presenting a thoroughgoing attempt to naturalize the imagery and militaristic language that had been used to describe strange sights in the sky. Popular perceptions of pointed weapons and towers in the air, Halley argued, were due to an illusion of perspective that made parallels seem to converge:

> Wherefore those Rays which arose highest above the Earth and were nearest the Eye, seemed to terminate in Cusps sufficiently acute, and have been for that supposed by the Vulgar to represent Spears. Others seen from afar, and perhaps not rising so high as the former, would terminate as if cut off with plains parallel to the Horizon, like truncate Cones or Cylinders: these have been taken to look like the Battlements and Towers on the Walls of Cities fortified after the ancient manner. Whilst others yet further off, by reason of their great Distance, good part of them being intercepted by the Interposition of the Convexity of the Earth, would only shew their pointed tops, and because of their shortness have gotten the Name of Swords.[54]

Every example of illegitimate figurative language highlighted in this passage was directly related to war. Although Halley himself was not above using military metaphors to describe the aurora, the most elaborate metaphors in his account, all specifically identified as subjective, convey a far different message. Halley described the onset of the aurora as a 'corona' or crown, then likened it to 'the Representation of Glory wherewith our Painters in Churchs surround the Holy Name of God', 'those radiating Starrs wherewith the Knights of the Most Noble Order of the Garter are adorned' and 'the Concave of the great Cupola of St. Paul's Church'.[55] Rather than armed conflict, the aurora visually represented God, Crown, Aristocracy and Church together in harmony.

In addition to Halley's works, one elaborate attempt to use natural philosophy to neutralize prodigies was Whiston's pamphlet on the aurora, *An Account of a Surprizing Meteor, Seen in the Air, March the 6th, 1715/16. at Night*.[56] The bulk of this pamphlet consisted of a compilation of narratives Whiston claimed to have received from correspondents in various parts of Britain describing their experience of the aurora. Most of these narratives employed the traditional device of natural-philosophical accounts of wonders, contrasting the philosophically educated correspondents with the uneducated who saw the aurora as a battle in the air or a divine sign. A correspondent from Oxford claimed:

> Already strange things are portended: I have met several who tell me they saw swords drawn, and Armies fighting in the Air: But as I was out my self, and saw almost the Whole, you may depend upon it there was nothing of this Nature, any further than large Rays of Light are like Broad Swords, and the playing of the streams within one another, their advancing, and intermingling, &c. may somewhat represent the Mustering of Soldiers.[57]

A correspondent from Edinburgh claimed that 'the Good Wives are making Dreadful Prognostications of what will follow this unusual sight', as was one from Huntington, 'to be certain the frightful circumstances of it will be multiplied with the addition of political remarks, as People stand affected'.[58]

When Whiston spoke in his own voice, he made explicit his argument against providentialism and the belief in battles in the air: such phenomena arose 'from the Fears, and Fancies, and Superstitions, and Prejudices of Vulgar and Injudicious Spectators'.[59] Only those celestial prodigies specifically prophesied by Christ, such as those preceding the fall of Jerusalem, could be considered providential. In 1719 Whiston published a very similar work relating to a blazing star of that year, *An Account of a Surprizing Meteor Seen in the Air March 19. 1718/19 at Night.* In it he specifically denied the apocalyptic relevance of the increase of celestial prodigies in recent years.[60] Whiston held to this view despite both his own belief in an imminent apocalypse and his hope for the fall of what he considered false religion and its replacement by true, that is Arian, Christianity.[61]

Despite the hard line taken by such leading natural philosophers as Halley and Whiston, not everyone viewed natural philosophy as incompatible with providential interpretation. An anonymous pamphlet, *The Black-Day, or, A Prospect of Doomsday. Exemplified in the Great and Terrible Eclipse, which will happen on Friday the 22d of April, 1715,* referred to the calculations of such respected natural philosophers as Halley, Whiston and Astronomer Royal John Flamsteed.[62] It used the standard story of a European conqueror impressing the natives with his ability to predict an eclipse in order to emphasize the superiority of those possessing natural philosophical understanding over the ignorant.[63] However, the pamphlet did not treat natural philosophical understanding as excluding providential and astrological interpretation. Despite its title, *The Black-Day* contained little apocalyptic material, though it did claim that great eclipses in the past had uniformly been followed by disasters. Referring back to the providential interpretations of the seventeenth century, *The Black-Day* included several stories of prodigies and disasters from the Civil War, including the claim that the execution of the king had been preceded by a lunar eclipse.[64] An astrological interpretation showed, however, that whatever the portents to Europe at large, the current eclipse portended good to Great Britain.[65]

'It . . . must of Necessity be a Prodigy': challenges to the natural-philosophical claim to a monopoly on prodigy explanation

Two significant works challenged natural philosophers' somewhat inadequate explanations of the aurora. The most forthright challenge to the natural philosophers' claim to exercise jurisdiction over the aurora was the anonymous pamphlet titled *An Essay Concerning the Late Apparition in the Heavens, on the Sixth of March.*

Proving by Mathematical, Logical, and Moral Arguments, that it could not have been produced by the Ordinary Course of Nature, but must of Necessity be a Prodigy. Humbly offer'd to the Consideration of the Royal Society. The other was the Tory Grubstreet hack and tavernkeeper Edward Ward's satirical poem *British Wonders: or A Poetical Description of the several Prodigies and Most Remarkable Accidents that have Happen'd in Britain since the Death of Queen Anne* (1717).[66] Neither work was explicitly Jacobite.

The anonymous pamphlet specifically disavowed interest in politics, pouring scorn on those who have 'divided the Heavens according to Party'.[67] It also denied knowledge of the specific event the wonder presaged.[68] Instead it presented itself as calling for a return to the tradition of using prodigies for moral refor-mation, the tradition characteristic of the prodigy writings of the 1690s. By appearing in the evening, 'the hour of repentance', the prodigy made its meaning clear.[69] The prodigy's appearance at London was also a rebuke of those in the provinces who dis-missed newspaper accounts of such occurrences.[70]

The author saw the natural philosophers as his or her princi-pal opponents in the mission of using the prodigy for reforma-tion, characterizing them as 'the Lucretiuses of the Age, you Modern Epicureans and Libertines', licentious materialists unwilling to acknowledge the divine power.[71] Rather than linking them as wonders, the author contrasted the mysterious lights with the recent eclipse, pointing out that while the eclipse indeed had a coherent natural-philosophical explanation, the lights did not. The eclipse, whose explanation had been widely dissemi-nated in works such as Halley's, therefore did not have a terrify-ing effect, even on the vulgar.[72] By contrast, the lights of 1716, which the author insisted belonged to the established providen-tial category of the comet, had been predicted by no one.[73] In dis-cussing the aurora, the author employed natural-philosophical arguments against common natural-philosophical explanations, pointing out that if the phenomenon had been caused by pent-up vapours – one popular explanation – it would have broken into a fire and burned itself out.[74]

The author of the essay preserved the distinction between the vulgar who viewed bizarre events as prodigies that called for repentance and the learned who assumed there was a natural explanation, but inverted its values, praising the 'Prudence among

the most illiterate of our People' in contrast to 'the general Stu-
pidity and Folly among the Learned', who despite their confidence
could not give a convincing natural explanation.[75] Those who
knowingly denied the prodigious nature of the eclipse committed
a sin against the Holy Ghost, and were fit targets of hell-fire.[76]

However, the author was not able to completely deny the
authority of natural philosophers to define the prodigious, as can
be seen in the decision, claimed in the title, to submit the pamphlet to the Royal Society, although there is no evidence that it
was in fact so submitted. (The copy now in the Royal Society
library was acquired in the nineteenth century.) Indeed, the
author's claims that there was no natural explanation for the phenomenon conceded that, if there was one, then like the eclipse it
was not a prodigy.

Ward's work shows the adaptation of the prodigy account
as a vehicle for satire and the independence of the satirical from
the natural-philosophical critique of providential prodigy belief.
British Wonders listed many disasters and prodigies following the
death of Queen Anne and the Hanoverian succession, including
a cattle plague, the Jacobite rebellion of 1715, and the solar eclipse
and aurora borealis. The satire mocked both dissenters, superstitious hypocrites who feigned virtue when threatened by a
prodigy, and then relapsed after it, and natural philosophers, who
used jargon to claim an ability to explain prodigious events they
did not really possess.[77] Ward used prodigies principally to challenge the pretension of natural philosophers to be able to explain
everything.[78]

> And Sporting Nature to amuse us
> Did Startling Novelties produce us
> Mocking our Archimedian Sons
> Of Art with strang Phaenomenons
> As puz'ling to our Math'maticians
> As new Distempers to Physicians
> Who, with their Terms of Art, oft hide
> Their Ign'rance to support their Pride
> Like Pedants, who to gloss their Errors
> Talk Latin to unlettered Hearers.[79]

Astrologers, another favourite target of Ward, were also mocked
as pretenders to a knowledge of the interpretation of prodigies
which they did not actually possess.[80]

Rejection or ambivalence characterized the treatment of providential prodigy interpretation by all sides in the political conflicts of the early eighteenth century. The wonder years signalled the end of the usefulness of the divine political prodigy as a category in educated society. So strong had the association between providential prodigy interpretation, vulgar superstition and Jacobitism become by the end of the reign of George II that Whigs like Henry Fielding could claim of the Jacobites: 'A River having too much or too little water in it, a Man born with an extraordinary Member, an Eclipse, a Comet, an Aurora Borealis, or any such ordinary or extraordinary phenomenon, is sufficient to support their drooping spirits.' In the same way, Samuel Johnson, not the most zealous supporter of the House of Hanover in the British kingdoms, could satirize 'Tom Tempest . . . a steady friend of the House of Stuart' as one who could 'recount the prodigies that have appeared in the sky . . . every year from the Revolution'.[81]

'Truth is of much cooler Contemplation': William Warburton's *Critical and Philosophical Enquiry Into the Causes of Prodigies and Miracles*

The contrast between, on the one hand, the anti-providentialism of the establishment Whig and future bishop William Warburton, expressed in his *A Critical and Philosophical Enquiry into the Causes of Prodigies and Miracles, as Related by Historians* (1727) and, on the other, the apocalyptic prodigy interpretation of the Arian heretic and natural philosopher William Whiston, expressed in his numerous writings, exemplifies the marginalization of providential prodigy interpretation in Georgian England. William Warburton, the future bishop of Gloucester, produced the most definitive statement of the anti-providential view of prodigies since Spencer's in his anonymous *Critical and Philosophical Enquiry*.[82] Warburton's work differed from Spencer's or the pamphleteers' of the wonder years in that its stated purpose was not that of combating the superstitious belief in omens and prodigies existing in the writer's own time, but rather that of explaining the prodigy belief of ancient, medieval and some more recent historians. Warburton wrote from the perspective of one who believed that the battle against providential prodigy interpretation had already been won in fields other than history. Throughout, he addressed himself to historians, and his *Critical and Philosophical Enquiry* took the form of an explanation of a previously existing phenomenon rather than an argument against current beliefs. While Warburton denounced contemporary historians as sensationalists, none of his specific examples of prodigy use was from his own time, although some early eighteenth-century historians, such as Laurence Eachard, had included prodigies in their narratives.[83]

Purifying history of prodigy stories was the eradication of a past error, specifically linked to the reform of other sciences from error – in particular, from medieval, and therefore Catholic, error.[84] The presence of prodigy accounts and miraculous material in histories dating from the Middle Ages was unsurprising, as nothing better could be expected from the time of monkish ignorance and superstition. Catholicism as 'superstition', however, was only a partially satisfying explanation: 'But Superstition, though one may allow it a very extended influence towards this Effect, and might give over the whole mob of Monkish Writers to its Tyranny, won't, I presume, account for so Universal a Practice in Men of all Religions, Times, and Temperatures.'[85] Warburton gave Livy as an example of a historian unaffected by Christianity in any form who yet used prodigies.[86] Explanations based on Catholic superstition were therefore incomplete, and needed to be supplemented with transhistorical explanations based on human psychology. The near universality of the belief in prodigies as historically significant events made its cumulative effects especially damaging:

> Prodigies and Portents have infected the best writings of Antiquity: and to have so blotted and deformed our modern Annals, that (with greater Justice than Polybius has observed it of the former) they may rather be called Tragedies, than Histories. How it comes to pass – that, while the other Sciences are daily Purging and Refining themselves from the Pollutions of superstitious Error, that had been collecting throughout a long Winter of Ignorance and Barbarism; History, still the longer it runs, contracts the more filth, and retains in it the additional Ordure of every Soil through which it has passed. How this happens, I say, is somewhat of difficult Disquisition.[87]

Warburton gave an explanation for the corruption of history similar to those given by Bacon, Spencer and the Royal Society propagandists for the persistence of vulgar errors in natural philosophy. The love of wonder, or 'Admiration', was one danger to historical accuracy, and was linked with 'enthusiasm': 'Admiration, we experience to be one of the most bewitching, enthusiastic Passions of the Mind: and every common Moralist knows; that it arises from Novelty and Surprize, the inseparable Attendants of Imposture.'[88] The very bizarreness of a lying prodigy appealed to this faculty of mind, which should be always suspected.

> But Truth (even of a new Discovery) is of much cooler Contemplation, as paying its court to the understanding only: by affording a regular view of its simple univocal original, with the Universal Relation, Dependance, and Harmony of its Parts. So Calm a Prospect often raises no emotion or but that of the lowest kind, which we call Approbation.[89]

The violence of this passion of 'admiration' could corrupt history both by unbalancing the historian's own mind and by leading the historian to load the historical narrative with prodigies 'to take advantage of this prevailing Propensity for lying wonders'.[90] Indeed, the violence of admiration also corrupted history through historians' tendency to concentrate on times of revolution rather than on more truly glorious times of peace, such as the recent reign of George I.[91]

Another reason Warburton gave for the prevalence of prodigies in historical writing was 'national Pride' – the desire to believe that one's own nation was a particular object of God's attention, whether that attention be benevolent or not. This vice linked modern Englishmen to the ancient Romans.[92]

Warburton's final reason for the prevalence of prodigies in historical writing was intellectual laziness, which led historians to reach for divine causation as an alternative to the hard work of finding 'real' causes.[93] Warburton made a possible punning reference to Nathaniel Crouch by asserting: 'Thus you see the constant need the Moderns have of the Aid and Support of Prodigies. Tis a Crouch they can't stir one Step without.'[94] If this pun was intentional, it was meant to associate prodigy-employing historians with popular credulity and ignorance, as represented by Crouch. Thus was providence reduced from the status of the guide and meaning of history to serve as a crutch for lazy historians – by a future bishop of the Church of England!

Warburton did not entirely eliminate prodigies and miracles from history. He made the usual exceptions for those associated with scripture and the first ages of the Church. Even false prodigies and miracles were admissible in history to the extent that they influenced historical actors.[95] Warburton also believed that some prodigies and miracles did continue to occur in post-biblical times, basing this belief on the 'universal consent' of humanity and God's omnipotence.[96]

Warburton echoed Baxter, Sprat and the prodigy compilers of the late seventeenth century in restricting legitimate contemporary miracles to those which uphold universal aspects of religion and morality, as opposed to the interests of a particular sect. As part of his mission to reform the writing of history, Warburton exalted this principle into part of the critical apparatus to be used by historians in evaluating alleged prodigies.

> He is to begin his Disquisition, by considering the End for which a Miracle is reported to be wrote. If, on Examination, he finds nothing but a private Interest, a religious sect, or Civil Party concerned in its Truth; he may here drop his Enquiry, and rest satisfied, that it is only the Game of Craft or Bigottry. But if he finds the End to be the Defence of the common Principles of Morality and Religion, let him go on; he has sufficient Reason to pursue his Enquiry, and whether he finds it Fact or no, he has the satisfaction to reflect, that this is an End worthy at least, of divine Interposition. But if undoubted Testimony proves some extraordinary Event, he is then carefully to Examine, whether it was truly Miraculous: If, for Instance human Affairs take some great and unexpected Turn, regularly conducted, and without the adequate Assistance of human Means; or if there be a real change in a Catholic Law of Nature, in which he is to take special Heed that one does not prove such a matter as is usually called a Judgement, or the other, merely an unusual Phenomenon. For if so, he here takes his Leave, and consigns one over to the old Women, and the other to the Virtuosi, otherwise he betrays his Presumption, and his Ignorance.[97]

Although Warburton were seems to accept the possibility of prodigies of punishment, or 'Judgements', he immediately revoked that acceptance by associating judgements with the standard figures of ridicule for popular credulity, old women. Unusual natural phenomena also hold no meaning for the historian, but are to be left to the accredited experts in that field, the natural philosophers, or 'virtuosi'. That the little legitimate scope the profane historian had for writing about prodigies might as well be none at all was shown by Warburton's fulsome praise of Sallust, who he claimed was the only ancient historian to omit prodigies from his narrative. This was particularly impressive in that the work of Sallust on which *Critical and Philosophical Enquiry* concentrated was written on a subject Warburton believed eminently suited to the inclusion of prodigies, the Catalinarian conspiracy. 'Now, what a fine opportunity was here of Introducing his story, in all the Blaze and Terror of anxious and disordered Nature?'[98] Remembering the long association of prodigies specifically with civil unrest, to which Warburton alludes, it is easy to see why he praised Sallust as one who, 'like another Hercules, subdued Monsters (i.e. Prodigies) in his cradle'.[99]

Warburton wished to retain the idea of a law-governed universe which would even include those supernatural miracles whose existence he, as an Anglican clergyman, could not and did not wish to deny. He had little interest in the distinction between prodigies and miracles and treated them as interchangeable, both being cases of divine intervention against natural law. Warburton rejected the claim that a miracle was 'an Arrest and Disturbance to the Laws of Nature'. Instead, a miracle was the result of God giving 'new Laws, to those Portions of Matter within the Sphere of the miracle'. This law-giving behaviour manifested God's 'stupendous Wisdom and Power', and also the inability of matter to violate natural law under any circumstance.[100]

The final phase of apocalyptic prodigy interpretation: William Whiston versus 'the sceptics of the town'

The growing isolation of those at the learned level who, unlike Warburton, continued to interpret prodigies providentially, whether their interpretations were political, apocalyptic or moralistic, can be seen in the case of William Whiston. Although Whiston had taken an anti-providential line in his astronomical writings in the 1710s, he eventually came to interpret the prodigies of the early eighteenth century in a strongly providential light. In his youth, Whiston had been greatly influenced by moralistic prodigy writings. He claimed that the story of John Duncalf, whose hands rotted after he had stolen a Bible (and who had provoked Simon Ford's scheme of magisterial prodigy story gathering), made a strong and lasting impression upon him as a child.[101] He also owned in his days at Oxford a copy of the Interregnum Puritan Samuel Clarke's compilation of judgements and prodigies, *A Mirrour or Looking-glasse for Saints and Sinners*.[102]

However, Whiston's own prodigy beliefs were not restricted to moralism. He also believed that the prodigies of his own day were heralds of the apocalypse. The connection between prodigies and the apocalypse was particularly marked in Whiston's case, as he accepted the Apocrypha's IV Esdras as properly belonging to the Old Testament canon, and employed it, as well as such classical texts from the traditional scriptural canon endorsing apocalyptic prodigy belief as Joel 2:30–1, to make his apocalyptic case. IV Esdras gave a picture of the approach of the apocalypse which involved a variety of spectacular prodigies, including monstrous births as well as the celestial apparitions prophesied in the canonical apocalyptic books.[103] One of the things that made William Whiston such a common target for satire was that he could be ridiculed both as a natural philosopher and as a providential and millenarian prodigy interpreter.

This apocalyptic belief required Whiston to completely reverse the positions taken in his anti-providential prodigy tracts of 1716 and 1719. Whiston became so convinced of the apocalyptic importance of the prodigious by the time of the composition of his *Memoirs* that he even adduced these same celestial phenomena of 1716 and 1719 as providential signs of the imminence of the apocalypse![104] He also contradicted his previous statement that the recent dramatic increase in celestial prodigies was not a herald of the apocalypse by asserting that, in fact, it was exactly that.[105] Whiston yielded to the temptation he had described and rejected in the 1716 tract, and used prodigies to construct an Arian providential history in which recent prodigies were connected with the toleration of Arianism in Britain, a beginning of the process of the restoration of primitive Christianity.[106]

As a believer in the providential and apocalyptic interpretation of prodigies, Whiston found himself increasingly isolated. Of course, providential prodigy belief was not the only thing denying Whiston any hope of acceptance by the Church of

England or by London's community of natural philosophers. Open and uncompromising Arianism led him to forfeit a career in the Church as well as admittance to the Royal Society.[107]

Whiston's intellectual isolation can be seen clearly in his analysis of the Mary Tofts case, in which a woman claimed to have given birth to a series of rabbits. The case evoked a variety of natural-scientific and satirical responses, but was not treated as a political or religious sign in the struggles of the day. Whiston himself was the exception, discussing Tofts in a specifically apocalyptic and providential context. He treated the monstrous birth as a fulfilment of the prophecy in IV Esdras that 'Monstrous Women will bring forth monsters'.[108] As part of his analysis of the Tofts case's cultural reception, Whiston expounded his theory of the decline of the providential interpretation of prodigies. For him, the central adversary of the acceptance of belief in the birth of the rabbits was not natural philosophy, but satirical ridicule:

> Neither did Mr. Ahlers, the King's Surgeon, nor Sir Richard Manningham, oppose Mr. Howard's, and Mr. St. Andre's Evidence, till the Thing was impudently laughed out of countenance, not in Surrey, where the scene lay, but at London, 30 Miles off, and till those that acted in this matter, or believed their Accounts, were unjustly made Sport of, by the Sceptics of the Town. Nor did the Woman herself ever confess a Fraud, till she was herself threatened with a painful Operation, and with Imprisonment; which fraud was impossible, because, upon Dissection, it was most evident, that many, at least, of those creatures that were taken from her, were not true or Natural Rabbets, but of prater-naturall production, which it was impossible for her to procure; had she been never so much disposed for it. Nor did the Surgeons or Man-midwives pretend to any Grounds of Suspicion till they found they were like to suffer greatly in their own Reputation and Practice, if they had supported that story any longer, which they were not willing to do, as any one may see in all their Retractations; of which sort of Confessions, like those made under Torture, I have no opinion at all.[109]

Whiston believed that following the correct natural-philosophical procedure – putting more weight on the testimony of Surrey eye-witnesses, heeding the results of the dissection – would have produced a providential interpretation. Instead, scepticism, satire and disbelief contributed to a situation where it was in the interest of all parties involved to deny the providential nature of the prodigy. These attitudes, linked to the debate on miracles and the increasing scepticism regarding the reality of witches, had, according to Whiston, become all but universal in England.

> The Way of Bantering Matters of Fact, that are disagreeable to Scepticks and Unbelievers, as whatsoever looks Supernatural or Miraculous always are, seem, after the Lord Shaftesbury and Mr. Collins, to have almost begun here with the Banter of this wonderful and supernatural production in Mary Toft, though it be now become a standing argument, since the writings of Dr. Middleton, against all such Facts as imply a Providence, and the Interposition of good Angels or wicked Demons in the Affairs of this World, which yet had been the constant Opinion, or rather Experience and Attestation of all Mankind, excepting the Sadducees and Epicureans, in all the past Ages of the World; till the present Age. And truly if these merry Infidels could as well banter off Eclipses, and Comets, and Northern Lights, and Balls of Fire, and Earthquakes, and their Effects, with the Like Facility as they now pretend to do ancient Histories, both Sacred and Profane, they would soon get clear of all Arguments for Divine Providence, and Divine Revelation, and would openly and universally throw off all the obligations of Religion.[110]

Whiston could quite easily have seen himself as a victim of these bantering, 'merry Infidels', for he had been a target of satire as an apocalyptic interpreter in the Mary Tofts literature. 'The learned Mr. Wh – on takes her to be the Whore of Babylon, with seven heads and ten Horns; which the Divines of our Church have always interpreted to be the Church of Rome.'[111]

Unsurprisingly, Whiston presented himself in his *Memoirs* as a lonely battler against the impiety of the age. As such, however interested he was in the prodigies preceding the imminent apocalypse, it would have been difficult for him to set up and maintain the elaborate network of prodigy reporters envisioned by the Poole and Turner projects, although he did make use of relatives and friends such as William Stukeley.[112] Nor did he have the political motivation of Ness or the compilers of the *Mirabilis Annus* tracts. However, the development of the newspaper and periodical press in the early to mid-eighteenth century offered an alternative form of prodigy gathering, in which the prodigy gatherer simply compiled transcriptions of press accounts of remarkable phenomena. Whiston did this in his *Memoirs*, referring to sources such as the *Gentleman's Magazine* in addition to long-established periodicals like *Philosophical Transactions*.[113]

As prodigy interpreters had been doing since Elizabethan times, Whiston sought as best he was able to announce the coming apocalypse by amassing stories of wonderful and dreadful prodigies. He was out of sympathy with his time, gathered no emulators, and was often considered a madman or an amusing eccentric rather than either a threat or an inspiration. His failure marks the end of providential and apocalyptic prodigy interpretation among learned Englishmen.

The public importance of prodigies continued to diminish throughout the first half of the eighteenth century, as satirists and journalists ridiculed providential interpretation. The intellectual hegemony of rational religion and natural philosophy in both the Church of England and the more respectable dissenting bodies such as the Presbyterians reinforced this tendency. By 1748 the leading dissenter Philip Doddridge, corresponding with his friend Henry Baker, was associating religious interest in prodigies with popular ignorance in tones identical to those of Anglicans: 'It was but a little while ago that we had a Calf produced in a Neighbouring Village with two heads and six Legs, which the ignorant Country People immediately brought to my house crying in a kind of rapture, "See the wondrous works of God" which one of them repeated to me more than twenty times almost in a breath.'[114]

Doddridge was speaking at the end of the long process by which prodigies had ceased to bear specific providential meanings for the English intellectual and political elite. 'Learned' prodigy interpretation as practised by people like Jessey and Ness was abandoned, and became something that political writers like Addison ridiculed their enemies for employing. As Doddridge testifies, belief that prodigies and monsters carried a divine message did persist among some of the lower classes, to the scorn of their betters. Males of the political nation were equally scornful of providential prodigy belief when displayed by women. Providential prodigy belief was now principally a class and gender marker, ascribed to those excluded from the charmed circle of England's rulers, rather than one which distinguished religious views.

Notes

1 The 1708 edition is titled *To Begin Harvest Three Days too soon rather than Two Days too Late or Sentences of the Dissenters, containing Relations of Pretended Judgements, Prodigies, and Apparitions, in Behalf of the Non-Conformists in Opposition to the Established Church.* Neither appears in the printed catalogue of Brydall's writings, *A Catalogue of the Tracts of Law and other Discourses written by John Brydall* (London, 1711).

2 *Oracles of the Dissenters* (London, 1708), 'Preface'.

3 *Oracles of the Dissenters*, pp. 51–2.

4 *Oracles of the Dissenters*, pp. 15–16, 25.

5 *Oracles of the Dissenters*, pp. 13–14, 34.

6 *Oracles of the Dissenters*, p. 25.

7 *Oracles of the Dissenters* (p. 34) had also charged the dissenters with involvement in the Fire of London, and connected this allegation to a prodigy story in *Mirabilis Annus Secundus*, but it was not central to the argument.

8 *A Protestant Monument, erected to the Immortal Glory of the Whiggs and the Dutch* (London, 1713).

9 Jonathan Swift, *An Elegy on Mr. Patrige, the Almanack-Maker, who died on the 29th of this Instant March, 1708* (London, 1708).

10 Bishops of the Church of England found by the Tories to be hostile were not immune from such attacks, however. One target of Tory wit was the Whig bishop of Worcester William Lloyd, known as a scholarly student of the Book of Revelations and a somewhat eccentric millenarian. For a satirical reference to him as a believer in portents and prodigies, see William Shippen, *Faction Displayed*, in *POAS*, vol. 6: 656.

11 Joseph Levine, *Dr. Woodward's Shield: History, Science, and Satire in Augustan England* (Berkeley, Los Angeles and London: University of California Press, 1977); and Richard Olson, 'Tory–High Church opposition to science and scientism in the eighteenth century: the works of John Arbuthnot, Jonathan Swift, and Samuel Johnson', in John G. Burke, ed., *The Uses of Science in the Age of Newton*, Publications of the Clark Library Professorship no. 8 (Berkeley, Los Angeles and London: University of California Press, 1983), pp. 171–204.

12 *Memoirs of the Extraordinary Life, Works, and Discoveries of Martinus Scriblerus*, ed. Charles Kerby-Miller (New Haven: Yale University Press for Wellesley College, 1950), pp. 143–53.

13 For one use of a providential prodigy in Whig journalism, see the discussion of a debate over a prodigy story in Lycosthenes's

Historia Ostentorum et Prodigiorum held at Rome between the supporters of the French king and England's ally the holy roman emperor: *A Postscript to the Post-Man*, Tuesday, March 14, 1704.

14 *Spectator*, no. 419 (Tuesday, July 1, 1712), cited in Donald Bond, ed., *The Tatler*, vol. 3: 572.

15 *Spectator*, no. 363 (Saturday, April 26, 1712), cited in Bond, ed., *The Tatler*, vol. 3: 359.

16 For the popular unrest surrounding George's accession and the Jacobite rising, see Paul Monod, *Jacobitism and the English People, 1688–1788* (Cambridge: Cambridge University Press, 1989), pp. 173–94; and Nicholas Rogers, 'Riot and popular Jacobitism in early Hanoverian England', in Eveline Cruickshanks, ed., *Ideology and Conspiracy: Aspects of Jacobitism, 1689–1759* (Edinburgh: John Donald, 1982), pp. 70–88.

17 For the aurora of 1716, see 'The earliest mention of the aurora borealis', *Nature*, 3 (November 17, 1870): 46–7; and Robert H. Eather, *Majestic Lights: The Aurora in Science, History, and the Arts.* (Washington: American Geophysical Union, 1980), pp. 52–3.

18 For standard astrological predictions that the eclipse would be the sign of unspecified disasters, see 'Astral Observations' and 'April', in the almanac *News From the Stars 1715*.

19 Mary, Countess Cowper, *Diary of Lady Cowper* (London: John Murray, 1864), pp. 90–1. For other dramatic descriptions of the aurora, see *Evening Post*, no. 1031 (March 13–15, 1716), and Notebooks of Whitelocke Bulstrode, vol. IV: 77 recto (Folser Library).

20 Whig adoption of authoritarian Tory arguments and, conversely, Tory adoption of libertarian Whig arguments are important themes in the intellectual history of the early eighteenth century. See J.P. Kenyon, *Revolution Principles: The Politics of Party, 1689–1720* (Cambridge: Cambridge University Press, 1975) and J.C.D. Clark, *English Society, 1688–1832: Ideology, Social Structure and Political Practice during the Ancien Régime* (Cambridge: Cambridge University Press, 1985), pp. 121–41.

21 *Freeholder*, no. 24 (March 12, 1716). See Joseph Addison, *The Freeholder*, ed. James Leheny (Oxford: Clarendon Press, 1979), p. 140.

22 *Freeholder*, no. 27 (March 23, 1716), in Leheny ed., p. 149.

23 Cowper, *Diary*, p. 92. Addison had earlier connected the mostly Whig newspapers of Charles II's reign to the early eighteenth-century writer of high Tory manuscript newsletters John Dyer through a shared interest in prodigies. *The Tatler*, 18 (May 21, 1709), cited in Bond, ed., *The Tatler*, vol. 1: 149–50. See also *The Tatler*, vol. 3: 121, and *The Guardian*, 58 (Monday, May 18, 1713).

24 *Freeholder*, no. 32 (April 9, 1716), in Leheny ed., p. 184.

25 Anthony Corbière to Horatio Walpole, March 9, 1716, quoted in J.H. Plumb, *Sir Robert Walpole: The Making of a Statesman* (London: Cresset Press, 1956), p. 221.

26 Countess Cowper, *Diary*, p. 91.

27 *The Flying Post*, no. 3634 (April 19–21, 1715). This letter was reprinted in the Whig annual *Annals of King George*, vol. 1 (London, 1716): 402–5.

28 *The Flying Post*, no. 3778 (March 20–22, 1715–16).

29 *The Flying Post*, no. 3634 (April 19–21, 1715).

30 Not all providentially minded Whigs were uneducated. For an example of a Whig official who in both his private writings and in public continued to view prodigies and other unusual natural phenomena in a providential context, see Notebooks of Whitelocke Bulstrode, vol. IV: fos 51–8, 77–85 (Folger Library): and the report of Bulstrode's charge to the Grand Jury of Middlesex in *Annals of King George*, vol. 4 (London, 1718): 396–7.

31 A more straightforward view of the aurora as a positive phenomenon may have been taken by a pamphlet advertised in the *Evening Post*, no. 1035 (March 22–24, 1716): *The Meteor a Good Omen, Prov'd by a parallel Instance in the 2d Year of Queen Elizabeth's Reign; Whereunto is Premis'd a brief Account of the Nature of Meteors in General*. The author is announced as 'H.H., Gent', but the work does not seem to have survived.

32 Ian Bostridge, *Witchcraft and its Transformations, c.1650–c.1750* (Oxford: Clarendon Press), pp. 132–6.

33 For Smith, see Bodeleian Rawlinson MS J, 'Biographical Notices of Oxford Writers', fos 2–12. Smith was a correspondent of Hans Sloane, Royal Society Letter Book Copies 19 pp. 212–13.

34 Elisha Smith, *The Superstition of Omens and Prodigies; with the Proper Reception, and Profitable Improvement. A Divinity Lecture upon the Surprizing Phaenomena of Light, March. 6. 1715. on the Sunday after* (London, 1715), p. 2.

35 Smith, *Superstition*, p. 1.

36 Joseph Burroughs, *A Sermon Occasion'd by the Total Eclipse of the Sun, Upon April the 22d, 1715* (London, 1715), p. 4.

37 Burroughs, *Sermon*, pp. 20–1.

38 William Matthews, ed., *The Diary of Dudley Ryder 1715–1717* (London: Methuen & Co., 1939), p. 213. Ryder encountered more Jacobite prodigy stories (pp. 314–15). He also related the story of a young man who had been stricken with paralysis on viewing the recent eclipse (pp. 317–18).

39 Thomas Hearne, *Remarks and Collections of Thomas Hearne*, vol. 5: 181; and *The Great Diurnall of Nicholas Blundell of Little Crosby, Lancashire*,

transcribed and annotated Frank Tyrer (Chester: Record Society of Lancashire and Chester, 1968–1972), vol. 2: 132, 161.

40 *The Diary of Henry Prescott*, ed. John Addy, 3 vols (Record Society of Lancashire and Cheshire, 1987–1997), vol. 2: 496–7.

41 *News from the Dead*, no. 4 (April 25–May 2, 1715): 36–8. For an attack on a shortlived Tory–Jacobite weekly called *The Orphan* as a vendor of subversive prodigy stories, see *The Weekly Journal* (March 24, 1716): 369. I have been unable to locate a copy of *The Orphan* or any further information about it.

42 Printed in *The Poetical Works of Richard Savage*, ed. Clarence Tracy (Cambridge: Cambridge University Press, 1962), pp. 19–25. Jacobites could also take revenge for the earlier Whig stories of bad omens at the accession of King James by recounting the story of the collapsing scaffolds at the coronation of King George: see the anonymous *On ye Thanksgiving Day* (Clarke Memorial Library).

43 For Savage's later mockery of providential prodigy-belief as 'vulgar', see *Poetical Works of Richard Savage*, pp. 123–240.

44 Rodney Baine, *Daniel Defoe and the Supernatural* (Athens: Georgia University Press, 1968), pp. 125–8, accepts with some hesitation the attribution of the pamphlet to Defoe, who was involved in a series of pamphlets on second sight. The most recent Defoe bibliography, by P.N Furbank and W.R. Owens, *A Critical Bibliography of Daniel Defoe* (London: Pickering & Chatto, 1998), generally very conservative in ascribing anonymous works to Defoe, lists the pamphlet as 'probably' by Defoe (pp. 156–7). Defoe did not always support providential prodigy-interpretation. See his periodical *A Review of the State of the British Nation*, IV, no. 80 (August 16, 1707) for his ridicule of the 'Old Women' who interpreted a recent rain of dead flies over London as a political sign, and his offering of an alternative natural-philosophical explanation. These flies may have been exploited as a validating prodigy by the French prophets: see Hillel Schwartz, *The French Prophets: The History of a Millenarian Group in Eighteenth-Century England* (Berkeley: University of California Press, 1980), p. 95; and *A Strange and Most Wonderful Relation of the Most Miraculous Swarms of Flies* (London, 1707).

45 (?)Daniel Defoe, *The Second-Sighted Highlander. Being Four Visions of the Eclipse, and Something of what may Follow* (London, 1715), p. 5.

46 *Second-Sighted Highlander*, p. 43.

47 *Second-Sighted Highlander*, pp. 14–19.

48 *Second-Sighted Highlander*, p. 43. For the response to the eclipse of popularizers of natural philosophy, see Alice N. Walters, 'Ephemeral events: English broadsides of early eighteenth-century solar eclipses', *History of Science*, 37 (1999): 1–43.

49 *Chit-Chat*, no. 2 (March 10, 1716), reprinted in Rae Blanchard, ed., *Richard Steele's Periodical Journalism 1714–1716* (Oxford: Clarendon Press, 1959), pp. 261–2. For another journalistic account which gave a natural-philosophical explanation based on the exhalation of vapours while condemning the superstition of both 'ignorant people' and 'the disaffected party', see the *Flying Post*, no. 3773 (March 8, 1715/16). For a recommendation of the value of natural philosophy and Whiston's lectures specifically for understanding the eclipse, see the comic essay paper *The Grumbler*, nos 10 (April 19–23, 1715) and 11 (April 22–26, 1715). The latter issue of this Whig effort also included ridicule of Jacobites and 'the People' as super- stitious and unlearned believers in prodigy. The *Grumbler* was edited and produced by the young Whig Thomas Burnet, the son of Bishop Gilbert Burnet.

50 Steele deferred to Whiston's authority as a natural philosopher on the subject of astronomical phenomena. See Blanchard, ed., *Steele's Periodical Journalism*, p. 262.

51 H.A. Feisenberger, ed., *Scientists: Sales Catalogues of Libraries of Eminent Persons no. 11* (London: Mansell with Sotheby Parke Bernet Publications, 1975), p. 250. In addition to addressing the public on the issue of the eclipse's political meaning, Halley also gave a tech- nical natural-philosophical report on the eclipse in *Philosophical Transactions*, 29, no. 343 (March–May 1715): 245–62. For the excite- ment as well as the 'amusement' produced in the community of natural philosophers by the eclipse, see Andrea Rusnock, ed., *The Correspondence of James Jurin (1684–1750) Physician and Secretary to the Royal Society* (Amsterdam-Atlanta: Editions Rodopi, 1996), p. 75.

52 Edmond Halley, *A Description of the Passage of the Shadow of the Moon over England, In the Total Eclipse of the Sun, on the 22d Day of April 1715 in the Morning* (London, 1715). Thoresby's correspondent John Baulter painted an even more unflattering caricature of lower-class credulity in connection with this eclipse, telling Thoresby 'your self would laugh to hear how full of admiration the common people are, that the conjurors should find out to a minute when the sun and moon should fight, and glad they were that the sun had not the better, for if victory had fallen to her ladyship's share they were sure the world world then be at an end': See W.C. Lancaster, ed., *Letters Addressed to Ralph Thoresby, F.R.S.*, Thoresby Society Publications no. 21 (Leeds: Thoresby Society, 1912), pp. 228–30.

53 *Annals of King George*, vol. 1: 399.

54 Edmond Halley, 'An Account of the late surprizing Appearance of the Lights seen in the Air, on the Sixth of March last; with an Attempt to explain the Principal Phaenomena thereof; As it was laid before

the Royal Society by Edmond Halley, J.V.D. Savilian Professor of
Geom. Oxon. and Reg. Soc. Secr.', *Philosophical Transactions*, 29, no.
347 (January–March 1716): 425. For another report on the aurora and
subsequent unusual celestial phenomena, see the following issue,
Philosophical Transactions, 29, no. 348 (April–June, 1716): 430–2. The
Royal Society continued to be a center for accounts of auroras and
other unusual celestial phenomena. Royal Society Letter Book
Copies 19, pp. 25–8. For Halley's analysis of the physical causes of
the aurora in terms of the eruption of vapours from the earth, see J.
Morton Briggs Jr, 'Aurora and enlightenment: eighteenth-century
explanations of the aurora borealis', *Isis*, 58 (1967): 491–4. Whitelocke
Bulstrode (Notebooks IV, 77: verso) gave a similar explanation. An
alternative natural-philosophical explanation of these scenes in the
air was that they were the magnified reflections of earthly events by
metallic vapours. This interpretation had been supported by
Athanasius Kircher, and was also known in England and Ireland.
See Birch, *History*, vol. 4: 416 and the minutes of the Dublin Philosophical Society, in Gunther, *Dr. Plot*, p. 172.

55 Halley, 'An Account', p. 407.

56 For discussion of this and other pamphlets by Whiston on unusual
natural phenomena, see Maureen Farrell, *William Whiston* (New
York: Arno Press, 1981), pp. 218–30. Whiston knew that auroras and
other spectacular phenomena interested people, and used them as a
hook for his public lectures on astronomical subjects at the Whig
bastion Button's Coffee-House and other venues. See the advertisement in *The Evening Post*, no. 1034 (March 20–22, 1716) and the *Daily
Courant*, nos 4488 (March 9, 1716) and 4493 (March 15, 1716). Earlier
Whiston, supporting himself financially in the competitive natural
philosophy market of London, had sold tickets to a viewing of the
eclipse: *The Post-Man*, no. 11050 (April 16–19, 1715).

57 Whiston, *Account of a Surprizing Meteor 1716*, pp. 33–4.

58 Whiston, *Account of a Surprizing Meteor 1716*, pp. 28, 49–50. For
others drawing a contrast between their own observations of
aurorae and those of the superstitious masses, see DWL MSS 12.107,
nos 239–42 and 24.23, fos 15–18.

59 Whiston, *Account of a Surprizing Meteor 1716*, p. 73. For Whiston's
apocalypticism, see James Force, *William Whiston: Honest Newtonian*
(Cambridge: Cambridge University Press, 1985). Whiston also
included (pp. 8–14) an extract from Pierre Gassendi's *Physics* which
denounced the belief in battles in the sky and providentialism in
connection with the aurora of 1621.

60 William Whiston, *An Account of a Surprizing Meteor Seen in the Air
March 19. 1718/19 at Night* (London, 1719), pp. 33–9. The early eigh-

teenth century was characterized by frequent and spectacular auroras. For a dismissal of the import of a similar phenomenon, see *Mercurius Politicus* (February 1717/18): 118–20. The 1719 aurora was also described in *Annals of King George*, vol. 5 (London, 1720): 418, with the comment that it had left 'behind it strange Impressions in the Minds of the Weak and Superstitious'.

61 Whiston, *Account of a Surprizing Meteor 1716*, pp. 73–7.

62 *The Black-Day, or, A Prospect of Doomsday. Exemplified in the Great and Terrible Eclipse, Which will happen on Friday the 22d of April, 1715* (London, 1715), Title Page.

63 *The Black-Day*, pp. 9–11.

64 *The Black-Day*, pp. 12–16. Curiously, the famous Black Monday solar eclipse of March 29, 1652, which had produced the largest outpouring of literature of any seventeenth-century eclipse, went entirely unmentioned.

65 *The Black-Day*, p. 23. For another Hanoverian interpretation of the eclipse, likening it to Britain's temporarily monarchless state between Anne's death and the arrival of George from Germany, see 'W.W.', *The Eclipse, A Poem in Commemoration of the Total Eclipse of the Sun. April 22. 1715* (London, 1715). 'W.W.' used the eclipse more as a poetical conceit than as a divine or astrological sign.

66 For Ward, see Howard William Troyer, *Ned Ward of Grubstreet: A Study of Sub-Literary London in the Eighteenth Century* (Cambridge: Harvard University Press, 1946).

67 *An Essay Concerning the Late Apparition in the Heavens, on the Sixth of March. Proving by Mathematical, Logical, and Moral Arguments, that it could not have been produced by the Ordinarly Course of Nature, but must of Necessity be a Prodigy. Humbly offer'd to the Consideration of the Royal Society* (London, 1716), p. 40. The book was advertised in *The Evening Post*, no. 1036 (March 24–7, 1716).

68 *Essay*, p. 37.

69 *Essay*, pp. 26–7.

70 *Essay*, p. 25.

71 *Essay*, p. 43.

72 *Essay*, pp. 22–3.

73 *Essay*, pp. 10–11.

74 *Essay*, pp. 14–16.

75 *Essay*, pp. 1–2.

76 *Essay*, pp. 24–5.

77 Edward Ward, *British Wonders: Or, A Poetical Description of the several Prodigies and Most Remarkable Accidents that have Happen'd in Britain since the Death of Queen Anne* (London, 1717), pp. 25–8, 52.

78 Using prodigies to challenge the knowledge-claims of organized

science has continued to the present day, particularly in the work of Charles Fort, whose examples of unexplainable events include many that would have earlier been considered prodigies such as armies in the sky or rains of frogs. See Charles Fort, *The Books of Charles Fort*, with an Introduction by Tiffany Thayer (New York: Published for the Fortean Society by Henry Holt & Company, 1941), pp. 457–8, 541–5.

79 Ward, *British Wonders*, p. 2.

80 Ward, *British Wonders*, pp. 3, 49.

81 Henry Fielding, *The Jacobite's Journal*, no. 25 (Saturday, May 21, 1748), and Samuel Johnson, *The Idler*, no. 10 (June 17, 1758), in *The Yale Edition of the Works of Samuel Johnson* (New Haven: Yale University Press), vol. 2: 34. The Reverend Richard Greaves, author of *The Spiritual Quixote* (London, 1773), a satire of Methodism actually written in the 1750s, similarly conflated providential prodigy belief and sentimental Jacobitism, along with popular superstition, in describing the comic rustic Jeremiah Tugwell. The passage specifically referred to the 1715 aurora. See Richard Greaves, *The Spiritual Quixote* (London, 1773), p. 24.

82 Considering his central position in mid-eighteenth century intellectual life, very little modern scholarly work has been done on Warburton. A.W. Evans, *Warburton and the Warburtonians: A Study in some Eighteenth-Century Controversies* (London: Oxford University Press, 1932), pp. 21–4, discusses the *Critical and Philosophical Enquiry* and prints part of a letter by Warburton concerning its composition. The most recent book-length study of Warburton is Robert Ryley, *William Warburton* (Boston: Twayne Publishers, 1984), which devotes little attention to the *Critical and Philosophical Enquiry*.

83 Eachard mentioned celestial prodigies in connection with the Civil War in *The History of England From the First Entrance of Julius Caesar and the Romans, To the Conclusion of the Reign of King James the Second, and the Establishment of King William and Queen Mary, Upon the Throne, in the Year 1688*, 3rd edition (London, 1720), pp. 542, 607. Providentially meaningful prodigies are also found in John Seller, *The History of England* (London, 1696), pp. 588, 602, 637, 644. Other historians, such as Sir William Temple, specifically repudiated the use of prodigies. See *Introduction to the History of England*, in *The Works of Sir William Temple, Bart. Complete in Four Volumes* (London, 1814), vol. 3: 194.

84 The antiquary William Stukeley quoted Warburton's *Critical and Philosophical Enquiry* specifically as an attack on the medieval scholarship of Hearne, pictured as a mere publisher of the rubbish of credulous monks. William Stukeley to Samuel Gale, October 25,

1727, in *The Family Memoirs of the Reverend William Stukeley* ed. W.C. Lukis (Durham: Surtees Society, 1880–85), vol. 1: 199.

85 William Warburton, *A Critical and Philosophical Enquiry into the Causes of Prodigies and Miracles, as related by Historians* (London, 1727), p. 3.

86 Some admirers tried to defend Livy against charges of superstitious prodigy belief. Thomas Hearne claimed that the 'Prodigies he relates were not all believed by himself, but that he related them as he found them in Annals': Hearne, *Remarks and Collections*, vol. 1: 334.

87 Warburton, *Critical and Philosophical Enquiry*, pp. 1–2.

88 Warburton, *Critical and Philosophical Enquiry*, p. 12.

89 Warburton, *Critical and Philosophical Enquiry*, p. 13.

90 Warburton, *Critical and Philosophical Enquiry*, p. 37. Note the continuing use of the phrase 'lying wonders', with its biblical echoes.

91 Warburton, *Critical and Philosophical Enquiry*, p. 46.

92 Warburton, *Critical and Philosophical Enquiry*, pp. 22–5.

93 Warburton, *Critical and Philosophical Enquiry*, p. 55.

94 Warburton, *Critical and Philosophical Enquiry*, p. 65.

95 Warburton, *Critical and Philosophical Enquiry*, p. 126.

96 Warburton, *Critical and Philosophical Enquiry*, pp. 121–3.

97 Warburton, *Critical and Philosophical Enquiry*, p. 124.

98 Warburton, *Critical and Philosophical Enquiry*, p. 78.

99 Warburton, *Critical and Philosophical Enquiry*, pp. 74–5.

100 Warburton, *Critical and Philosophical Enquiry*, pp. 123.

101 William Whiston, *Memoirs of the Life and Writings of Mr. William Whiston Containing Memoirs of Several of his Friends Also*, 2 vols, 2nd edition, corrected (London, 1753), vol. 1: 6–7. Soon after the publication of the first edition of Whiston's memoirs, there was a republication of the Ford–Illingworth account of Duncalf with the material from Whiston's memoirs appended, *A Genuine Account of the Man, Whose Hands and Legs Rotted off, In the Parish of Kings-Swinford in Staffordshire, where he Died, June 21, 1677* (London, ?1750).

102 Maureen Farrell, *William Whiston* (New York: Arno Press), pp. 49–55.

103 Whiston, *Memoirs*, vol. 2: 17, 21–9.

104 Whiston, *Memoirs*, vol. 2: 132.

105 Whiston, *Memoirs*, vol. 2: 48–55.

106 Whiston, *Memoirs*, vol. 1: 205.

107 Whiston's prodigy belief was not a necessary consequence of his theology. One somewhat more discreet Arian Church of England clergyman and friend of Whiston, Samuel Clarke, attacked the whole idea of looking to the world for divine signs: Samuel Clarke, *The Works of Samuel Clark* (London, 1738), pp. 461–71.

108 Whiston, *Memoirs*, vol. 2: 108–10, in a passage that included other recent monsters as well. The Tofts case is narrated in S.A. Seligman,

'Mary Toft – the rabbit breeder', *Medical History*, 5 (1961): 349–60. The most recent investigation of the Tofts case, Dennis Todd's *Imagining Monsters: Miscreations of the Self in Eighteenth-Century England* (Chicago: University of Chicago Press, 1995), p. 94, identifies Whiston as the only person to connect the event to fanatical or enthusiastic religion. For belief in the actuality of the rabbit-birth combined with reluctance to appear 'a Propogator of wonders', see Royal Society Letter Book Copies 19, pp. 133–5. For analyses of the satirical and other literature surrounding it, see Todd, *Imagining Monsters*; Lisa Cody, 'The doctor's in labour: or a new whim wham from Guildford', *Gender and History*, 4 (1992): 175–96; and William A. Eddy, 'The anatomist dissected – by Lemuel Gulliver', *Modern Language Notes*, 41 (1926): 330–1. For newspaper interest in Tofts and monstrous births generally, see Geoffrey Alan Cranfield, *The Development of the Provincial Newspaper 1700–1760* (Oxford: Clarendon Press, 1962; reprinted Westport, CT: Greenwood Press, 1978), p. 73.

109 Whiston, *Memoirs*, vol. 2: 115–17. Whiston made a similar argument regarding Mary Tofts in *Memoirs*, vol. 2: 108–10.

110 Whiston, *Memoirs*, vol. 2: 119–20.

111 *A Philosophical Enquiry into the Wonderful Coney-warrent, Lately Discovered at Godalmin near Guilford in Surrey, Being an Account of the Birth of Seventeen Rabbits Born of a Woman at Several Times, and She Still Continues in Strong Labour, at the Bagnio in Leicester-Fields* (London, 1726), p. 2.

112 Whiston, *Memoirs*, vol. 2: 48–55.

113 Whiston, *Memoirs*, vol. 1: 377–8.

114 *Calendar of the Correspondence of Philip Doddridge DD, 1702–1751*, ed. Geoffrey Nuttall, (London: Northants Record Society, 1979), pp. 265–6. For Baker's reply recounting a similar incident, see p. 269.

Conclusion: from reverence to ridicule

The period of almost 100 years from the Poole project to Whiston's *Memoirs* was marked by the severing of a particular connection between the human, natural and spiritual worlds: the providential prodigy.[1] Not only was the connection severed, but belief in prodigies as humanly and divinely meaningful events now stigmatized the holder. It was seen as characteristic of superstitious, uneducated and unenlightened people, such as the poor, country folk and women. Indeed, a belief in the mere occurrence of some kinds of prodigies – rains of frogs or battles in the sky, for example – was now considered superstitious. The problem of the incapacity of the Church of England to function as a gate-keeper of the miraculous had been solved initially by government censorship and repression in the 1660s, and eventually by the creation, and self-creation, of an institutionalized natural-philosophical elite which in effect denied the supernatural cause or the immediate political meaning of any anomalous natural events.

The logical culmination of this cultural marginalization of the prodigious was the argument of the Scottish philosopher and historian David Hume, in *An Enquiry Concerning Human Understanding* (1748), that certain events were of their very nature not to be believed by a rational mind, no matter what the number, credibility or status of their witnesses. Hume claimed that it would always be more likely that a witness is lying or deceived than that a law of nature be violated. Although this argument is usually treated in the context of the debate on miracles,

Hume explicitly declared that it was directed against 'accounts of miracles and prodigies'.[2] In fact, his argument had been anticipated in one of the Mary Tofts tracts:

> Suppose one were to see a Letter from Battersea, importing that a woman there had been delivered of five Cucumbers, or indeed a hundred Letters, would that lead a man of Sense to believe any thing, but, either that the People who wrote those Letters had been grossly impos'd upon themselves, or intended to impose upon him. Either of these two things may, and do happen every Day; but it was never known, that ever any Creature brought forth any one Creature of a species in all respects different from it self, much less five or seventeen such creatures; for which therefore, an man of common sense, much more a penetrating and quick-sighted Anatomist, should look upon all such Letters with the utmost contempt.[3]

The evolution of the position that was to become Hume's had been closely linked to the religious and political struggles of the seventeenth century and the need for legitimation of groups of intellectuals and divines. From the shadowy producers of the *Mirabilis Annus* tracts to the natural philosophers of the Royal Society to the Tory journalists of the Exclusion period, a common attitude toward prodigies served as one bond uniting the members of intellectual factions. The fact that prodigies occupied a liminal position between a variety of intellectual realms – natural philosophy, politics, astrology and religion – made them a particularly active site of contention, a contention which eventually overturned providentialism.

The development of this new attitude toward the providential meaning and, eventually, the mere occurrence of prodigies can be divided into two phases. In the first, beginning in the Civil War and definitively established during the *Mirabilis Annus* controversy, difference of opinion as to the providential meaning of prodigies was one of the marks of a religious division between Anglicans and Protestant dissenters, belief in the providential meaning of prodigies being stigmatized by Anglicans as characteristic of 'fanatics'. Spencer's *Discourse Concerning Prodigies*, and associated works by divines and natural philosophers, completely denied the providential relevance of prodigies. The second phase, chronologically overlapping with the first, emerged in the culture of natural philosophy, expanding into the political world by the early eighteenth century. In this phase, belief in the providential meaning of prodigies was defined as 'superstitious' and treated as a class marker, dividing a sceptical upper class and intelligentsia from a lower class described as credulous. It was also defined as dividing sceptical men from credulous women. Individual men of the educated classes, such as Whiston, dissented from this consensus, but it was clearly dominant. By 1727 Warburton's *Critical and Philosophical Enquiry on the Causes of Prodigies and Miracles* was able to treat past belief in the providential prodigy as self-evidently absurd. By his time, the realms of politics, religion and science were no longer connected through prodigies.

Notes

1 Similar early-Enlightenment events took place in France. See B. Robert Kreiser, *Miracles, Convulsions, and Ecclesiastical Politics in Early Eighteenth-Century Paris* (Princeton: Princeton University Press, 1978) for the controversy concerning the Jansenist-alleged miracles surrounding St Medard, in which State and Church authorities promoted a sceptical and anti-supernatural view in an attempt to neutralize miracles associated with the religious and political opposition.

2 David Hume, *Enquiries Concerning the Human Understanding and Concerning the Principles of Morals*, ed. L.A. Selby-Bigge, 2nd edition (Oxford: Clarendon Press, 1962), p. 110. For historical discussions of the origins of Hume's arguments in terms of the debate on miracles, see Robert M. Burns, *The Great Debate on Miracles: From Glanville to David Hume* (Lewisburg: Bucknell University Press, 1981), and Fred Wilson, 'The logic of probabilities in Hume's argument against miracles', *Hume Studies*, 15 (1989): 255–75.

3 'Lemuel Gulliver', *The Anatomist Dissected, or the Man-Midwife Finely Brought to Bed* (Westminster, 1727), pp. 5–6. The position articulated by Hume and 'Gulliver' is dominant in our own time. For the impotence of witnesses' testimony to establish the existence of phenomena considered anomalous, such as the earthly presence of extraterrestial spacecraft, see Ron Westrum, 'Social intelligence about anomalies: the case of UFOs', *Social Studies of Science*, 7 (1977): 271–302.

Bibliography

Primary sources

Manuscript sources: Great Britain

Cambridge, Cambridge University Library
MS Dd.III.64, no. 61: 'A Designe for the Registring of Illustrious Providences'
MS Dd.III.64, no. 62: 'Of Mr. Poole's Design'
MS Mm. VI. 50 fo. 1*
MS Oo.VI.115
Additional MS 1: Correspondence of John Strype

London, British Library
Additional MSS 10116–17: Thomas Rugge, 'Mercurius Politicus Reviv'd, or Diurnall'
Additional MS 15948: John Evelyn Correspondence
Additional MS 45675: Hall Sermon Notebook
Additional MS 61903: Diary and Commonplace Book of Peter Le Neve
Harleian MSS 6430: Letterbook of Nathaniel Wanley
Sloane MSS 5246: James Plessis du Paris, 'A Short History of Human Prodigious and Monstrous Births, of Dwarfs, Sleepers, Giants, Strong Men, Hermaphrodites, Numerous Births, and Extream Old Age &c'
Thomason Collection

London, Doctor Williams Library
Richard Baxter Correspondence
Morrice MS P. Entering Book of Roger Morrice

MS 12.40 (Blackmore Papers), Item no. 5: 'A Brief Narrative of an Apparition of a great number of horsemen seen on a common called Kefeny-cord near unto Montgomery upon the 20th day of December 1661'
MSS 12.107, nos 239–42 and 24.23 fos 15–18: Accounts of Auroras

London, Public Record Office
State Papers 29 (Charles II)
State Papers 44 (Entry Book)

London, Royal Society
Boyle Letters
Classified Papers
Letter Book Copies
Register Book Copies

Oxford, Bodeleian
Ashmole MS 242
Ashmole MS 423
Ashmole MS 371
Ashmole MS 546
Rawlinson MS J: Biographical Notices of Oxford Writers
Tanner MS vol. 49, fo. 96: Letter of Thomas Holdsworth to William Sancroft, April 6, 1661

Sheffield, University of Sheffield Library
The Hartlib Papers. Via CD-Rom

Manuscript sources: North America

Los Angeles, William Andrews Clark Memorial Library
Jacob Allestry, 'Some Observations'
On ye Thanksgiving Day
John Bolles, 'Observations Politicall and Civil'
Newsletters 1682–1710

San Marino, Huntington Library
Hastings MSS
   3340: Letter of Jean Gailhard to the earl of Huntingdon
   5721: Letter of Knyvett Hastings to the earl of Huntingdon
   10653–64: Letters of Thomas Salusbury
   13083: Letter of Thomas Watson, bishop of St David's, to the Earl of Huntingdon

15179: Letter of John Lesley, bishop of Clogher, to Archbishop Bramhall
15511: Letter of Thomas Parnell to Sir George Rawdon
15978: Letter of Joseph Warren to Dame Isabella Graham
Huntington MS 30659: Newsletters 1690–1710

Washington, DC, Folger Library
V.a.299: John Ward, 'A book on purpose for such things as are of common
    use and observation not in physic or divinity but promiscuous'
V.a.403: 'Notes on Sermons, 1680–1681'
V.b.110: Commonplace Book of Henry Oxenden
W.a. 127–30: Notebooks of Whitelocke Bulstrode

Periodicals

Athenian Mercury
Athenian News, or Dunton's Oracle
British Mercury
Daily Courant
Domestick Intelligence
Evening Post
Flying Post
Gentleman's Journal: or the Monthly Miscellany
Gentleman's Magazine
Grumbler
Heraclitus Ridens
Impartial Protestant Mercury
Intelligencer
Kingdom's Intelligencer
London Gazette
Loyal Protestant, and True Domestick Intelligence
Man in the Moon
*Memoirs for the Curious: Or, an Account of What Occurs that's Rare, Secret,
    Extraordinary, Prodigious, or Miraculous, through the World; Whether in
    Nature, Art, Learning, Policy, or Religion*
Memoirs for the Ingenious, Or the Universal Mercury
Mercurius Aulicus
Mercurius Britanicus
Mercurius Democritus
Mercurius Politicus
Mercurius Publicus
Moderate Mercury
News from the Dead
Observator

Perfect Diurnall
Philosophical Collections
Philosophical Transactions
Post-Angel
Post-Man
Protestant Courant
Publick Occurences Truly Stated
Review of the State of the British Nation
Royal Diurnall
Smith's Protestant Intelligence
True Protestant Mercury
Weekly Journal
Weekly Pacquet of Advice from Rome
Weekly Post

Other primary printed sources

Addison, Joseph. *The Drummer*. London, 1716.
——*The Freeholder*, ed. James Leheny. Oxford: Clarendon Press, 1979.
Age of Wonders, or Miracles are not Ceased. London, 1660.
Annals of King George. Six volumes. London, 1716–1721.
Aubin, Ronald, ed. *London in Flames London in Glory*. New Brunswick: Rutgers University Press, 1943.
Aubrey, John. *The Natural History and Antiquities of the County of Surrey*. London, 1719.
'R.B.' (Nathaniel Crouch). *Admirable Curiosities, Rarities, and Wonders in England, Scotland, and Ireland*. London, 1682.
——*The General History of Earthquakes*. London, 1694.
——*The Surprizing Miracles of Nature and Art*. London, 1683.
——*Wonderful Prodigies of Judgement and Mercy*. London, 1682.
Bacon, Francis. *Novum Organum*, ed. Thomas Fowler. Oxford: Clarendon Press, 1878.
——*The Twoo Bookes of Francis Bacon Of the proficiencies and advancement of Learning, divine and humane*. London, 1605.
Bainbridge, John. *An Astronomicall Description of the Late Comet from the 18 of November 1618 to the 16 of December Following*. London, 1618.
Batman, Stephen. *The Doome, Warning all Men to the Judgement: Wherein are contayned all the strange Prodigies that hapned in the Worlde, with divers secrete figures of Revelations tending to Mannes' stayed conversion towardes God*. London, 1581.
Baxter, Richard. *The Certainty of the World of Spirits*. London, 1691.
——*Reliquiae Baxterianae*. ed. Matthew Sylvester. London, 1696.
——*The Saints' Everlasting Rest*. London, 1650.

Beard, Thomas. *The Theatre of God's Judgements*. London, 1597.

Bedford, Thomas. *A True and Certaine Relation of a Strange-Birth*. London, 1635.

Behn, Aphra. *A Pindarick on the Death of our Late Sovereign, with an Ancient Prophecy on his Present Majesty*. London, 1685.

Bentley, Richard. *The Folly and Unreasonableness of Atheism*. Fourth edition, corrected. London, 1699.

Beverley, Thomas. *Evangelical Repentance Unto Salvation not to be Repented Of*. London, 1693.

Biblioteca Furleiana. Rotterdam, 1714.

Birch, Thomas. *History of the Royal Society of London for improving of natural knowledge*. Four volumes. London, 1756–1757.

The Black-Day, or, A Prospect of Doomsday. Exemplified in the Great and Terrible Eclipse, Which will happen on Friday the 22d of April, 1715. London, 1715.

Blanchard, Rae, ed. *Richard Steele's Periodical Journalism 1714–1715*. Oxford: Clarendon Press, 1959.

The Blazing-Star, or, a Discourse of Comets. London, 1664.

A Blazyng Starre seen in the West at Totneis in Devonshire, on the Fourteenth of this instant November, 1642. Wherin is Manifested how Master Ralph Ashley, a Deboyst Cavalier, Attemted to Ravish a Young Virgin, the Daughter of Mr. Adam Fisher, Inhabiting neare the said Towne. Also how at that Instant, a Fearful Comet Appeared, to the Terrour and Amazement of all the Country Thereabouts. Likewise Declaring how He Persisting in his Damnable Attemt, was Struck with a Flaming Sword, which Issued from the Comet, so that he Dyed a Fearfull Example to al his Fellow Cavaliers. London, 1642.

Blundell, Nicholas. *The Great Diurnall of Nicholas Blundell of Little Crosby, Lancashire*. Transcribed and annotated by Frank Tyrer. Chester: Record Society of Lancashire and Chester, 1968–72.

Blundell, William. *A Cavalier's Note Book*, ed. Reverend T. Ellison Gibson. London: Longman, Green & Co., 1880.

Bold, Henry. *On the Thunder Happening after the Solemnity of the Coronation of Charles the II*. London, 1661.

Bond, Donald, ed. *The Tatler*. Three volumes. Oxford: Clarendon Press, 1987.

Booker, John. *Telescopium Uranicum 1662*. London, 1662.

Boyle, Robert. *A Free Enquiry into the Vulgarly Receiv'd Notion of Nature*. London, 1686.

——*The Works of the Honourable Robert Boyle*, ed. Thomas Birch. Six volumes. London, 1772.

Bramston, John. *The Autobiography of Sir John Bramston, K.B*. Camden First Series no. 32. London: Camden Society, 1845.

Brinckmair, L. *The Warnings of Germany*. London, 1638.

Burnet, Gilbert. *Bishop Burnet's History of His Own Time*. 2nd edition, enlarged. Six volumes. Oxford: At the University Press, 1833.

Burroughs, Joseph. *A Sermon Occasion'd by the Total Eclipse of the Sun, Upon April the 22d, 1715*. London, 1715.

Butler, Samuel. *Characters*, ed. with an Introduction and notes by Charles W. Daves. Cleveland: Press of Case Western Reserve University, 1970.

——*Hudibras* ed. John Wilders. Oxford: Oxford University Press, 1967.

Calendar of the Clarendon State Papers.

Calendar of State Papers, Domestic.

A Catalogue of the Tracts of Law and other Discourses written by John Brydall. London, 1711.

Centlivre, Susannah. *The Basset-Table*. London, 1705.

Chambrun, Pineton de. *The History of the Persecutions of the Protestants by the French King in the Principality of Orange*. London, 1689.

A Character of a Coffee-House. London, 1665.

Childrey, Joshua. *Britannia Baconica*. London, 1660.

——*Indago Astrologica*. London, 1652.

A Choice Collection of Wonderful Miracles, Ghosts, and Visions. London, 1681.

Cicero, Marcus Tullius. *De Divinatione.*

Clark, Samuel. *The Works of Samuel Clark*. London, 1738.

Clarke, Robert. *The Lying Wonders, or rather the Wonderful Lyes*. London, 1660.

Clarke, Samuel. *A Mirrour, or Looking-glasse for Saints and Sinners*. London, 1645.

——*A Mirrour, or Looking-Glasse for Saints and Sinners*. Second edition. London, 1654.

Cokayne, George. *Divine Astrology*. London, 1658.

——*Flesh Expiring, and the Spirit Inspiring in the New Earth*. London, 1648.

Coley, Henry. *Merlini Anglici Ephemeris 1684*. London, 1704.

——*Nuncius Coelestis, or the Starry Messenger for 1682*. London, 1682.

A Collection of Papers Relating to the Present Juncture of Affairs in England. [London], 1688.

Cowley, Abraham. *Poemata Latina*. London, 1668.

——*The Second and Third Parts of the Works of Mr. Abraham Cowley*. London, 1689.

Cowper, Countess Mary. *Diary of Lady Cowper*. London: John Murray, 1864.

Croese, Gerard. *The General History of the Quakers*. London, 1696.

Cudworth, Ralph. *The True Intellectual System of the Universe*. London, 1678.

A Declaration of a Strange and Wonderful Monster. London, 1646.

(?) Defoe, Daniel. *The Second-Sighted Highlander. Being Four Visions of the Eclypse, And something of what may Follow.* London, 1715.

'Democritus'. *The Petitioning-Comet: or a Brief Chronology of all the Famous Comets, and their Events, that happen'd from the Birth of Christ, to this very day. Together with a Modest Enquiry into this Present Comet.* London, 1681.

Derham, William. *Physico-Theology: Or, a Demonstration of the Being and Attributes of God, from his works of Creation.* Third edition. London, 1714.

A Dialogue Between a Whig and a Jacobite, Upon the Subject of the Late Rebellion, and the Execution of the Rebel-Lords, &c. occasion'd by the Phaenomenon in the Skie, March 6, 1715–16. London, 1716.

Doddridge, Philip. *Calendar of the Correspondence of Philip Doddridge DD 1702–1751*, ed. Geoffrey Nuttall. Northants Record Society vol. 29. London: Northants Record Society, 1979.

Doolittle, Samuel. *A Sermon Occasioned by the Late Earthquake Which happen'd in London, And other places on the Eighth of September 1692. Preached to a Congregation in Reading.* London, 1692.

Dryden, John. *Threnodia Augustalis.* London, 1685.

Dunton, John. *The Life and Errors of John Dunton.* London, 1705.

Eachard, Laurence. *The History of England From the First Entrance of Julius Caesar and the Romans, To the Conclusion of the Reign of King James the Second, and the Establishment of King William and Queen Mary, Upon the Throne, in the Year 1688.* Third edition. London, 1720.

Edward, John. *Cometomantia, or A Discourse of Comets.* London, 1684.

Edwards, Thomas. *The Second Part of Gangraena.* London, 1646.

Eniantos Terastios, Mirabilis Annus, or the Year of Prodigies and Wonders. London, 1661.

An Essay Concerning the Late Apparition in the Heavens, on the Sixth of March. Proving by Mathematical, Logical, and Moral Arguments, that it could not have been produced by the Ordinarly Course of Nature, but must of Necessity be a Prodigy. Humbly offer'd to the Consideration of the Royal Society. London, 1716.

Evelyn, John. *Diary and Correspondence of John Evelyn*, ed. William Bray. Four volumes. London: G. Bell, 1889–91.

——*The Diary of John Evelyn*, ed. E.S. DeBeer. Six volumes. Oxford: Clarendon Press, 1955.

An Exact and True Relation of the Wonderfull Whirle-Wind. London, 1660.

A Fair Warning for Pride: By a Foal which is Lately said to come into the World with a Top-Knot on its Head of Several Colours, at Chelcknom in Glocester-Shire (np, nd).

The Farmers Wifes Complaint against the Ladys Commodes and Topknots (np, nd).

Fielding, Henry. *The Jacobite's Journal,* in Henry Fielding. *The Jacobite's Journal and Related Writings,* ed. W.B. Coley. Oxford: Wesleyan University Press, 1975.

Fleetwood, William. *An Essay upon Miracles. In two Discourses.* London, 1701.

Ford, Simon. *A Discourse Concerning God's Judgements.* London, 1678.

Fort, Charles. *The Books of Charles Fort,* with an Introduction by Tiffany Thayer. New York: Published for the Fortean Society by Henry Holt & Co., 1941.

Foxe, John. *Acts and Monuments, with a Life of the Martyrologist, and Vindication of the Work,* ed. Reverend George Townsend. Eight volumes. New York: AMS Press, 1965.

Franks, Augustus and Herbert Gruber, eds., with Edward Hawkins, compiler. *Medallic Illustrations of the History of Great Britain and Ireland to the Death of George II.* London: Trustees of the British Museum, 1885.

Gadbury, John. *A Brief Examination of that Nest of Sedition and Phanatick Forgeries.* London, 1661.

——*De Cometis.* London, 1665.

——*Dies Novissimus, or Dooms-Day not so Near as Dreaded.* London, 1664.

——*Ephemeris, or, a Diary Astronomical, Astrological, and Meteorological, For the Year of our Lord 1661.* London, 1661.

——*Ephemeris, or, a Diary Astronomical, Astrological, and Meteorological, For the Year of Our Lord 1679.* London, 1679.

——*Ephemeris, or, a Diary Astronomical, Astrological, and Meteorological, For the Year of Our Lord 1681.* London, 1681.

——*Ephemeris, or, a Diary Astronomical and Astrological, For the Year of Our Lord 1680.* London, 1680.

——*Ephemeris, or, a Diary Astronomical and Astrological, For the Year of Our Lord 1685.* London, 1685.

——*Ephemeris, or, a Diary Astronomical and Astrological, For the Year of Our Lord 1695.* London, 1695.

——*Natura Prodigiorum.* London, 1660.

——*Natura Prodigiorum.* Second edition. London, 1665.

——*Philastrogus Knavery Epitomized.* London, 1652.

Gibbon, John. *Dux Bonis Omnibus Appelans. The Swans Welcome to his Royal Highness the Duke. Or, Some Remarks upon that Note-worthy Passage, Mentioned in the True Domestick Intelligence, Dated Octob. 14. 1679. Concerning a Company of Swans, More than Ordinary Gathered Together, at his Royal Highness's Landing.* (np), 1679.

——*Prince-Protecting Providences: or A Collection of Some Historical Passages, Relating how Several Princes and Personages, (Born for Great Actions) have had Miraculous Preservations. Made Publick upon Occasion of the Late Memorable (and Miraculous) Deliverance of His Royal Highness, James, Duke of York.* London, 1682.

Glanvill, Joseph. *Essays upon Several Important Subjects in Philosophy and Religion.* London, 1676.

——*Philosophia Pia; or a Discourse of the Religious Temper, and Tendencies of the Experimental Philosophy, Which is profest by the Royal Society.* London, 1671.

——*Some Philosophical Considerations Touching the Being of Witches and Witchcraft.* London, 1667.

Goodman, Godfrey. *The Fall of Man, or the Corruption of Nature, Proved by the Light of our Natural Reason.* London, 1616.

'Gorion, Joseph Ben'. *A Compendious and most marveilous History of the Jewes Commonwealth.* London, 1588.

A Great Wonder in Heaven. London, 1642.

Greaves, Richard. *The Spiritual Quixote.* London, 1773.

Greene, John. 'The Diary of John Greene', ed. E.M. Symons, *English Historical Review,* 43 (1928): 385–94, 598–604; 44 (1929): 106–17.

Grew, Nehemiah. *The Anatomy of Plants.* [London] 1682.

'Gulliver, Lemuel'. *The Anatomist Dissected, or the Man-Midwife Finely brought to Bed.* Westminster, 1727.

Gunther, R.T., ed. *Dr. Plot and the Correspondence of the Philosophical Society of Oxford.* Early Science in Oxford XII. Oxford: For the Subscribers, 1939.

——*Life and Letters of Edward Lhwyd.* Early Science in Oxford XIV. Oxford: For the Subscribers, 1945.

——*The Philosophical Society.* Early Science in Oxford IV. Oxford: For the Subscribers, 1925.

'G.V.'. *An Account of a Child born at Iurbick in Darbyshire, the 19th of January 1694 with a Top-knot and Rowle On its Head, of Several Colours.* London, 1694.

Hakewill, George. *An Apologie of the Power and Providence of God in the Government of the World.* Oxford, 1627.

Hall, A. Rupert and Marie Boas Hall, eds. *The Correspondence of Henry Oldenburg.* Eleven volumes. Madison: University of Wisconsin Press and London: Mansell, 1965–77.

Halley, Edmond. *A Description of the Passage of the Shadow of the Moon over England, In the Total Eclipse of the Sun, on the 22d Day of April 1715 in the Morning.* London, 1715.

Hatton. *Correspondence of the Family of Hatton,* ed. Edward Maunde Thompson. Camden Society New Series nos 22, 23. London: Camden Society, 1878.

Historical Manuscripts Commission *Dudley and Delisle MSS*: VI.

——*Duke of Leeds MSS.*

——*Salisbury MSS*: XIX.

Hearne, Thomas. *Remarks and Collections of Thomas Hearne*. ed. C.E. Doble. Oxford Historical Society vols 2, 3, 5, 7, 13, 34, 42, 43, 50, 65, 67, 72. Oxford: Oxford Historical Society, 1885–1921.

Henry, Philip. *Diaries and Letters of Philip Henry*, ed. Matthew Henry Lee. London: Kegan, Paul, Trench & Co., 1882.

Heywood, Oliver. *The Rev. Oliver Heywood B.A., 1630–1712. His Autobiography, Diaries, Anecdote and Event Books*, ed. J. Horsfall Turner. Four volumes. Brighouse, 1882–85.

Hill, John. *An Allarm to Europe by a late Prodigious Comet seen November and December, 1680*. London (nd).

Hobbes, Thomas. *The English Works of Thomas Hobbes of Malmesbury*, ed. William Molesworth. Eleven volumes. London: John Bohn, 1839.

Holwell, John. *Catastrophe Mundi: or Europe's Many Mutations until the Year 1701*. London, 1682.

——*A New Prophecy*. London, 1679.

——*Remarkable Observations on the Comet, in the Year 1680*. London, 1682.

Hooke, Robert. *The Diary of Robert Hooke*, ed. Henry Robinson and Walter Adams. London: Taylor & Francis, 1935.

——*Posthumous Works*, ed. Richard Waller. London, 1705.

Howard, Henry. *A Defensative Against the Poyson of Supposed Prophesies*. London, 1583.

Hughes, Lewis. *Certain Grievances, or, the Popish Errors and Ungodlinesse of so much of the Service-Book as is Antichristian*. (np), 1642.

Hume, David. *Enquiries Concerning the Human Understanding and Concerning the Principles of Morals*, ed. L.A. Selby-Bigge. 2nd edition. Oxford: Clarendon Press, 1962.

Hutchinson, Francis. *An Historical Essay Concerning Witchcraft*. London, 1718.

Illingworth, James. *A Genuine Account of the Man, Whose Hands and Legs Rotted Off, in the Parish of Kings-Swinford in Staffordshire, where he died, June 21, 1677*. London, (?)1750

——*A Just Narrative of the Man whose Hands and Legs rotted off: in the Parish of Kings-Swinford, in Staffordshire*. London, 1678.

Isidore of Seville. *Etymologiae*.

Jackson, Thomas. *A Collection of the Works of that Holy Man and Profound Divine Thomas Jackson*. London, 1653.

——*The Eternal Truth of Scriptures*. London, 1613–14.

——*A Treatise Concerning the Signes of the Times*. Oxford, 1637.

——*The Works of the Reverend and Learned Divine, Thomas Jackson*. Three volumes. London, 1673.

Jeake, Samuel. *An Astrological Diary of the Seventeenth Century*, ed. Michael Hunter and Annabel Gregory. Oxford: Clarendon Press, 1988.

Johnson, Samuel. *The Idler* in *The Yale Edition of the Works of Samuel Johnson*. New Haven: Yale University Press, 1958–90.

Josephus, Flavius. *The Jewish War*.

Josselin, Ralph. *The Diary of Ralph Josselin*, ed. Alan Macfarlane. Records of Social and Economic History New Series no. 3. London: Oxford University Press for the British Academy, 1976.

Josten, C.H., ed. *Elias Ashmole (1617–1692): His Autobiographical and Historical Notes, His Correspondence, and Other Contemporary Sources Related to His Life and Work*. Five volumes. Oxford: Clarendon Press, 1966.

Jurin, James. *The Correspondence of James Jurin (1684–1750) Physician and Secretary to the Royal Society*, ed. Andrea Rusnock. Amsterdam–Atlanta: Editions Rodopi, 1996.

Keach, Benjamin. *Distressed Sion Relieved*. London, 1689.

—— *Sion in Distress: or the Groans of the Protestant Chruch*. London, 1681.

Kennett, White. *A Register and Chronicle Ecclesiastical and Civil*. London, 1728.

Kerby-Miller, Charles, ed. *Memoirs of the Extraordinary Life, Works, and Discoveries of Martinus Scriblerus*. New Haven: Yale University Press for Wellesley College, 1950.

Kerr, Russel J. and Ida Coffin Duncan, eds. *The Portledge Papers*. London: J. Cape, 1928.

King, William. *The Transactioneer*. London, 1700.

Knox, Robert. *An Historical Relation of the Island of Ceylon in the East-Indies*. London, 1681.

Lancaster, W.T., ed. *Letters addressed to Ralph Thoresby FRS*. Publications of the Thoresby Society no. 21. Leeds: The Thoresby Society, 1912.

The Last Words and Sayings of the true Protestant Elm-Board. London, 1682.

L'Estrange, Roger. *Considerations and Proposals in Order to the Regulation of the Press*. London, 1663.

—— *A Modest Plea both for the Caveat and the Author of it*. London, 1661.

—— *Truth and Loyalty Vindicated*. London, 1662.

Letters Written by Eminent Persons in the Seventeenth and Eighteenth Centuries, ed. John Walker. London, 1813.

Lilly, William. *Merlini Anglici Ephemeris 1662*. London, 1662.

—— *Merlini Anglici Ephemeris 1663*. London, 1663.

—— *Merlini Anglici Ephemeris 1680*. London, 1680.

—— *William Lilly's History of his Life and Times*. London, 1822.

Lloyd, Davis. *Wonders no Miracles*. London, 1666.

Lloyd, Owen. *The Panther-Prophecy*. London, 1661.

Locke, John. *The Correspondence of John Locke*, ed. E.S. DeBeere. Eight volumes. Oxford: Clarendon Press, 1976–1989.

The London Ladies Vindication of Top-Knots (np, nd).

Lord, George DeF. (general editor) *Poems on Affairs of State*. Seven volumes. New Haven: Yale University Press, 1963–75.

The Lord's Loud Call to England. London, 1660.

Ludlow, Edmund. *Memoirs*, ed. C.H. Firth. Oxford: Clarendon Press, 1894.

——*A Voyce From the Watch Tower*, ed. A.B. Worden. Camden Society Fourth Series no. 21. London: Camden Society, 1978.

Luther, Martin. *The Signs of Christ's Coming*. London, 1661.

Luttrell, Narcissus. *A Brief Historical Relation of State Affairs from September 1678 to April 1714*. Six volumes. Oxford: Oxford University Press, 1857.

Lycosthenes, Conrad. *Historia Ostentorum et Prodigiorum*. Basel, 1557.

Macpike, Eugene Fairfield, ed. *Correspondence and Papers of Edmond Halley*. New York: Arno Press, 1975. Reprint of 1932 Oxford edition.

Magrath, J.R., ed. *The Flemings in Oxford*. Oxford Historical Society vols 44, 62, 79. Oxford: Oxford Historical Society 1904–24.

Marsin, M. *An Answer to Dr. Whitby*. London, 1701.

——*The Near aproach of Christ's Kingdom*. London, 1696.

——*Some of the chief heads of the Most Miraculous Wonders*. London, 1694.

Martindale, Adam. *The Life of Adam Martindale written by Himself*, ed. Reverend Richard Parkinson. Chetham Society no. 4. Manchester: Chetham Society, 1845.

Mather, Increase. *Angelographia*. Boston, New England, 1696.

——*An Essay for the Recording of Illustrious Providences*. Boston, New England, 1684.

The Mather Papers. Collections of the Massachusetts Historical Society Fourth Series no. 8. Boston: Massachusetts Historical Society, 1868.

Merlin Reviv'd: or, an Old Prophecy Found in a Manuscript in Pontefract Castle in York-Shire. London, 1681.

Milton, John. *Paradise Lost*. London, 1667.

Mirabilis Annus Secundus or the Second Part of the Second Year's Prodigies. [London] 1662.

Mirabilis Annus Secundus; or, the Second Year of Prodigies. [London] 1662.

A Miracle of Miracles. London, 1649.

Miraculum Signum Coeleste: A Discourse of those Miraculous Prodigies, that have been Seen since the Birth of our Blessed Lord and Saviour Jesus Christ with a Chronological Note of such Eminent Accidents, Which have Immediately Ensued the Appearance of Every of Them (np) 1658.

(Montagu, Charles and Matthew Prior) *The Hind and the Panther Transvers'd*. London, 1687.

More Last Words and Sayings of the True Protestant Elm-Board (np) 1682.

More, Henry. *The Immortality of the Soul*. London, 1659.

Morton, John. *The Natural History of Northamptonshire*. London, 1712.

A Monstrous Birth. London, 1657.

The Mystery of Ambras Merlins, Standardbearer Wolf, and last Boar of Cornwall. London, 1683.

A Narrative of the Late Extraordinary Cure Wrought in an Instant upon Mrs. Eliz. Savage, (Lame from her Birth) Without the Using of any Natural Means. London, 1694.

Ness, Christopher. *An Astrological and Theological Discourse upon this Present Great Conjunction.* London, 1682.

—— *The Devil's Patriark.* London, 1683.

—— *A Distinct Discourse and Discovery of the Person and Period of Antichrist.* London, 1679.

—— *A Full and True Account of the late blazing star.* London, 1680.

—— *A Key (with the Whip) to open the Mystery of Iniquity of the Poem Called, Absalom and Achitophel.* London, 1682.

—— *The Lord Stafford's Ghost, or A warning to traitors, with his prophecie concerning the blazing star.* London, 1680.

—— *A Philosophical and Divine Discourse Blazoning upon this Blazing Star.* London, 1681.

—— *A Protestant Antidote against the Poyson of Popery.* London, 1679.

—— *The Signes of the Times.* London, 1681.

—— *A Strange and Wonderful Trinity; or, a Triplicity of Stupendious Prodigies, consisting of a Wonderful Eclipse, as well as of a Wonderful Comet, and of a Wonderful Conjunction. London.* 1683.

—— *A True Account of this Blasing-Star.* London, 1682.

Newcome, Henry. *Diary of the Reverend Henry Newcome*, ed. Thomas Heywood. Chetham Society no. 18. London: Chetham Society, 1849.

New News of a Strange Monster found in Stow Woods near Buckingham of Human Shape, with a Double Heart, and no Hands; a Head with Two Tongues, and no Brains. London, 1679.

News From the Stars 1715 (London, 1715).

A New Song, on the Strange and Wonderful Groaning Board. London, 1682.

Newton, Isaac. *The Correspondence of Isaac Newton*, ed. H.W. Turnbull. Seven volumes. Cambridge: Cambridge University Press for the Royal Society, 1961.

The New Yeares Wonder. London, 1642.

Nicolson, Marjorie Hope, ed. *The Conway Letters: The Correspondence of Anne, Viscountess Conway, Henry More, and their Friends.* Revised edition with an Introduction and new material, ed. Sarah Hutton. Oxford: Clarendon Press, 1992.

Notes Conferr'd: or a Dialogue Betwixt the Groaning Board, and a Jesuit. London, 1682.

Old Stories which were the Fore-runners of the Revolution in Eighty-Eight, Reviv'd. London, 1719.

Parker, Samuel. *History of His Own Time*. London, 1730.

Partridge, John. *Vox Lunaris, Being a Philosophical and Astrological Discourse of Two Moons which were seen at London and the parts Adjacent, June the Eleventh, 1679*. London, 1679.

Pepys, Samuel. *The Diary of Samuel Pepys*, ed. R.C. Latham and W. Matthews. Eleven volumes. Berkeley and Los Angeles: University of California Press, 1970–1983.

——*Further Correspondence of Samuel Pepys 1662–1679*, ed. J.R. Tanner. London: G. Bell & Sons, 1929.

——*The Pepys Ballads in Facsimile*, ed. W.G. Day. Five volumes. Cambridge: D.S. Brewer, 1987.

A Perfect Narrative of the Phanaticke Wonders Seen in the West of England. London, 1660.

The Phanaticke's Plot Discovered. London, 1660.

A Philosophical Enquiry into the Wonderful Coney-warrent, lately discovered at Godalmin near Guilford in Surrey, being an account of the birth of seventeen rabbits born of a woman at several times, and she still continues in strong Labour, at the Bagnio in Leicester-Fields. London, 1726.

Pinney, John. *Letters of John Pinney 1679–1699*, ed. Geoffrey Nuttall. London: Oxford University Press, 1939.

Plot, Robert. *Enquiries to be propounded to the most Ingenious of each County in my Travels through England and Wales, in order to their History of Nature and Arts* (np, nd).

——*The Natural History of Oxfordshire*. Oxford, 1677.

——*The Natural History of Staffordshire*. Oxford, 1686.

Poor Robin's Opinion of the present Blazing-Star. London, 1677.

A Practical Discourse on the late Earthquakes, with An Historical Account of Prodigies and their Various Effects, by a Reverend Divine. London, 1692.

Prescott, Henry. *The Diary of Henry Prescott*, ed. John Addy. Record Society of Lancashire and Chester vols 127, 132, 133. Chester: Record Society of Lancashire and Chester, 1987–97.

Proposals for a National Reformation of Manners. London, 1694.

The Protestant Almanac for 1685. London, 1685.

A Protestant Monument, erected to the Immortal Glory of the Whiggs and the Dutch. London, 1713.

'J.D.R., French Minister'. *The Earth Twice Shaken Wonderfully*. London, 1693/94.

——*Observations upon Three Earthquakes*. London, 1692.

'Rationalis, Theophilus'. *Multum in Parvo, aut Vox Veritatis: Wherein The Principles, Practices, and Transactions of the English Nation: But More Especially and in Particular By Their Representatives Assembled in Parliament Anno Domini 1640, 1641: As also 1680, 1681. Are Most faithfully*

Examined, Collected and Compared together for the Present Seasonable Use, Benefit and Information of the Publick. London, 1681.

Ray, John. *The Correspondence of John Ray.* ed. Edwin Lankester. London: Ray Society, 1848.

——*Further Correspondence of John Ray.* ed. R.T. Gunther. London: Ray Society, 1928.

——*Miscellaneous Discourses Concerning the Dissolution and Changes of the World.* London, 1692.

——*The Wisdom of God Manifested in the Works of Creation.* London, 1691.

A Real Vindication of Dr. B——from the Base and Scandalous Affronts put upon him in the Scurrilous Pamphlets. London, 1682.

A Relation of Several Hundred of Children and Others that Prophesie and Preach in their Sleep, &c. First Examined and Admired by several Ingenious Men, Ministers and Professors of Philosophy at Geneva, and sent from thence in two letters to Rotterdam. London, 1689.

Rollins, Hyder, ed. *Cavalier and Puritan: Ballads and Broadsides Illustrating the Period of the Great Rebellion 1640–1660.* New York: New York University Press, 1923.

——*The Pack of Autolycus: or, Strange and Terrible News of Ghosts, Apparitions, Monstrous Births, Showers of Wheat, Judgements of God, and other Prodigious and Fearful Happenings as told in Broadside Ballads of the Years 1624–1693.* Cambridge, MA: Harvard University Press, 1927.

——*A Pepysian Garland.* Cambridge, Harvard University Press, 1934.

The Royall Legacies. London, 1649.

Ryder, Dudley. *The Diary of Dudley Ryder,* ed. William Matthews. London: Methuen & Co., 1939.

Sad Newes from the Eastern Parts. London, 1646.

Savage, Richard. *The Poetical Works of Richard Savage,* ed. Clarence Tracy. Cambridge: Cambridge University Press, 1962.

A Second and Most Exact Relation of those Sad and Lamentable Accidents, which happened in and about the Parish Church of Wydecombe neere the Dartmoores, in Devonshire, on Sunday the 21 of October last, 1638. London, 1638.

Seller, John. *The History of England.* London, 1696.

Serrarius, Petrus. *An Awakening Warning.* Amsterdam, 1662.

Shadwell, Thomas. *The Virtuoso.* London, 1676.

Signes and Wonders from Heaven. London, 1645.

Signes from Heaven: or Several Apparitions. London, 1646.

Smith, Elisha. *The Superstition of Omens and Prodigies, with the Proper Reception, and Profitable Improvement. A Divinity Lecture upon the Surprizing Phaenomena of Light, March. 6. 1715. on the Sunday after.* London, 1715.

Smith, Francis. *An Account of the Injurious Proceedings of Sir George Jeffreys*

Kt., Late Recorder of London Against Francis Smith, Bookseller. London, 1680.

A Sober Vindication of the Reverend Dr. and the Harmless Board Late Glew'd Together in a Profane Pasquil. London, 1682.

The Somersetshire Wonder: Being a True Relation of a Cow within 8 mile of Bathe, who Brought forth a Calf, with the Likeness of a Womans Head-Dress, being a Commode, near Half a Yard high, which Calf will be Shortly Brought to the Tower of London, there to be Exposed to all Curious Spectators (np, nd).

Spencer, John. *A Discourse Concerning Prodigies*. Cambridge, 1663.

——*A Discourse Concerning Vulgar Prophecies*. Cambridge, 1665.

——*The Righteous Ruler*. Cambridge, 1660.

Sprat, Thomas. *History of the Royal Society*. Facsimile reprint of London 1667 edition, with Introduction and Notes by Jackson Cope and Harold Whitmore Jones. St. Louis: Washington University Studies, 1959.

A Strange and Lamentable Accident. London, 1642.

Strange and True Newes from Gloucester. London, 1660.

A Strange and True Relation of Several Wonderful and Miraculous Sights. London, 1661.

Strange and Wonderful News from Holbitch in Lincoln-Shire. London, 1693.

Strange and Wonderful News from Southwark. London, 1684.

Strange and Wonderful Prophecies and Predictions Taken from the Apparition of the late Dreadful Comet, The Last Wonderful Ecclips, and the Great and Signal Conjunction of Jupiter and Satwin in the Fiery Trigon. London, 1682.

A Strange and Wonderful Relation of the Most Miraculous Swarms of Flies. London, 1707.

Strange Newes from the West. London, 1661.

Strange News from Barkshire of an Apparition of Several Ships and Men in the Air, which Seemed to the Beholders to be Fighting. They were Seen by the Carrier of Cirencester and his Company, as they were upon the Road coming for London, near Abingdon, on Tuesday the 26th of August, 1679 (np, nd).

Strange News from France. London, 1678.

Strange News from Lemster in Hertfordshire. London, 1679.

Strange News from Oxfordshire: Being a True and Faithful Account of a Wonderful and Dreadful Earthquake that Happened in those Parts on Monday the 17th of this Present September, 1683. London, 1683.

Stukeley, William. *The Family Memoirs of the Reverend William Stukeley*, ed. W.C. Lukis. Surtees Society nos 73, 76, 80. Durham: Surtees Society: 1880–85.

Suetonius, *Lives of the Caesars*.

Swift, Jonathan *An Elegy on Mr. Patrige, the Almanack-Maker, who died on the 29th of this Instant March, 1708*. London, 1708.

Tanner, John. *Angelus Britannicus 1681*. London, 1681.

Temple, William. *The Works of Sir William Temple, Bart. Complete in Four Volumes*. London, 1814.

(Terrill, Edward) *The Record of a Church of Christ in Bristol*, ed. Roger Haydon. Bristol Record Society's Publications no. 27. Bristol: Bristol Record Society, 1974.

Thoresby, Ralph. *The Diary of Ralph Thoresby*, ed. Reverend Joseph Hunter. London: H. Colburn and R. Bentley, 1830.

To Begin Harvest Three Days too soon rather than Two Days too Late or Sentences of the Dissenters, containing Relations of Pretended Judgements, Prodigies, and Apparitions, in Behalf of the Non-Conformists in Opposition to the Established Church. London, 1708.

Tong, Ezerel. *The Northern Star the British Monarchy*. London, 1680.

Townshend, Henry. *The Diary of Henry Townshend of Elmley Lovett. 1640–1663*, ed. J. Willis Bund. London: Worcester History Society, 1920.

Trevelyan, Sir Walter Caverly and Sir Charles Edward Trevelyan, eds. *Trevelyan Papers Part III*. Camden Society Old Series no. 105. London: Camden Society, 1872.

A True and Perfect Account of the Miraculous Sea-Monster. London, 1674.

A True and Perfect Relation of Elizabeth Freeman of Bishops Hatfield in the County of Hertford, Of a Strange and Wonderful Apparition which Appeared to Her Several Times, and Commanded Her to Declare a Message to His Most Sacred Majesty. London, 1680.

The True Figure of that Great Eclipse of the Sun. London, 1699.

A True Relation and Description of the Strange and Prodigious Blazing Comett Seen in the Heavens. London, 1680.

A True Relation of a very strange and Wonderfull thing that was heard in the Air, October the twelfth. London, 1658.

A True Relation of Some Passages at Madrid. London, 1655.

A True Relation of Strange and Wonderful Sights seen in the Air. London, 1656.

A True Relation of Those Sad and Lamentable Accidents, which happened in and about the Parish Church of Withycombe in the Dartmoores, in Devonshire, on Sunday the 21. of October last, 1638. London, 1638.

Turner, William. *A Compleat History of the most Remarkable Providences, Both of Judgement and Mercy, which have hapned in the Present Age*. London, 1697.

—— *An Essay on the Works of Creation*. London, 1695.

—— *The History of All Religions in the World*. London, 1695.

Tutchin, John. *The Earth-Quake of Jamaica, Describ'd in a Pindarick Poem* London, 1692.

Twysden, Isabella. 'The diary of Isabella Twysden'. *Archaeologia Cantiana* 51 (1939): 113–36.

The Vanity of Female Pride. London, 1691.

A Very Strange, but True Relation of the Raining of a Showre of Blood at Shewall in the Parish of Stoake Idith in the County of Hereford, on the 16th Day of this Instant July, 1679. The Examination whereof was taken upon Oath the 18th of this Instant July before Richard Hopton Esq. One of His Majesties Justices of the Peace for the Said County. London, 1679.

Vicars, John. *Dagon Demolished.* London, 1660.

——*A Looking-glasse for Malignants.* London, 1643.

——*The Looking-Glasse for Malignants, Enlarged.* London, 1645.

——*Prodigies and Apparitions.* London, 1642.

Voetius, Gisbert. *De Signis.*

Vox Infantis. London, 1649.

Warburton, William. *A Critical and Philosophical Enquiry into the Causes of Prodigies and Miracles, as Related by Historians.* London, 1727.

Ward, Edward. *British Wonders: Or, A poetical Description of the several Prodigies and most Remarkable Accidents that have happen'd in Britain since the Death of Queen Anne.* London, 1717.

——*The London Spy.* Two volumes. London, 1698–1700.

Weems, James. *The Workes in Four Volumnes.* London, 1637.

Wetenhall, Edward. *A Judgement of the Comet.* Dublin, 1682.

W.G. (William Greene) *Memento's to the World.* London, 1680.

Whiston, Edward. *The Life and Death of Mr. Henry Jessey.* (?)London, 1671.

Whiston, William. *An Account of a Surprizing Meteor, Seen in the Air, March the 6th, 1715/16.* London, 1716.

——*An Account of a Surprizing Meteor seen in the Air March 19. 1718/19 at Night.* London, 1719.

——*Memoirs of the Life and Writings of Mr. William Whiston Containing Memoirs of Several of his Friends also.* Two volumes. 2nd edition, corrected. London, 1753.

Wodrow, Robert. *Analecta, or Materials for a History of Remarkable Providences mostly relating to Scotch Ministers and Christians.* Maitland Club no. 60. [Edinburgh]: Maitland Club, 1842–43.

The Wonderful Blazing Star: with the dreadful Apparition of two Armies in the Air. London, 1681.

Wood, Anthony. *Athenae Oxonienses: an exact history of all the writers and bishops who have had their education in the most ancient and famous University of Oxford, from the fifteenth year 1500, to the end of the year 1690 representing the birth, fortune, preferment, and death of all those authors and prelates.* Two volumes. London: 1691–92.

——*History and Antiquities of the University of Oxford,* ed. John Gutch. Oxford, 1792.

——*The Life and Times of Anthony Wood,* ed. Andrew Clark. Five volumes. Oxford: Oxford Historical Society, 1891–1907.

Woodcock, Thomas. 'Extracts from the Papers of Thomas Woodcock (ob. 1695)', ed. G.C. Moore, in *Camden Miscellany XI*, Camden Third Series no. 13. (London: Camden Society, 1907, pp. 49–89.)

Woodward, Josiah. *An Account of the Rise and Progress of the Religious Societies in the City of London, etc. And of the Endeavours for Reformation of Manners that have been Made therein. The Second edition, enlarged.* London, 1698.

Worthington, John. *The Diary and Correspondence of Dr. John Worthington,* ed. James Crossley. Chetham Society vols 13, 36, 114. Manchester: Chetham Society, 1847–86.

'W.W.' *The Eclipse, A Poem in Commemoration of the Total Eclipse of the Sun. April 22. 1715.* London, 1715.

Yonge, James. *The Journal of James Yonge (1647–1721), Plymouth Surgeon,* ed. F.N.L. Poynter. London: Longmans, 1963.

Secondary sources

Published works

Altick, Richard D. *The Shows of London.* Cambridge, MA: Harvard University Press, Belknap Press, 1978.

Ashcraft, Richard. *Revolutionary Politics and Locke's Two Treatises of Government.* Princeton: Princeton University Press, 1986.

Ashworth, William. 'Natural history and the emblematic world view', in David Lindberg and Robert Westman, eds. *Reappraisals of the Scientific Revolution.* Cambridge: Cambridge University Press, 1990, pp. 303–32.

Axon, William E.A. 'Welsh folk-lore of the seventeenth century', *Y Cymmrodor,* 21 (1908): 113–31.

Bahlmann, Dudley W.R. *The Moral Revolution of 1688.* New Haven: Yale University Press, 1957.

Baine, Rodney. *Daniel Defoe and the Supernatural.* Athens, GA: Georgia University Press, 1968.

Ball, Bryan. *A Great Expectation: Eschatological Thought in English Protestantism to 1660.* Studies in Christian Thought no. 12. Leiden: E.J. Brill, 1975.

Barnes, Robin Bruce. *Prophecy and Gnosis: Apocalypticism in the Wake of the Lutheran Reformation.* Stanford: Stanford University Press, 1988.

Bazerman, Charles. *Shaping Written Knowledge: The Genre and Activity of the Experimental Article in Science.* Madison: University of Wisconsin Press, 1988.

Bell, Maureen. 'Elizabeth Calvert and the "confederates"', *Publishing History,* 32 (1994): 5–49.

Bostridge, Ian. *Witchcraft and its Transformations, c.1650–c.1750*. Oxford: Clarendon Press, 1997.

Boylan, Michael. 'Henry More's space and the spirit of nature', *Journal of the History of Philosophy*, 18 (1980): 395–405.

Brady, David. '1666: The year of the beast', *Bulletin of the John Rylands Library of Manchester*, 61 (1979): 314–36.

Brandt, William J. *The Shape of Medieval History: Studies in Modes of Perception*. New Haven and London: Yale University Press, 1966.

Briggs, J. Morton Jr. 'Aurora and enlightenment: eighteenth-century explanations of the aurora borealis', *Isis*, 58 (1967): 491–503.

Brooke, John Hedley. *Science and Religion: Some Historical Perspectives*. Cambridge: Cambridge University Press, 1991.

Brownley, Martine Watson. 'Sir Richard Baker's Chronicle and later seventeenth century English historiography', *Huntington Library Quarterly*, 52 (1989): 481–500.

Brumberg, Joan. *Fasting Girls: The History of Anorexia Nervosa*. Cambridge, MA: Harvard University Press, 1988.

Buell, Llewelyn. 'Elizabethan portents: superstition or doctrine?', in *Essays Critical and Historical Dedicated to Lily B. Campbell*. New York: Russell and Russell, 1968. Reprint of Berkeley: University of California Press, 1950.

Burke, Peter. *Popular Culture in Early Modern Europe*. London: Harper & Row, 1978.

—— 'Popular culture in seventeenth century London', *London Journal*, 3 (1977): 143–62.

—— 'A survey of the popularity of ancient historians, 1450–1700', *History and Theory*, 5 (1966): 135–52.

Burns, Robert M. *The Great Debate on Miracles: From Joseph Glanville to David Hume*. Lewisburg: Bucknell University Press, 1981.

Burns, William E. 'Signs of the times: Thomas Jackson and the controversy over prodigies in the reign of Charles I', *The Seventeenth Century*, 11 (1996): 21–33.

—— '"The terriblest eclipse that hath been seen in our days": Black Monday and the debate on astrology during the interregnum', in Margaret J. Osler, ed. *Rethinking the Scientific Revolution*. Cambridge: Cambridge University Press, 2000.

Burtt, Edwin Arthur. *The Metaphysical Foundations of Modern Science*. Atlantic Highlands, NJ: Humanities Press, 1980. Reprint of 1932 edition.

Camporesi, Piero. *Bread of Dreams: Food and Fantasy in Early Modern Europe*, trans. David Gentilcore. Cambridge: Polity Press, 1989.

Capp, Bernard. *English Almanacs: Astrology and the Popular Press, 1500–1800*. Ithaca: Cornell University Press, 1979.

——*The Fifth Monarchy Men: A Study in Seventeenth Century English Millenarianism*. London: Faber, 1972.

Céard, Jean. 'The crisis of the science of monsters', trans. Constance Spreen, in Phillipe Desan, ed. *Humanism in Crisis: The Decline of the French Renaissance*. Ann Arbor: University of Michigan Press, 1991, pp. 181–205.

——*La nature et les prodiges: l'insolite au 16e siècle, en France*. Series travaux d'humanisme et renaissance no. 158. Geneva: Droz, 1977.

Champion, J.A.I. *The Pillars of Priestcraft Shaken: The Church of England and its Enemies, 1660–1730*. Cambridge: Cambridge University Press, 1992.

Christian, William A. *Apparitions in Late Medieval and Renaissance Spain*. Princeton: Princeton University Press, 1981.

Clark, J.C.D. *English Society, 1688–1832: Ideology, Social Structure, and Political Practice during the Ancien Régime*. Cambridge: Cambridge University Press, 1985.

Clark, Stuart. *Thinking with Demons: The Idea of Witchcraft in Early Modern Europe*. Oxford: Clarendon Press, 1997.

Claydon, Tony. *William III and the Godly Revolution*. Cambridge: Cambridge University Press, 1996.

Clucas, Stephen. 'Samuel Hartlib's Ephemerides, 1635–59, and the pursuit of scientific and philosophical manuscripts: the religious ethos of an intelligencer', *The Seventeenth Century*, 6 (1991): 33–55.

Cody, Lisa. 'The doctor's in labour: or a new whim wham from Guildford', *Gender and History*, 4 (1992): 175–96.

Cohn, Norman. *The Pursuit of the Millenium*. New York: Oxford University Press, 1970. Revised and expanded edition.

Contamine, Phillipe. 'Prodige et propagande: Vendredi 20 Août 1451, de 7h à 8h du matin: le Ciel de Bayonne', in Bernard Ribemont, ed. *Observer, Lire, Ecrire le Ciel au Moyen Age*, Collection Sapience no. 1. Paris: Klinksieck, 1991, pp. 63–86.

Cope, Jackson I. *Joseph Glanville: Anglican Apologist*. St. Louis: Washington University Studies, 1956.

Courtines, Leo Pierre. *Bayle's Relations with England and the English*. New York: Columbia University Press, 1938.

Cragg, G.R. *From Puritanism to the Age of Reason*. Cambridge: Cambridge University Press, 1950.

Cranfield, Geoffrey Alan. *The Development of the Provincial Newspaper 1700–1760*. Westport, CT: Greenwood Press, 1978. Reprint of Oxford: Clarendon Press, 1962.

Cressy, David. 'De la fiction dans les archives? Ou le monstre de 1569', *Annales: Économies, Sociétés, Civilisations*, 48 (1993): 1309–29.

Crosby, Thomas. *The History of the English Baptists*. Four volumes. London, 1738.

Curry, Patrick. *Prophecy and Power: Astrology in Early Modern England.* London: Princeton University Press, 1989.

Daniels, R. Balfour. *Some Seventeenth-Century Worthies in a Twentieth-Century Mirror.* Chapel Hill: University of North Carolina Press, 1940.

Daston, Lorraine. 'Baconian facts, academic civilty, and the prehistory of objectivity', *Annals of Scholarship,* 8 (1991): 337–63.

—— 'Marvelous facts and miraculous evidence in early modern Europe', *Critical Inquiry,* 18 (autumn, 1991): 93–124.

—— and Katherine Park. *Wonders and the Order of Nature, 1150–1750.* New York: Zone Books, 1998.

Dear, Peter. 'Miracles, experiments, and the ordinary course of nature', *Isis,* 81 (1990): 663–83.

—— 'Narratives, anecdotes, and experiments: turning experience into science in the seventeenth century', in Peter Dear, ed. *The Literary Structure of Scientific Argument: Historical Studies.* Philadelphia: University of Pennsylvania Press, 1991.

—— 'Totius in verba: rhetoric and authority in the early Royal Society', *Isis,* 76 (1985): 145–61.

Delameau, Jean. *Sin and Fear: The Emergence of a Western Guilt Culture 13th–18th Centuries,* trans. Eric Nicholson. New York: St. Martin's Press, 1990.

Donagan, Barbara. 'Godly choice: Puritan decision making in seventeenth-century England', *Harvard Theological Review,* 76 (1983): 307–34.

Douglas, Mary. *Natural Symbols.* Second edition. New York: Pantheon Books, 1982.

Duffy, Eamon. 'Valentine Greatrakes, the Irish stroker: miracle, science and orthodoxy in Restoration England', in Keith Robbins, ed. *Religion and Humanism,* Oxford: Basil Blackwell, 1981. Studies in Church History no. 17.

Durston, Chris. 'Signs and wonders and the English Civil War' *History Today,* 37 (1987): 22–8.

Eather, Robert H. *Majestic Lights: The Aurora in Science, History, and the Arts.* Washington: American Geophysical Union, 1980.

Eddy, William A. 'The anatomist dissected – by Lemuel Gulliver', *Modern Language Notes,* 41 (1926): 330–1.

Engehausen, Frank. 'Luther und die Wunderzeichen: Eine englische Übersetzung der Adventpostille im Jahr 1661', *Archiv für Reformationsgeschicte* (Archive for Reformation History), 84 (1993): 276–88.

Evans, A.W. *Warburton and the Warburtonians: A Study in Some Eighteenth-Century Controversies.* London: Oxford University Press, 1932.

Farrell, Maureen. *William Whiston.* New York: Arno Press, 1981.

Findlen, Paula. 'Jokes of nature and jokes of knowledge: the playfulness of scientific discourse in early modern Europe', *Renaissance Quarterly*, 43 (1990): 292–331.

Force, James. *William Whiston: Honest Newtonian*. Cambridge: Cambridge University Press, 1985.

Foucault, Michel. *The Order of Things*. New York: Vintage Press, 1979.

Frank, Joseph. *The Beginnings of the English Newspaper 1620–1660*. Cambridge, MA: Harvard University Press, 1961.

Friedman, Jerome. *The Battle of Frogs and Fairford's Flies: Miracles and the Pulp Press during the English Revolution*. New York: St. Martin's Press, 1993.

Furbank, P.N. and W.R. Owens. *The Canonisation of Daniel Defoe*. New Haven: Yale University Press, 1988.

Furbank, P.N. and W.R. Owens. *A Critical Bibliography of Daniel Defoe*. London: Pickering and Chatto, 1998.

Gascoigne, John. *Cambridge in the Age of the Enlightenment: Science, Religion and Politics from the Restoration to the French Revolution*. Cambridge: Cambridge University Press, 1989.

Genuth, Sara Schechner. *Comets, Popular Culture, and the Birth of Modern Cosmology*. Princeton: Princeton University Press, 1997.

Gillespie, Neal. 'Natural history, natural theology, and social order: John Ray and the "Newtonian ideology"', *Journal of the History of Biology*, 20 (1987): 1–51.

Golinski, J.V. 'A noble spectacle: phosphorus and the public culture of science in the early Royal Society', *Isis*, 80 (1989): 11–39.

Graham, Walter. *English Literary Periodicals*. New York: Thomas Nelson & Sons, 1930.

Greaves, Richard. *Deliver Us from Evil: The Radical Underground in Britain 1660–1663*. New York: Oxford University Press, 1986.

——*Enemies Under His Feet: Radicals and Nonconformists in Britain 1664–1677*. Stanford: Stanford University Press, 1990.

——*Saints and Rebels: Seven Nonconformists in Stuart England*. Macon, GA: Mercer University Press, 1985.

——*Secrets of the Kingdom: British Radicals from the Popish Plot to the Revolution of 1688–1689*. Stanford: Stanford University Press, 1992.

Greene, Robert A. 'Henry More and Robert Boyle on the spirit of nature', *Journal of the History of Ideas*, 23 (1962): 451–74.

Guerlac, Henry and M.C. Jacob. 'Bentley, Newton, and Providence', *Journal of the History of Ideas*, 28 (1967): 307–18.

Haley, K.H.D. *The First Earl of Shaftesbury*. Oxford: Clarendon Press, 1968.

Hall, David D. *Worlds of Wonder, Days of Judgement: Popular Religious Belief in Early New England*. New York: Alfred A. Knopf, 1989.

Harris, Tim. *London Crowds in the Reign of Charles II: Propaganda and Politics from the Restoration to the Exclusion Crisis*. Cambridge: Cambridge University Press, 1987.

Harris, Tim, Mark Goldie and Paul Seaward, eds. *The Politics of Religion in Restoration England*. Oxford: Basil Blackwell, 1990.

Harris, Victor. *All Coherence Gone*. Chicago: University of Chicago Press, 1949.

Hart, A. Tindal. *William Lloyd 1627–1717: Bishop, Politician, Author and Prophet*. London: Society for the Promotion of Christian Knowledge, 1952.

Hart, W.H. *Index Expurgatorius Anglicanus*. London, 1872–78.

Hepburn, Ronald W. 'George Hakewill: the virility of nature', *Journal of the History of Ideas*, 16 (1955): 135–50.

Hesse, Mary B. 'Hooke's philosophical algebra', *Isis*, 57 (1966): 67–83.

Henry, John. 'The Scientific Revolution in England', in Roy Porter and Mikulas Teich, eds. *The Scientific Revolution in National Context*. Cambridge: Cambridge University Press, 1992.

Heyd, Michael. 'The new experimental philosophy: a manifestation of "enthusiasm" or an antidote to it?', *Minerva*, 25 (1987): 423–40.

——'The reaction to enthusiasm in the seventeenth century: towards an integrative approach', *Journal of Modern History*, 53 (1981): 258–80.

Hill, Christopher. *Antichrist in Seventeenth Century England*. Oxford: Clarendon Press, 1971.

——*Change and Continuity in Seventeenth-Century England*. London: Weidenfeld & Nicholson, 1974.

——*Intellectual Origins of the English Revolution*. London: Oxford University Press, 1965.

——'New contributions to seventeenth-century social history', *Journal of British Studies*, 32 (1993): 76–83.

Hooker, Edward N. 'The purpose of Dryden's *Annus Mirabilis*', *Huntington Library Quarterly*, 10 (1946): 49–67.

Hull, William. *Benjamin Furly and Quakerism in Rotterdam*. Swarthmore: Swarthmore College, 1941.

Hunter, J. Paul. *Before Novels: The Cultural Contexts of Eighteenth Century English Fiction*. New York and London: W.W. Norton & Co., 1990.

Hunter, Michael. *Establishing the New Science: The Experience of the Early Royal Society*. Woodbridge: Boydell Press, 1989.

——*Science and Society in Restoration England*. Cambridge: Cambridge University Press, 1981.

Hutchison, Keith. 'Supernaturalism and the mechanical philosophy', *History of Science*, 21 (1983): 297–333.

Jacob, James. *Henry Stubbe, Radical Protestantism and the Early Enlightenment*. Cambridge: Cambridge University Press, 1983.

——*Robert Boyle and the English Revolution*. Studies in the History of Science no. 3. New York: Burt Franklin, 1977.

——and Margaret Jacob. 'The Anglican origins of modern science: the metaphysical foundations of the Whig Constitution', *Isis*, 71 (1980): 251–67.

Jacob, Margaret. *The Cultural Meaning of the Scientific Revolution*. Philadelphia: Temple University Press, 1988.

——*The Newtonians and the English Revolution 1689–1720*. Ithaca: Cornell University Press, 1976.

JFHS. 'Giles Calvert's Publishing Career', *Journal of the Friends' Historical Society*, 35 (1938): 45–9.

Jones, Eldred. *The Elizabethan Image of Africa*. Charlottesville: The University Press of Virginia for the Folger Shakespeare Library, 1971.

Jones, J.R. *The First Whigs: The Politics of the Exclusion Crisis 1678–1683*. University of Durham Publications. London: Oxford University Press, 1961.

Jones-Davies, M.T. ed. *Monstres et Prodiges au Temps de la Renaissance*. Centre de recherchés de la Renaissance no. 5. Paris: Diffusion J. Touzot, 1980.

Kaplan, Barbara Beigun. 'Greatrakes the stroker: the interpretations of his contemporaries', *Isis*, 73 (1982): 178–85.

Kenyon, J.P. *The Popish Plot*. London: Heinemann, 1972.

——*Revolution Principles: The Politics of Party, 1689–1720*. Cambridge: Cambridge University Press, 1977.

Kitchin, George. *Sir Roger L'Estrange*. London: K. Paul, Trench, Trubner & Co., 1913.

Knox, R. Buick, ed. *Reformation, Conformity, and Dissent: Essays in Honour of Geoffrey Nuttall*. London: Epworth Press, 1977.

Kreiser, B. Robert. *Miracles, Convulsions, and Ecclesiastical Politics in Early Eighteenth-Century Paris*. Princeton: Princeton University Press, 1978.

Kubrin, David. 'Newton and the cyclical cosmos: providence and the mechanical philosophy', *Journal of the History of Ideas*, 28 (1967): 325–6.

Lamont, William M. *Richard Baxter and the Millenium: Protestant Imperialism and the English Revolution*. London: Croom Helm, 1979.

Leonard, John. 'To warn proud cities: a topical reference in Milton's airy knights' simile (*Paradise Lost* 2533–8)', *Renaissance and Reformation*, 19 (1995): 63–71.

Lerner, Robert. *The Powers of Prophecy: The Cedars of Lebanon Vision from the Mongol Onslaught to the Dawn of the Enlightenment*. Berkeley and Los Angeles: University of California Press, 1983.

Levine, Joseph. *Dr. Woodward's Shield: History, Science, and Satire in Augustan England*. Berkeley, Los Angeles, and London: University of California Press, 1977.

Lindberg, David C. and Ronald L. Numbers, eds. *God and Nature: Historical Essays on the Encounter Between Christianity and Science*. Berkeley and Los Angeles: University of California Press, 1986.

Love, Harold. *Scribal Publication in Seventeenth-Century England*. Oxford: Clarendon Press, 1993.

Macdonald, Michael and Terence R. Murphy. *Sleepless Souls: Suicide in Early Modern England*. Oxford: Clarendon Press, 1990.

MacGillivray, Royce. 'The Use of Predictions in Seventeenth Century Historians', *Cithara*, 8 (November, 1968): 54–63.

Manuel, Frank. *The Religion of Isaac Newton*. Oxford: Clarendon Press, 1974.

Martin, Julian. *Francis Bacon, the State and the Reform of Natural Philosophy*. Cambridge: Cambridge University Press, 1992.

Masters, R. *Master's History of the College of Corpus Christi and the Blessed Virgin Marie in the University of Cambridge with additional matter and a Continuation to the Present Time by John Lamb D.D. Master of the College*. Cambridge: Cambridge University Press, 1831.

Mayer, Robert. 'Nathaniel Crouch, bookseller and historian: popular historiography and cultural power in late seventeenth-century England', *Eighteenth-Century Studies*, 27 (1994): 391–419.

McEwen, Gilbert D. *The Oracle of the Coffee House: John Dunton's Athenian Mercury*. San Marino: Huntington Library, 1972.

McKeon, Michael. *Politics and Poetry in Restoration England: The Case of Dryden's 'Annus Mirabilis'*. Cambridge, MA: Harvard University Press, 1975.

Mendyk, Stan A.E. *'Speculum Britanniae': Regional Study, Antiquarianism, and Science in Britain to 1700*. Toronto, Buffalo and London: University of Toronto Press, 1989.

Merchant, Carolyn. *The Death of Nature: Women, Ecology, and the Scientific Revolution*. San Francisco: Harper & Row, 1980.

Middlekauf, Robert. *The Mathers: Three Generations of Puritan Intellectuals 1596–1728*. New York: Oxford University Press, 1971.

Monod, Paul Kléber. *Jacobitism and the English People, 1688–1788*. Cambridge: Cambridge University Press, 1989.

Muddiman, J.G. *The King's Journalist 1659–1689: Studies in the Reign of Charles II*. Reprints of Economic Classics, New York, Augustus M. Kelley, 1971. Reprint of London: John Lane The Bodley Head, 1923.

Mulligan, Lotte. 'Robert Boyle, "right reason", and the meaning of metaphor', *Journal of the History of Ideas*, 55 (1994): 235–57.

—— 'Robert Hooke and certain knowledge', *The Seventeenth Century*, 7 (1992): 151–69.

Nature. 'The earliest mention of the aurora borealis', *Nature*, 3, no. 17 (1870): 45–6.

Newton, Theodore F.M. 'The mask of Heraclitus: a problem in Restoration journalism', *Harvard Studies and Notes in Philology and Literature*, 16 (1934): 145–60.

Niccoli, Ottavia. *Prophecy and People in Renaissance Italy*, trans. Lydia Cochrane. Princeton: Princeton University Press, 1990.

Oakley, Francis. 'Christian theology and the Newtonian science: the rise of the concept of the laws of nature', *Church History*, 30 (1961): 433–57.

——*Omnipotence, Covenant, and Order: An Excursion in the History of Ideas from Abelard to Leibniz*. Ithaca: Cornell University Press, 1984.

Olson, Richard. 'Tory–high church opposition to science and scientism in the eighteenth century: the works of John Arbuthnot, Jonathan Swift, and Samuel Johnson', in John Burke, ed. *The Uses of Science in the Age of Newton*. Publications of the Clark Library Professorship UCLA no. 8. Berkeley, Los Angeles and London: University of California Press, 1983, pp. 171–204.

Parel, Anthony J. *The Machiavellian Cosmos*. New Haven and London: Yale University Press, 1992.

Park, Katherine. 'Bacon's "enchanted glass"', *Isis*, 75 (1984): 290–302.

——and Lorraine J. Daston. 'Unnatural conceptions: the study of monsters in France and England', *Past and Present*, 92 (August, 1981): 20–54.

Parker, Derek. *Familiar to All: William Lilly and Astrology in the Seventeenth Century*. London: Jonathan Cape, 1975.

Plumb, J.H. *Sir Robert Walpole: The Making of a Statesman*. London: Cresset Press, 1956.

Popkin, Richard. 'Hartlib, Dury and the Jews', in Mark Greengrass, Michael Leslie and Timothy Raylor, eds. *Samuel Hartlib and Universal Reformation: Studies in Intellectual Communication*. Cambridge: Cambridge University Press, 1994.

——'Predicting, prophesying, divining and foretelling from Nostradamus to Hume', *History of European Ideas*, 5 (1984): 117–35.

Raven, Charles. *English Naturalists from Neckham to Ray*. Cambridge: Cambridge University Press, 1947.

——*John Ray, Naturalist*. Cambridge: Cambridge University Press, 1950.

Reay, Barry, ed. *Popular Culture in Seventeenth-Century England*. London: Croom Helm, 1985.

Redwood, John. *Reason, Ridicule, and Religion: The Age of Enlightenment in England 1660–1750*. London: Harvard University Press, 1976.

Rogers, Nicholas. 'Riot and popular Jacobitism in early Hanoverian England', in Eveline Cruickshanks, ed. *Ideology and Conspiracy: Aspects of Jacobitism, 1689–1759*. Edinburgh: John Donald, 1982.

Rollins, Hyder E. *Analytical Index to the Ballad-Entries in the Stationers' Registers 1557–1709*. Hatboro, PA: Tradition Press, 1967.

Rostenberg, Leona. *Literary, Political, Scientific, Religious, and Legal Publishing, Printing and Bookselling in England 1551–1700: Twelve Studies*. New York: Burt Franklin, 1965.

Rousseau, G.S. ' "Wicked Whiston" and the Scriblerians: another ancients–modern controversy', *Studies in Eighteenth Century Culture*, 17 (1987): 17–44.

Rumsey, Peter Lockwood. *Acts of God and the People, 1620–1730*. Studies in Religion no. 2. Ann Arbor: UMI Research Press, 1984.

Rusche, Harry. 'Merlini Anglici: astrology and Propaganda from 1644 to 1651', *English Historical Review*, 80 (1965): 322–33.

—— 'Prophecies and propaganda, 1641–1651', *English Historical Review*, 84 (1969): 752–70.

Ryley, Robert. *William Warburton*. Boston: Twayne Publishers, 1984.

Schaffer, Simon. 'Natural philosophy and public spectacle in the eighteenth century', *History of Science*, 21 (1983): 1–43.

Schaffer, Simon and Steven Shapin. *Leviathan and the Air-Pump: Hobbes, Boyle, and the Experimental Life*. Princeton: Princeton University Press, 1985.

Schutte, Anne Jacobson. ' "Such monstrous births": a neglected aspect of the antinomian controversy', *Renaissance Quarterly*, 38 (1985): 85–106.

Scott, Jonathan. *Algernon Sidney and the Restoration Crisis*. Cambridge: Cambridge University Press, 1991.

Schwartz, Hillel. *The French Prophets: The History of a Millenarian Group in Eighteenth-Century England*. Berkeley: University of California Press, 1980.

—— *Knaves, Fools, Madmen, and that Subtle Effluvium: A Study of the Opposition to the French Prophets in England 1706–1710*. University of Florida Monographs, Social Sciences, no. 62. Gainesville: University Presses of Florida, 1978.

Schwoerer, Lois. 'Propaganda in the revolution of 1688–89', *American Historical Review*, 82 (1977): 843–74.

Scribner, Robert W. 'The Reformation, popular magic, and the "disenchantment of the world" ', *Journal of Interdisciplinary History*, 23 (1993): 475–94.

Seligman, S.A. 'Mary Toft – the rabbit breeder', *Medical History*, 5 (1961): 349–60.

Shapin, Stephen. 'Pump and circumstance: Robert Boyle's literary technology', *Social Studies of Science*, 14 (1984): 481–520.

—— *A Social History of Truth: Civility and Science in Seventeenth-Century England*. Chicago: University of Chicago Press, 1994.

Shapiro, Barbara. *Probability and Certainty in Seventeenth-Century England*. Princeton: Princeton University Press, 1983.

Somerville, C. John. *Popular Religion in Restoration England*. University of Florida Monographs, Social Sciences, no. 59. Gainesville: University Presses of Florida, 1977.

——*The Secularization of Early Modern England*. New York and Oxford: Oxford University Press, 1992.

Speck, W.A. 'Political Propaganda in Augustan England'. *Transactions of the Royal Historical Society*, Fifth Series, 22 (1972): 17–32.

Spurr, John. 'The Church, the societies, and the moral revolution of 1688', in John Walsh, Colin Haydon and Stephen Taylor, eds. *The Church of England c.1689–c.1833: From Toleration to Tractarianism*. Cambridge: Cambridge University Press, 1993

——*The Restoration Church of England, 1646–1689*. New Haven and London: Yale University Press, 1991.

Stearns, Bertha-Monica. 'The first English periodical for women', *Modern Philology*, 28 (1930): 45–59.

Steneck, Nicholas. 'Greatrakes the stroker: the interpretations of historians', *Isis*, 73 (1982): 161–77.

Stewart, Larry. *The Rise of Public Science: Rhetoric, Technology and Natural Philosophy in Newtonian Britain, 1660–1750*. Cambridge: Cambridge University Press, 1992.

Sutherland, James. *The Restoration Newspaper and its Development*. Cambridge: Cambridge University Press, 1986.

Tester, S.J. *A History of Western Astrology*. Woodbridge: Boydell Press, 1987.

Thomas, Keith. *Religion and the Decline of Magic*. New York: Charles Scribner's Sons, 1971.

Todd, Dennis. *Imagining Monsters: Miscreations of the Self in Eighteenth-Century England*. Chicago: University of Chicago Press, 1995.

Troyer, Howard William. *Ned Ward of Grubstreet: A Study of Sub-Literary London in the Eighteenth Century*. Cambridge, MA: Harvard University Press, 1946.

Vander Molen, Ronald. 'Providence as mystery, providence as revelation: Puritan and Anglican modifications of John Calvin's doctrine of providence', *Church History*, 47 (1978): 27–47.

Van der Wall, Ernestine G.E. 'The Amsterdam millenarian Petrus Serrarius (1600–1699) and the Anglo-Dutch circle of Philo-Judaists', in J. Van den Berg and Ernestine G.E. van der Wall, eds. *Jewish–Christian Relations in the Seventeenth Century: Studies and Documents*. International Archives of the History of Ideas 119. Dordrecht: Kluwer Academic Publishers, 1988.

Van de Wetering, Maxine. 'Moralizing in Puritan natural thought: mysteriousness in earthquake sermons', *Journal of the History of Ideas*, 43 (1982): 417–38.

Vickers, Brian. 'Critical reactions to occult sciences during the Renaissance', in Edna Ullman Margalit, ed. *The Scientific Enterprise: The Bar Hillel Colloquium: Studies in History, Philosophy and Sociology of Science,* vol. 4. Boston Studies in the Philosophy of Science no. 146. Dordrecht: Kluwer Academic Publishers, 1992.

—— 'The Royal Society and English prose style: a reassessment', in *Rhetoric and the Pursuit of Truth: Language Change in the Seventeenth and Eighteenth Centuries*. Papers heard at a Clark Library Seminar, 8 March 1980. Los Angeles: William Andrews Clark Memorial Library, 1985, pp. 1–76.

——ed. *Occult and Scientific Mentalities in the Renaissance*. Cambridge: Cambridge University Press, 1984.

Walker, D.P. 'The cessation of miracles', in Ingrid Merkel and Allen Debus eds. *Hermeticism and the Renaissance*. Washington: Folger Library, 1988.

Walker, J. 'The censorship of the press during the reign of Charles II', *History*, 35 (1950): 219–38.

Walsham, Alexandra. *Providence in Early Modern England*. Oxford: Oxford University Press, 1999.

Walters, Alice N. 'Ephemeral events: English broadsides of early eighteenth-century solar eclipses', *History of Science*, 37 (1999): 1–43.

Walton, Michael T., Robert M. Fineman and Phyllis J. Walton. 'Of monsters and prodigies: the interpretation of birth defects in the sixteenth century', *American Journal of Medical Genetics*, 47 (1993): 7–13.

Ward, Benedicta. *Miracles and the Medieval Mind: Theory, Record, and Event 1000–1215*. Philadelphia: University of Pennsylvania Press, 1982.

Warmington, Andrew. 'Frogs, toads and the Restoration in a Gloucestershire village', *Midland History*, 14 (1989): 30–42.

Watt, Tessa. *Cheap Print and Popular Piety 1550–1640*. Cambridge: Cambridge University Press, 1991.

Webster, Charles. *The Great Instauration: Science, Medicine and Reform, 1626–1660*. London: Duckworth, 1975.

Westfall, Richard. *Science and Religion in Seventeenth Century England*. New Haven: Yale University Press, 1958.

Westrum, Ron. 'Social intelligence about anomalies: the case of UFOs', *Social Studies of Science*, 7 (1977): 271–302.

Whiting, C.E. *Studies in English Puritanism from the Restoration to the Revolution 1660–1688*. Publications for the Church Historical Society New Series no. 5. London: Society for the Promotion of Christian Knowledge, 1931.

Wiles, R.M. *Freshest Advices: Early Provincial Newspapers in England*. Columbus: Ohio State University Press, 1965.

Wilson, Dudley Butler. *Signs and Portents: Monstrous Births from the Middle Ages to the Enlightenment*. London and New York: Routledge, 1993.

Wilson, Fred. 'The logic of probabilities in Hume's argument against miracles', *Hume Studies*, 15 (1989): 255–75.

Winship, Michael. *Seers of God: Puritan Providentialism in the Restoration and Early Enlightenment*. Baltimore: Johns Hopkins University Press, 1996.

Worden, Blair. 'Providence and politics in Cromwellian England', *Past and Present*, 109 (November, 1985): 55–99.

Wurzbach, Natascha. *The Rise of the English Street Ballad 1550–1650*, trans. Ganya Walls. Cambridge: Cambridge University Press, 1990.

Zambelli, Paola, ed. *'Astrologi Hallucinati': Stars and the End of the World in Luther's Time*. Berlin and New York: Walter de Gruyter, 1986.

Zook, Melinda S., *Radical Whigs and Conspiratorial Politics in Late Stuart England*. University Park: Pennsylvania State University Press, 1999.

Zwicker, Steven N. *Lines of Authority: Politics and English Literary Culture, 1649–1689*. Ithaca: Cornell University Press, 1993.

Unpublished Ph.D. dissertations

Arnold, Ken. 'Cabinets for the curious: practicing science in early modern English museums'. Princeton University, 1991.

Bowden, Mary Ellen. 'The Scientific Revolution in astrology: the English reformers, 1558–1686'. Yale University, 1974.

Crist, Timothy. 'Francis Smith and the opposition press in England, 1660–1688'. Cambridge University, 1977.

Genuth, Sara Schecner. 'From monstrous signs to natural causes: the assimilation of comet lore into natural philosophy'. Harvard University, 1988.

Index

Note: 'n.' after a page reference indicates the number of a note on that page.